The Illustrated

ENCYCLOPEDIA

of KNOWLEDGE

❁ VOLUME 1 ❁

The Illustrated

ENCYCLOPEDIA

of KNOWLEDGE

❁ A,a–Amm ❁

The EDUCATIONAL BOOK GUILD, Inc.

HOW TO USE THIS ENCYCLOPEDIA

IN THIS ENCYCLOPEDIA there are articles on many thousands of different subjects—more than can be found in any other encyclopedia of its kind. These articles are arranged in alphabetical order. When a subject may have two or more different names, the editors have selected the name that most people will look up.

WHEN A WORD is printed in SMALL CAPITALS, it means there is a separate article on that subject. This other article will give you more information on the subject about which you are reading.

AN ARTICLE on a country or city is followed by a paragraph giving official population and other figures and information, so that you may find it quickly. Population figures for the United States are based on the census of 1950, and for foreign places are based on United Nations figures for 1952 or later.

FOR NAMES AND WORDS that are hard to pronounce, see the GUIDE TO PRONUNCIATION in the last volume.

Prepared and Edited by

THE NATIONAL LEXICOGRAPHIC BOARD

ALBERT H. MOREHEAD, *Chairman and General Editor*

LOY C. MOREHEAD, *President*

LOYD F. GEHRES, GEOFFREY MOTT-SMITH, DONALD D. WOLF, WALDEMAR VON ZEDTWITZ, *Vice-Presidents.* GRACE ROBERTSON, *Secretary.* WILLIAM C. CAMPBELL, GEORGE H. COPELAND, HAROLD J. BLUM.

STAFF for The ILLUSTRATED ENCYCLOPEDIA

DONALD D. WOLF, *Vice-President in Charge*

HAROLD J. BLUM, BETSY MACLEAN, ARNOLD ROMNEY, ARTHUR DIENER, SHELDON KRANZ, JAMES T. MOREHEAD, MARGOT L. WOLF, JANE MC-DOWELL, RICHARD FORWARD, DOROTHY CULBERTSON, JACK LUZZATTO

Drawings by RAFAELLO BUSONI
Typographic Design by ANDOR BRAUN

CONTRIBUTORS and CONSULTANTS

JOHN G. ALBRIGHT
Professor of Physics
University of Rhode Island

ANGUS M. WOODBURY
Head, Department of Vertebrate Zoology
University of Utah
Project Director, Wildlife Research
Dugway Proving Ground, Utah

DAVID L. DEJARNETTE
Archaeological Museum, Mound State
  Monument
Alabama

MARIO A. PEI
Professor of Romance Philology
Columbia University

PAUL HENLE
Professor and Chairman, Department of
  Philosophy
University of Michigan

LOUIS S. CHASE, M.D.
Assistant Professor of Psychiatry
Tufts Medical School;
Instructor, Harvard and Boston Universities

WILLIAM W. HOWELLS
Professor of Anthropology
University of Wisconsin

LEROY A. MARTIN
President
Tennessee Wesleyan University

vii

THE REV. PATRICK J. FLYNN, C.S.P.
Director, Paulist Information Center
New York City

THE REV. JOHN J. KEATING, C.S.P.
Assistant Director, Paulist Information
Center
New York City

THE REV. EMIL G. KRAELING
Professor (retired)
Union Theological Seminary

LLOYD R. WYLIE
Professor of Astronomy
Wittenberg College

CLAUDE E. ZOBELL
Professor of Microbiology
Scripps Institution of Oceanography
University of California

LYLE W. R. JACKSON
Professor of Silviculture
University of Georgia

HAROLD C. VORIS, M.D.
Clinical Professor of Neurologic Surgery
Loyola University

CAPT. JAMES B. DONNELLY, U.S.N. Ret.
Research Institute
Temple University

ERWIN RAISZ
Lecturer in Cartography
Institute of Geographical Exploration
Harvard University

ELMO N. STEVENSON
President
Southern Oregon College

EDWARD B. DANSON
Assistant Professor of Anthropology
University of Arizona

CAPT. R. S. BARNABY, U.S.N. Ret.
Chief, Aeronautics Section
Franklin Institute, Philadelphia

CHESTER L. VINCENT
Professor of Horticulture
State College of Washington

JULES W. LEAF, D.D.S.
Assistant Professor of Dental Surgery
New York University

CLAUD C. MARION
Professor of Agriculture
Maryland State College

GEORGE A. CRABB, JR.
Supervisor, Michigan Hydrologic Research
Station
United States Department of Agriculture

GEORGE M. SAVAGE
Associate Professor of Theater Arts
University of California at Los Angeles

LOREN RAY HEIPLE
Head, Department of Civil Engineering
University of Arkansas

A. PAUL WISHART
Former Assistant Professor of Geology
University of Tennessee

WALTER C. BURKHART
Professor of Bacteriology
University of Georgia

BROTHER AMANDUS LEO, F.S.C.
Dean of Engineering
Manhattan College

ROBERT S. GRIFFIN
Chairman, Department of English and
Speech
University of Nevada

FRANK E. SORENSON
Chairman, Department of Educational
Services
University of Nebraska

TEMA SHULTS CLARE
Assistant Professor of Botany
University of Southern California

LUCY MARY MALTBY
Director of Home Economics
Corning Glass Works

ELLSWORTH C. DOUGHERTY
Research Associate in Zoölogy
Lecturer in Physiology
University of California

WILLARD H. ELLER
Professor and Chairman, Department of
    Physics
University of Hawaii

SIGISMOND DER. DIETTRICH
Head, Department of Geography
University of Florida

HOWARD DWIGHT SMITH
University Architect
Ohio State University

JOHN G. HERNDON
Professor of Public Finance
Haverford College

HUGH J. MEANS
Professor and Chairman, Department of
    Radiology
Ohio State University

E. L. BOWSHER
Superintendent of Schools
Toledo Board of Education

STANLEY G. KNIGHT
Professor of Bacteriology
University of Wisconsin

IRA LA RIVERS
Assistant Professor of Biology
University of Nevada

RICHARD L. CAYLOR
Professor of Biology
Delta State College

LEON LOYAL WINSLOW
Director of Art Education
Baltimore Public Schools

MALCOLM E. CAMPBELL
Dean, School of Textiles
North Carolina State College

FRANCES HEINTZ
Assistant Professor of Home Economics
Wayne University

ELSA KOSKINEN
Assistant Professor of Home Economics
Wayne University

ELY CULBERTSON
Chairman, Citizens' Committee for United
    Nations Reform

CHESTER HALE
The Chester Hale School of Ballet

ALBERT LEEDS STILLMAN
The Berwind-White Coal Mining Company

BERTRAM LEBHAR, JR.
Director, Radio Station WMGM
(Bert Lee, Radio and TV Sportscaster)

JOSEPH SCHWARTZ
Westcott & Thomson
Philadelphia

EDWIN J. POLLOCK
Sports Editor
Philadelphia Bulletin

PABLO M. YNSFRAN
Professor, Institute of Latin-American
    Studies
University of Texas

DONALD J. HART
Dean, School of Business Administration
University of Idaho

BERNARD DAVIS
National Philatelic Museum
Philadelphia

BENJAMIN E. MAYS
President
Morehouse College

A or a

Our first bit of "learning" is our ABC's, so it might be said that the first thing we learn is the letter A. Originally this letter was a picture. When men first started to write, they used pictures instead of letters to express what they wanted to say. First it was a picture of an ox. Then it became a letter like this: ◁ . In the alphabet of the ancient Phoenicians, which was developed more than a thousand years before the birth of Christ, the word for ox was *aleph* and it was represented by a letter that looks like this: ∀ —can't you see the ox's horns? The ancient Greeks turned it around. This made it A, which they called *alpha,* and so it has come down through the centuries to us.

This was originally the A pronounced as in *far,* or *father*—what we call the "Italian a." It is very fitting that this should be the first letter in our alphabet, for it is the most natural sound a human being can make. It is the sound that comes out when we simply open our mouths and make a sound; to make any other sound we have to change the position of the mouth or lips or tongue.

In our English language, this letter can be pronounced in several other ways. We call it the "long a" in a word like *blade,* and the "short a" in a word like *man.* The word *awe* is still another *a* sound, heard in the words *water* and *fall.* In *vary* and *fare, a* has a sound very much like *e* in *there.* In *alone* it is much more of an "uh" sound.

At the top of this page, you will see the a's from four different languages, in the box with the capital A. At the far left is the original Phoenician *aleph,* or ox, the one the Greeks turned upside down. Next to it is the same letter in Hebrew, the language in which much of the Bible was written. At the right of the capital A is the Greek *alpha* that grew out of it. Finally, at the far right, there is the "German black-letter" capital A, used in many German books.

Read also the article ALPHABET.

Aa

Almost anywhere you look on a map of Europe, you are likely to see a river called "the Aa." There are forty rivers in Europe with this name. Most of them are small, and none is very important. They got their name from the old language spoken by the Germanic peoples thousands of years ago, in which the sound "aa" (like the sound you use for a sheep's baa, but without the *b*) meant "flowing water."

Aachen

Aachen is an important city in West Germany. It has a population of about 175,000, which makes it about the size of New Haven, Connecticut, or Tulsa, Oklahoma, and there are many factories there, but mostly Aachen is important because of the part it has played in history. The great emperor Charlemagne was born there. Beginning more than a thousand years ago, and for hundreds of

1

German Tourist Office

In the "chapel of Charlemagne" at Aachen,
32 emperors and kings have been crowned.

Dutch-speaking settlers of South Africa called it aardvark (which in Dutch means "earth pig") because it looks like a small, ugly pig, though its ears and tail are longer than a pig's. The aardvark's long snout can be poked deep into anthills, and its long tongue is so sticky that the ants stick to it and very few escape. In South Africa the aardvark is considered good to eat and is hunted for its meat.

American Museum of Natural History

The aardvark hunts at night. He breaks open anthills with his thick, heavy claws.

years after that (until the year 1531), the coronations of the emperors of the Holy Roman Empire (the great realm of the German states in Europe) were held in the chapel of Aachen's famous castle. Much of this castle, and of the beautiful cathedral beside it, was destroyed in World War II.

The French call the city Aix-la-Chapelle (which means "springs at the chapel") because there are fine springs there and because of the famous chapel. For a few years, from 1801 to 1814, the city belonged to France. The treaties ending two wars were signed here, and there is a separate article about them: see AIX-LA-CHAPELLE.

AACHEN. Population, 175,000 (1953 estimate). Location, North Rhine-Westphalia province, West Germany.

aardvark

The aardvark is an animal that lives in South Africa and lives by eating ants. It is also called an *anteater;* but the

aardwolf

The aardwolf is a small animal about the size of a fox, which is found in South Africa. Its name means "earth wolf," and it burrows in the ground. The aardwolf is related to the African hyena, and like the hyena it is a very timid animal. It hides during the day, but ventures out during the night in search of food. It eats other small animals and white ants.

Aaron

Aaron was the first High Priest of the Jews, and this was so important that for more than a thousand years no one could be a Jewish priest unless he was descended from Aaron. Yet Aaron, like many important men, had earlier made great mistakes and later repented.

As you can read in the Bible, in the Book of Exodus, Aaron was the older brother of Moses, the hero who led the Jewish people out of Egypt where they had been slaves. Moses' speech was slow and hard to understand, so God gave Aaron the task of speaking for him. When Moses went into Sinai to receive instructions of God, Aaron made a golden calf and let the people worship it, in defiance of the Ten Commandments. God punished Aaron and the people, but Aaron repented and in time he was forgiven. He married Elisheba, and his son Eleazar became High Priest after him. The mountain on which Aaron died became known as the Mount of Aaron. It is now called Mount Hor.

abacus

The abacus is the earliest "adding machine" known to history. It has been used for thousands of years, especially in oriental countries, and it is still much used in China, Japan, and other countries. The colored beads strung on wires on the side of a baby's play pen are an abacus, and nearly everyone has seen one though very few know what it is.

There are several forms of abacus. The one shown in the picture is a Chinese abacus, which they call a *swanpan* or reckoning-board. The beads above the middle bar are called *quints* and count 5 each when pushed down to the bar; the beads below count 1 each when pushed up to the bar. Each wire strung with beads is called a *column* because it represents one column of figures. Suppose the operator of an abacus wants to record the number 7; in the extreme right-hand column he pushes down one upper bead and pushes up two of the lower beads. In the second column from the right these would count 70; in the third column, 700; and so on. The operator actually does the arithmetic in his head, step by step, and records it on the abacus as he goes along, just as we do with pencil and paper (and in fact abacuses were used in prehistoric times, before men could write), but it is faster with an abacus than with pencil and paper.

A Chinese expert compares his abacus with one of the newest, most complicated electronic calculating machines. With long practice, one can do arithmetic at lightning speed on an abacus, and in very large numbers—the beads on the abacus shown in the picture total 1,050,558,755. A few years ago a Chinese bookkeeper with an abacus won a race against an electric calculating machine (but not the kind of electronic machine shown in this picture).

International News Photo

American Museum of Natural History

The pieces of jewelry shown on the left were cut from an abalone shell like the one on the right.

abalone

The abalone is a shellfish that lives in warm, shallow ocean waters. It is found in great quantities along the shores of California and other Pacific states, where it is very popular as food. Unlike oysters and clams, but like the snail, the abalone has only one shell, but this shell is large (several inches long) and very useful, since the inside is "mother-of-pearl" from which buttons and jewelry are made, and the uncut shell may be used as an ashtray, bowl, or ornament.

Abbey, Edwin Austin

Edwin Austin Abbey was one of the principal American painters of the last

hundred years. He was born in Philadelphia in 1852. Every year thousands of persons visit the Boston Public Library to see his most famous work, "The Quest of the Holy Grail," a huge painting in 15 sections. He is one of three Americans who have been commissioned to paint the coronation of an English king—"the crowning of Edward VII" in 1901. He died in 1911.

abbey

An abbey is the home, including all the grounds and buildings, of a community of men or women who have devoted themselves to a religious life, not as priests or ministers but as monks or nuns. The head of such a community is called an *abbot* if a man, or an *abbess* if a woman. The abbey usually includes a building built around a large courtyard called a cloister. In this building the monks or nuns have their tiny rooms, called cells, in which they live, study, work, and pray. There is also a church or chapel in which religious services are held. Westminster Abbey in London, the famous church where the kings and queens of England are crowned, used to be part of such a religious community. Other religious faiths have abbeys, but the most famous ones are Christian. Read also CONVENT and MONASTERY.

A.B.C. Powers

Argentina, Brazil and Chile, three of the largest South American countries, are usually called the "A.B.C. Powers" when they act together in any international matter. Each is an independent country, of course, and there is no actual political connection between them.

Abd-el-Krim

In North Africa, where most of the people are Mohammedans but have long been under French or Spanish control, Abd-el-Krim was a leader of his people, the Riffs, and other natives of Morocco. He was born in 1880, led his first revolution in 1920, and was successful until 1925, when French and Spanish armies combined to defeat him. In 1926 he surrendered and was exiled to Réunion, an island in the Indian Ocean owned by France, but in 1947 he escaped and began again to work for North African independence.

abdication

A king is said to abdicate when he

British Railways

ABBEYS

The abbey of this cathedral in Wales once owned thousands of acres of land. Drawing at right shows what is inside the walls. The big building, with the nave, choir, and tower, is the cathedral. Each cellarium is a storeroom. The monks have little cells, or rooms, in which they live. In the chapel they worship and pray. The refectory is a large dining hall. The abbot has a private apartment and offices. The open space in the center is surrounded by cloisters, or covered walks. See picture below.

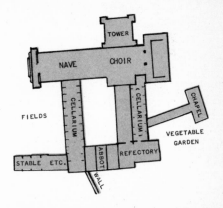

Spanish Tourist Bureau

signs a paper by which he agrees that he will not be, and will not try to be, king any longer. A king may do this for any number of reasons; some kings have done it because they wanted to devote their lives to religious service, some because they felt they had failed as rulers and wanted their people to have a better king. In the most famous case of our times, Edward VIII of England abdicated (and became the Duke of Windsor) because he could not keep his throne and also marry the woman he wanted to. Nearly always, however, kings abdicate only because they are forced to. In former centuries no man could remain king very long unless the nobles of his country wanted him, and in our age a majority of the whole population must want him.

Abdications have been very numerous in this century. Emperor William II of Germany abdicated after his country lost World War I; King Alfonso XIII of Spain had to abdicate in 1931 because his people wanted a republic. Often a king abdicates in favor of his son, as did King Carol of Rumania in 1940, King Leopold of Belgium in 1951, and King Farouk of Egypt in 1952. In 1948 a queen, Wilhelmina of the Netherlands, abdicated so that her daughter Juliana could become queen; Wilhelmina did not have to abdicate, because the people of the Netherlands loved her, but being a king or queen is a very hard job, and Queen Wilhelmina, who was old and tired, thought her daughter would be better for the people. There are separate articles on all these kings and queens.

abdomen

The abdomen is the front section of the body, between the chest and the hips; it is the part we usually call "the stomach," but actually it includes much more than the stomach. In medical terms, it is the area from the *thorax,* or chest, to the *pelvis,* or place where the

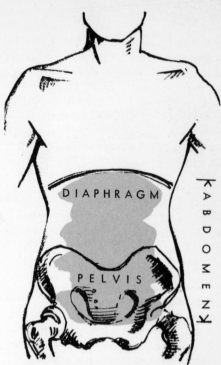

The abdomen holds many of our vital organs (meaning that we cannot live without them), and nature has protected it well. The diaphragm is a wall of muscle. The pelvis is a broad, flat bone that is joined to the hips.

body joins the legs. The muscles of the abdomen are thick and heavy, forming a sort of wall to protect the "abdominal cavity" within which lie the liver, kidneys, stomach, bladder, spleen, intestines, and gall bladder. These are described in separate articles and in the article on the HUMAN BODY.

Other animals that, like men, have backbones—they are called *vertebrate* animals—have abdomens like the human one. In creatures of other kinds, the area where the food is digested is called the abdomen. An octopus, for example, has an abdomen in one of its eight tentacles (which we usually call "arms"). So has the starfish. The abdomen of an ant is its large rear section, behind the section on which its legs grow.

Abel

Adam and Eve, the first man and woman, had Cain as their first son and Abel as their second son. Abel was a shepherd. He was also the first man ever to be murdered. In the Bible, chapter 4 of the Book of Genesis, it is told that Abel's offering of lambs pleased the Lord more than Cain's offering of garden produce, and Cain killed Abel in jealous anger.

Abelard

One of the favorite romantic stories of all time is that of Heloise and Abelard. Peter (or, in French, *Pierre*) Abelard was a real person, born in France in the year 1079, nearly 900 years ago. He was a scholar and a schoolteacher, and he fell in love with Heloise when she was his pupil. The uncle of Heloise, named Fulbert, was canon, or head, of the Cathedral of Notre Dame in Paris, a man of great influence; and he did not approve of Abelard. After Abelard and Heloise were secretly married, Fulbert hired a gang of cutthroats to attack Abelard and mutilate him. Thinking himself unfit to remain the husband of Heloise, Abelard retired to the monastery of St. Denis and became a monk. Heloise also sought a religious life, becoming an abbess. They wrote beautiful letters to each other for the rest of their lives, and their names have since been used as an example of love and devotion. Abelard lived on till 1142 and continued to study and write on philosophy. He and Heloise are buried together in Paris.

Abelard himself took Heloise to the Convent of the Paraclete, and made her the abbess. See the article on Abbeys.

Aberdeen

Aberdeen is the third-largest city in Scotland. It has a population of about 190,000, making it about the same size as Tulsa, Oklahoma. It is an important harbor, located on the North Sea at the mouth of the River Dee. There are fine granite quarries in that section, and Aberdeen is sometimes called "the Granite City" because of its many buildings made of white granite, including famous St. Machar Cathedral. There are also iron foundries, and large herring and salmon fisheries. Aberdeen is the capital of Aberdeen (or Aberdeenshire) County.

Aberdeen is also the name of an important city in South Dakota, with a population of 21,000; and a town in Maryland named Aberdeen is near the Proving Grounds of the U.S. Army.

abolitionists

Ever since slavery has been practiced on earth, there have been people who opposed it as a wicked practice and wanted to abolish it. In the United States, in the period from about 1830 until the Civil War ended slavery, those who worked and spoke most vigorously against slavery were called abolitionists. Some were of the North, some

John Brown is being taken out to be hanged, after he tried to free the slaves and failed. All the colored people in this picture were slaves, in what is now the state of West Virginia. They loved John Brown.

of the South. They held meetings, published booklets, made speeches on street corners, and formed political parties to fight slavery. William Lloyd Garrison was one of the most active abolitionists in his writing and speaking; John Brown went even farther and tried to free the slaves by force. The abolitionists were much persecuted. Slave-owners opposed them, of course, and hired ruffians to attack them; but there were many others, who had no strong feelings of their own about slavery, who were violently opposed to abolitionism because they feared it might lead to war. They threw stones at abolitionist speakers, broke up their printing presses, and burned their pamphlets. Eventually the question of slavery did lead to war, and after the Civil War ended there was no further need for an abolitionist movement.

Aboukir

Aboukir is a village in Egypt and also the name of a bay below the village, where the great river Nile meets the Mediterranean Sea. Here the great British naval hero, Horatio Nelson, defeated a French fleet in 1798 and prevented Napoleon from gaining control of all North Africa for France. This was the famous Battle of the Nile. The present population of Aboukir is about 7,000. Its name is also spelled Abukir. See NAPOLEONIC WARS and NELSON.

abracadabra

Abracadabra, a word that in ancient times was carved upon charms and amulets to keep evil spirits away. About 2,000 years ago, some people thought this was a magic word, and that no illness, trouble, or evil could harm them if they wore a necklace or bracelet with "ABRACADABRA" carved on it. Now the word means just a kind of hocus-pocus, or nonsense, such as when children pretend that an ordinary stick becomes a magic wand if they wave it about and say "Abracadabra!" See CHARMS.

Abraham

Abraham is called "the father of the Jews." It was to him, as told in the Bible (Book of Genesis), that God first revealed Himself and made the covenant by which the Jews were to become the chosen people. Originally named Abram, Abraham then assumed his new name, which means "father of many." Abraham was married to Sarah, and both were old; Sarah was too old to hope to have any more children. But the Lord promised the land of Canaan to the descendants of a son of Abraham and Sarah, and by a miracle Sarah did have another son in her old age, named Isaac. God then ordered Abraham to offer the life of this son, Isaac, as a sacrifice. Abraham's faith was so great that he was prepared to obey, but an angel appeared and stopped him, for it was only a test of his faith and his faith had been proved.

Abraham, Plains of

Just outside the city of Quebec, in Canada, on the top of a hill with steep sides, is a high level field called the Plains of Abraham. Here, in 1759, the English general Wolfe defeated the French general Montcalm in a battle that decided the last of the French and Indian Wars. The result was important to North Americans, because if the battle had gone the other way the language and background of a majority of our people might have been French instead of English. In 1948 the Plains of Abraham became a Canadian National Park, and visitors to Quebec should see it. Read also the article on the FRENCH AND INDIAN WARS.

Canadian Information Office

A monument in the city of Quebec keeps alive the memory of General James Wolfe, who won Canada for the English king.

abrasives

Abrasives are materials used to abrade, which means to rub off. Grinding and polishing are done with abrasives. Grindstones used to sharpen axes, sandpaper used to make wood smooth, scouring powders, steel wool, silver polish, the side of a match box, and even rubber erasers, all contain abrasives.

There are many abrasive materials. Some are very hard, some are much softer. Diamond is the hardest of all, and many diamonds that are not good enough to use in jewelry are used as abrasives. Other abrasives are silicon carbide, a manufactured abrasive; corundum, which includes rubies and sapphires; emery, garnet, sandstone, flint, pumice, and rouge. These are crushed and put through sieves that separate the finer and the coarser grains. The grains may then be mixed with a paste or soap; or baked with clay, as a brick is, to make a grinding wheel; or stuck onto a sheet of paper or cloth with glue, as sandpaper is.

A person who needs an abrasive decides which to use by considering the work it is expected to do. He may select a hard or soft, coarse or fine-grained abrasive to suit this use. Coarse grains are used where a lot of material is to be ground away. Fine grains are used for polishing.

The man is using an abrasive wheel to sharpen huge saws with which lumber is cut. This is called "gumming" the saw. The top saw has to be sharpened once every day, the bottom saw four times every day.

Carborundum Company

The tomb of Absalom, built nearly 3,000 years ago, can still be seen in the Kidron Valley near Jerusalem, which was the capital city of his father, King David.

Absalom

Absalom was the third son of King David; his story, as told in the Bible (II Samuel), is a great example of the love of a father for his son. Absalom was far from being a good son or a good man. He murdered his brother Amnon. He led a revolt to throw his father off the throne and make himself the king instead. But when David's armies defeated the rebels, and Absalom was killed in the battle, David wept, and cried, "O my son Absalom, my son, my son Absalom! would God I had died for thee, O Absalom, my son, my son!"

absolute zero

The absence of all heat, however little, is called absolute zero. Of course, everyone is familiar with "zero weather" and knows it is very cold, but there is still a great deal of heat left. Otherwise it could not become even colder and fall "below zero." Absolute zero is the stage at which it could not become any colder. On the Fahrenheit thermometer that most of us use, this would be more than 459 degrees below zero! On the centi-grade thermometer more often used in science, it is more than 273 degrees below zero. (The exact figures are: $-459.72°$ F.; $-273.16°$ C.)

As long as there is any heat at all, there is some motion, if only of the tiny molecules that make up all matter. Absolute zero is the point at which all motion ceases. Such coldness can only be imagined; it could never be proved, because the presence of someone near enough to observe it would provide enough heat to raise the temperature. Read also the articles on TEMPERATURE and THERMOMETER.

absorption

When one kind of matter changes its nature and becomes part of another kind of matter, it is said to be absorbed, and the process is called *absorption*. Our bodies absorb the food we eat, or at least the nourishing part of it; a piece of bread or a dish of spinach actually becomes flesh and blood and bone, this being called *digestive absorption*. A plant absorbs water, and minerals dissolved in water, through its roots; it absorbs carbon dioxide, a gas that is part of the air, through its leaves. These processes are more fully described in the articles on DIGESTION and METABOLISM and PHOTOSYNTHESIS.

Another kind of absorption is the one we see daily when wet hands are dried on a towel. The water is absorbed, or soaked in, by the fibers of which the towel is made. After that, as the towel dries in the air, the water is once again absorbed, this time into the air by the process known as EVAPORATION.

Even light can be absorbed, as is explained in the article on LIGHT, and it is this kind of absorption that makes us see colors. If a material will absorb every color except blue, for instance, then when light shines on it the other colors will be absorbed and the blue will be reflected back into our eyes, becoming the only color we can see. A material that absorbs almost no light looks white to us; a material that absorbs nearly all the light that strikes it looks black.

Heat offers a good example of absorption. When any two things touch, the one that is colder will absorb heat from the one that is warmer—and will keep on absorbing heat until the two things have the same temperature. It does not matter whether it is a solid, a liquid or a gas (the air is a gas) that does the touching. When a pan is put on a fire it absorbs heat from the fire and becomes hot. Any food in the pan then absorbs heat from the pan and becomes hot, which cooks it.

A striking example is found in the way ice cream freezes in an old-fashioned ice-cream freezer. At first, the ice cream is a liquid. It is put in a container and surrounded by ice. Salt is put on the ice, and this makes the ice melt. The ice, upon melting, becomes water, which is warmer than ice. The fact that it is warmer means that it is absorbing heat from somewhere. Part of the heat it absorbs comes from the air around the freezer, but much of the heat comes

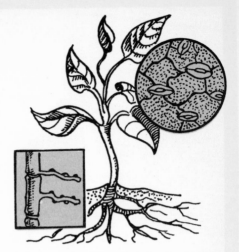

Plants absorb water though tiny hairlike roots. You can see, in the square box at the left, how these tiny hairs grow off the root. The circle shows how the leaves have pores, or openings, for absorbing carbon dioxide from the air.

from the liquid "ice cream" inside the container. In fact, this liquid loses so much heat that it becomes cold enough to freeze, and turns into solid ice cream.

Abydos

Two ancient cities were named Abydos, but the one we remember best was on the Asiatic side of the Dardanelles strait, the narrow body of water between Greece and Asia Minor. Across this strait, which was then called the Hellespont, Leander swam every night (in the story of HERO AND LEANDER), from Abydos to Sestos. It was also at this Abydos that Xerxes built a bridge of boats to carry his army across the water.

The other Abydos was in Egypt, and archaeologists have discovered in its ruins many ancient writings, ornaments, and buildings from times hundreds of years before the birth of Christ.

abyss

The word *abyss* has several meanings. It means "the bottomless pit,"

ABYSSAL FISH

1

2

All Photos Amer. Mus. of Nat. Hist.

1. This deep-sea fish looks like an eel, but has its eyes set in the front like headlights. It is about 2½ feet long.

2. The angler fish is one of the ugliest and strangest of all creatures. It is a big fish, 3 to 5 feet long, and it lives by killing and eating other fish. Its spine grows out of its nose to form a sort of fishing hook that attracts other fish. Its beard is believed to glow in the black waters of the deep sea.

3. This is another kind of big angler fish. The bony rod sticking out from it is not so much like a fishhook, but when another fish bites at it, the angler fish gobbles him up.

4. This is another kind of angler fish, with a feathery kind of "fishhook" growth on its head.

3

4

because in the Greek language it actually meant "without a bottom." But it is also used to describe the bottom of the ocean where the water is more than a mile deep. At this depth hardly anything is the same as it is in shallower waters.

No plants grow on the ocean bottom at such depths, and there is no light at all, because the rays of the sun cannot reach farther than a few hundred feet through the water.

Until very recently, scientists in their bathyspheres could not go so far down, but they could still let down traps and bring up abyssal fish for study. These are quite different from fish that swim near the surface. Many of them have no eyes (with no light, they do not need them). The mouths and teeth of these fish are very large, as they have to be to gather in enough food, for there are no schools of small fish and no sea plants for them to feed on. The water is icy cold. The pressure is tremendous, because of the weight of all the water above. A single quart of water weighs almost two pounds, and in the abyss even a small fish has several tons of water resting on it. Such pressure would immediately kill a fish accustomed to shallower water. Because they are so strangely unlike the fish we know, abyssal fish seem hideously ugly to us.

Abyssinia, a former name for Ethiopia. See ETHIOPIA.

acacia

The acacia is a small tree or a shrub that grows wild in tropical countries and is raised in greenhouses farther north because of its beautiful flowers. The wood of some acacia trees makes fine furniture; the sap of some acacias is very sweet-smelling and is used in making perfumes, and besides gives us "gum arabic," the sticky substance that makes gum drops "chewy" and is also used in making some glues.

Australian Information Service

Acacia is the national flower of Australia. The flowers on this tree grow several more feet above the girl's head.

academy

The first academy was a grove of trees, used as a public park, in the city of Athens in ancient Greece. It was named more than 2,300 years ago for a great Greek warrior, Academus, one of the athletes who used the park.

The Greek philosopher Plato, the wisest man of his time, used to stroll in this grove with his pupils, teaching them. Because of this, they called Plato and his followers "the Academy," and ever since that time the word has been used to mean a school or other institution of learning, or a group of learned men who form an association for study. When a boy goes away to school, he is likely to go to a military academy, and in this case "academy" means "high school." Officers of the United States Army are trained at the United States Military Academy at West Point, and officers of the United States Navy are trained at the United States Naval Academy at Annapolis, and here "academy" means "college." A great writer, or artist, or architect, or geographer, may be elected to an "Academy," and in this case the word means a society, or club. This kind of academy is always a society of very distinguished men, and it is an honor to be elected to one.

The most famous of these academies is the French Academy. It is more than 300 years old, and can never have more than forty members, who are called the "forty Immortals." These men of the French Academy have decided for hundreds of years what is proper in speaking and writing the French language, and they have helped many sciences to advance. Other countries have distinguished academies too. In the United States there is the American Academy of Arts and Letters, which never has more than fifty members. It never became as well known in this country as the French Academy is in France and throughout the world.

Academy Awards

The Academy of Motion Picture Arts and Sciences was founded in 1927, to encourage the making of better motion pictures. Every year it gives prizes

Audrey Hepburn won the Academy Award in 1954 as "best actress," for her performance in *Roman Holiday*.

Acme

to those who have done the best work in making pictures, whether they were actors or actresses, or photographers, or producers, or directors, or anyone else who contributed to the writing, playing or making of the picture. Every year, each company nominates the persons that it thinks should win the prizes, from among those who made its own pictures. There is a board of governors of the Academy that elects the prize-winners, and every year they have a big banquet at which the prizes are awarded to these winners. A television broadcast of this banquet pays most of the Academy's expenses. Each prize is a little statue with the figure of a man on top of it. One of the first actresses who won one of these statues nicknamed the little man "Oscar," and the name has stuck. Ever since, winning an Academy Award has been known as "winning an Oscar."

Acadia

The part of Canada that is now Nova Scotia and Prince Edward Island, and also a part of the province of New Brunswick and the state of Maine in the United States, was once called Acadia and belonged to France. That was more than 200 years ago. About 12,000 French people had come over, just as the Pilgrims had come to Massachusetts, and had made homes for themselves there.

Then in 1755, during the French and Indian Wars between England and France, the English made more than half of these French people move from Acadia to parts of what is now the United States. The poet Henry Wadsworth Longfellow wrote one of his finest poems, called "Evangeline," about these unhappy thousands who had to leave their homes and move hundreds of miles away. His poem is about a girl named Evangeline, and the young man she was to marry, named Gabriel. Gabriel was one of those sent away. Evan-

Nova Scotia Bureau of Information

The picture above shows the place, in what is now Nova Scotia, where the French-speaking Acadians landed when they first came to America nearly 300 years ago. It is now a beautiful fishing village called Terence Bay, near Halifax, the capital of Nova Scotia. In Kings County, Nova Scotia, thousands of tourists visit the statue of Evangeline (shown in the picture at the right). Behind it stands the beautiful, ivy-covered Grand Pré church. This part of Canada is cool and pleasant in the summer.

geline followed him, hoping to find him. She went to Louisiana, where many of the Acadians had gone, but could not find him there; then she went all the way to Michigan looking for him, and finally to Philadelphia. There she finally found him, but both were very old and he was dying.

The name of Acadia lives on in the nickname of many Louisiana descendants of the Acadians who went there, called "Cajuns" (which is just a mispronunciation of "Acadians"), and also in the Acadian National Park, which visitors to the very northernmost part of Maine may see.

accidents

An accident is something that happens unexpectedly to hurt a person. If you hit somebody and he hits you back and hurts you, that is not an accident because you should have expected it. But if you climb on a rickety chair to reach something, and the chair lets you fall and hurt yourself, that is called an accident because you did not expect it—at least, it is supposed that if you had expected to fall you would not have climbed on the chair.

In the United States alone, nearly 100,000 persons are killed in accidents every year, and for every one person who dies in an accident there are about 100 who are hurt in accidents but do not die. This means there must be nearly ten million Americans who are hurt in accidents every year. The biggest group of those who are killed, about 35,000, die in automobile accidents of one kind or another, and the second biggest group, about 25,000, die as a result of accidents at home. Floods, hurricanes, earthquakes, and other acts of nature are not classed as accidents.

Long ago, there were many people who believed that accidents were the will of God and could not be prevented. Since then they have learned that most accidents are not accidents at all, but happen because someone is careless. There will always be some accidents, but nearly all accidents could be prevented if people were more careful. Yet during World War II, more people were hurt by accidents in the United States than were injured in battle.

An organization called the National Safety Council, with headquarters in Chicago, spends all its time trying to teach people how to be more careful and avoid accidents. Big factories, automobile companies, and many others who are interested in preventing accidents at work and on the road, spend millions of dollars every year to prevent accidents. They have a good reason to do this. When a worker in a factory is hurt, the factory produces less and makes less money. Automobile accidents and home accidents, too, keep people away from work and cost the whole country money in lost time as well as in doctors' bills and hospital expenses.

Everyone, men and women, boys and girls, will be better off if there are fewer accidents. The pictures on these pages show some of the ways to avoid accidents.

Riding bicycles on highways need not cause accidents if traffic rules are carefully obeyed, but these riders should be in single file at the side of the street.

All Photographs by National Safety Council

Small children put everything in their mouths; nothing like cleaning fluids or medicines or other household materials should be left where a child can get to them.

The picture below shows that it isn't safe to step into the street when a car is moving on it, even if the street seems fairly empty. A driver has various "blind spots" and he cannot see anything in those blind spots. In the picture, the driver of the car in front cannot see any of the men, and he cannot see the car behind him. They are all in his "blind spots."

Young children are never safe in the kitchen alone. This little girl might get a bad burn. If she turns the gas on and it does not light, it might kill her. Standing on a chair is dangerous, too.

Boys who hold on to the back of cars or trucks like this often have bad accidents. If the truck stops suddenly or makes a sudden turn, the bicycle will go flying.

The driver did not stop where the sign told him to. He will be lucky if he does not have a bad accident.

A YEAR'S ACCIDENTS

What They Mean to People

 96,000 ACCIDENTAL DEATHS

 9,600,000 INJURIES
Each disabling the victim
for at least 2 days

 350,000 PERMANENT INJURIES
Ranging from partial use of a finger
to blindness or complete crippling

What They Cost in Money

OVER $3 BILLION WAGE LOSS

Through temporary disability, lowered earning power, permanent loss of earning power

$1.3 BILLION IN INSURANCE COSTS

For administration and claim processing only

$2.3 BILLION PROPERTY LOSS

From motor vehicle accidents and fires

$600 MILLION MEDICAL EXPENSES

For doctors' and hospital fees

$1.5 BILLION INDIRECT COSTS

Losses in property, production, etc., in occupational accidents

Total Monetary Costs . . . $8.7 Billion

CHART BY GRAPHICS INSTITUTE, N.Y.C.

accordion

The accordion is a musical instrument that is popular throughout the world. It is made of a bellows between two boxlike ends, and a number of metal reeds (flat, flexible pieces of metal) that vibrate to sound different notes when air blows across them. Opening or closing the bellows creates the flow of air, and the player has a keyboard, like a piano keyboard, that he plays with his right hand to sound the notes, and a number of buttons that he operates with his left hand to make chords. Because of its piano keyboard, the instrument is often called a *piano accordion*. For many years, accordions had no keyboards, but only buttons to press.

The accordion is a new instrument, as musical instruments go; it is less than 150 years old. For fifty years or more, it was manufactured chiefly in Paris, and considered little more than a toy.

The concertina is a simple form of accordion, and easier to play than the large ones.

From that modest start it grew into a very complex instrument—the largest accordions have as many as 120 buttons and up to 50 keys—and an accordion player can give a concert all by himself. There are small accordions that are quite easy to play, but the big piano accordions cannot be played well without both talent and practice.

An accordion player can give a concert all by himself. This one is playing at Dublin Stadium, in Ireland, at a festival of Folk Dancing. He has a "piano accordion."

Irish Tourist Bureau

Accounting

All manufacturing, banking and business depends on good accounting.

accounting

An accountant goes over the bookkeeping records of a business to find out how much the business is actually worth, and how much money it is making, and (very often) how it could make more money. His profession is called *accountancy,* or, more often, *accounting.* The first step in accounting is bookkeeping (and there is a separate article on BOOKKEEPING in a later volume), but accounting only begins there. The bookkeeper sets down the figures that show how much money a business has taken in and how much it has spent, but the accountant tells what the figures mean.

Very few people realize how big a part the accountant has played in the growth of the United States. Until about 100 years ago, accounting was not a very important or very well developed profession. This means it is a very young profession, considering that there have been doctors for thousands of years and lawyers for almost as long. Then, as businesses grew bigger and bigger, and government laws grew more and more complex, the need for accounting grew. The general public would not invest in a big business unless it had a system for proving that their money was being spent wisely. Ac-

countants provided this system. A big business with dozens of branches and thousands of employees would be in a constant mess if it were not for accounting systems to show exactly how its money was being spent and with what success, and accountants worked out the system for that too. Alfred P. Sloan, for many years head of General Motors Corporation, one of the biggest businesses in the world, once said that good accounting is the backbone of successful business.

Accounting is a profession, which means that the person who practices it must have special education. An accountant must know much more than bookkeeping. He must know the principles of analyzing bookkeeping records —that is, taking every separate item and discovering exactly what it means. He must know a great deal of law as it applies to businesses, especially tax laws and laws relating to an employer's duty to his employees. Many accountants have their own offices and work for several different companies, going from one to the other to examine and analyze their books; this is called public accounting, and the accountant who practices it must know a great deal about the actual operation of many different kinds of business, and must pass an examination that makes him a Certified Public Accountant.

FINANCIAL STATEMENTS

The accountant shows the result of business operations by what is called a balance sheet. A balance sheet is divided into two parts. In one part is shown everything a company owns, whether in money or in things that are worth money. These are its assets. In the other part of the balance sheet, the accountant sets down everything the company owes, or must eventually be prepared to pay. These are the company's liabilities. The difference between the assets and the liabilities is the company's net worth. This balance sheet, or financial statement, shows a company's net worth on some particular date that is the end of an

The accountant prepares a "financial statement" or "balance sheet" to show how much a company is worth, but often it is hard for anyone but a businessman to understand it. Turn the page and see how the Corn Exchange Bank of New York made a simpler statement.

Courtesy Corn Exchange Bank of N. Y.

REPORT OF THE CONDITION OF THE
Corn Exchange Bank, New York

RESOURCES.

Specie		$6,537,537.51
Other currency authorized by the Laws of the United States		908,343.10
Cash items, viz.:		
Exchanges and checks for next day's clearings	$25,545,000.36	
Other cash items	5,632,293.51	
		31,177,293.87
Due from The Federal Reserve Bank of New York		29,215,820.84
Due from approved reserve depositaries		300,000.00
Due from other banks, trust companies and bankers		2,283,381.83
Stock and bond investments, viz.:		
Public securities	$64,215,856.78	
Private securities	34,610,129.72	
		98,825,986.50
Loans and discounts secured by bond and mortgage, deed or other real estate collateral		497,556.35
Loans and discounts secured by other collateral		43,085,518.63
Loans, discounts and bills purchased not secured by collateral		32,166,997.32
Own acceptances purchased		583,951.40
Overdrafts		24,423.64
Bonds and mortgages owned		14,964,858.76
Real estate, viz.:		
Bank buildings		7,527,240.49
Customers' liability on acceptances (see liabilities, per contra)	$2,631,384.33	
Less anticipations	111,446.14	
		2,519,938.19
Accrued interest entered on books at close of business on above date		1,950,693.27
Total		$272,569,541.70

LIABILITIES.

Capital stock		$10,000,000.00
Surplus:		
Surplus fund	$10,000,000.00	
Undivided profits	4,767,891.04	
		14,767,891.04
Deposits:		
Preferred, as follows:		
Due New York State Savings Banks	$8,235,906.43	
Due New York State Savings and Loan Associations, Credit Unions and Land Bank	258,146.91	
Other deposits due as executor, administrator, guardian, receiver, trustee, committee or depositary	207,964.03	
Other deposits secured by a pledge of assets	1,264,300.00	
Not preferred, as follows:		
Deposits subject to check	187,546,685.91	
Time deposits, certificates and other deposits, the payment of which cannot legally be required within thirty days	4,140,094.83	
Demand certificates of deposit	413,539.20	
Deposits withdrawable only on presentation of pass-books	27,046,948.97	
Cashiers' checks outstanding, including similar checks of other officers	1,432,672.96	
Certified checks	6,035,468.89	
Unpaid dividends	3,698.00	
Due trust companies, banks and bankers	7,351,910.04	
Extend total deposits		243,937,336.17
Acceptances of drafts payable at a future date or authorized by commercial letters of credit		2,631,384.33
Reserves for taxes, expenses, etc.	$437,093.40	
Accrued interest entered on books at close of business on above date	278,953.47	
Estimated unearned discounts	516,883.29	
		1,232,930.16
Total		$272,569,541.70

accounting period. If between one accounting period and another a company's net worth grows, then during that period the company has made money; if its net worth becomes less, the company has lost money or has paid out its profits.

It is not possible to tell what a company is worth merely from how much cash and other assets it has. That is one of the important things accounting has taught business over the course of the years. Suppose a publisher of magazines sells a million subscriptions for $3.00 each and takes in $3,000,000, which he has in cash in the bank. It might seem that he has an income of $3,000,000 from this, but the accountant shows that it is not so; in fact, the $3,000,000 goes on the publisher's balance sheet as a liability, not as an asset, even though it is cash in the bank. That money belongs to the subscribers until the publisher has finished sending them their magazines. Every time he sends each subscriber one issue of the magazine, the accountant takes $\frac{1}{12}$ of the $3,000,-000, or $250,000, and shows it as income. The rest still is owed to the subscribers. Such money is called deferred income, and cash that is actually on hand but must be held for a particular purpose is called a reserve.

Again, suppose a man buys a truck and goes into the trucking business. The truck cost him $4,000. At the end of the year, he has taken in $10,000 from his charges for trucking, and has spent only $5,000, which makes it seem that he has a $5,000 profit. But the accountant knows that in four years the truck will wear out and he will have to buy another one. So the accountant takes off one-fourth of the $4,000 he spent for the truck, and reduces his profit by $1,000. That is called depreciation.

The basic principles of accounting are quite simple, but the businesses it serves have become so complex that years of study are required to learn the profession well. A young man who wants to be an accountant, after studying in college, usually works in the offices of an experienced accountant as a "junior." He does not make a high salary as a junior, but he keeps on learning until he can himself become a Certified Public Accountant and open his own office. Many accountants specialize, just as doctors do, on one or more particular phases of accounting, spending most of their time as cost accountants or as consultants in some business or profession.

AUDITING

Every accountant is an auditor. In one sense, however, auditing is a special branch of accounting. The auditor examines the accounts of a company to make sure they are correct. This is important in government organizations from the mighty Federal Government of the United States down to the tiniest town, because taxpayers want to be sure their money is being spent honestly and intelligently. It is important in businesses, because the stockholders, who are the real owners, turn the control over to just a few persons—directors and officers—and they too want to know that their investment is being protected.

When an accountant makes a careful audit, he investigates everything personally. If the company's records show that it has a million dollars worth of merchandise on hand to be sold, the accountant goes and looks at it. If the company's books show that certain persons owe it money, the accountant "verifies" these accounts—that is, he gets in touch with the persons concerned and finds out from them that they really do owe the money. Years ago, before accounting was developed to its present state, it was not unusual for investors in a business to be cheated by the managers of the business. Today that has been stopped, due to accounting. .

COST ACCOUNTING

The cost accountant analyzes the

This is an advertisement in which the Corn Exchange Bank of New York arranged its financial statement so it would be easier for people to understand. See also page 21.

money a company is spending so that he knows exactly how much it costs the company to perform every operation of its business. For example, if the company is manufacturing chewing gum, he will tell them not only that each piece of chewing gum costs them, say, one-fifth of a cent; but exactly how much every operation that goes into the making of the chewing gum costs, down to hundredths or thousandths of a penny.

Manufacturers in particular want to know this, so they will know how much to charge for their products to give them a fair profit. In addition, the cost accountant is often able to point out savings that will allow them to increase their profits and reduce their selling price to the public. The fact that Americans can buy so much good merchandise at such low prices is in many cases due to savings that have been pointed out by accountants. In some unusual cases, an accountant has saved a manufacturer money by raising the level of a workman's bench a few inches so that the workman would not have to stoop so low to get to his work, and would not become so tired and work less well toward the end of the day; or by spacing machines differently to make them more convenient; or by showing that the cost of shipping raw materials to the factory would make it worthwhile to build another factory closer to where the materials are; or in any of thousands of other ways.

TAX ACCOUNTING

Taxes have become so many and so large that every business has to consider taxes before it makes any plans. There may be as many as a dozen tax forms to fill out, all of them complicated, and all of them required on a certain date, and the accountant must know about all of them. There may be reasons why a company should wait a year before adding a new building or new machine to its properties, or an equally good reason why the company should do it immediately, solely because of the way the decision will affect the taxes it pays.

Then, there are individuals who are not really in business at all but are bewildered by the complications of tax forms and who go to accountants to get help in making out their income taxes. Tax accountants very often save their clients more money in reduced taxes than they charge in fees.

In many aspects of tax accounting, the accountant is engaged in work resembling a lawyer's work. There are special tax courts, and many accountants argue cases before these courts just as lawyers do.

These are usually cases in which the government has demanded a tax higher than the taxpayer thinks he should pay, and the accountant's job is to prove to the court that the taxpayer is right.

Aceldama

After Judas had betrayed Jesus, as told in the New Testament (in the 27th chapter of the Gospel of Matthew), he repented. He gave back the 30 pieces of silver that he had been paid, and he hanged himself. The 30 pieces of silver were used to buy a field that had belonged to a potter (a maker of pottery) and Judas was buried there. In the first chapter of the Book of Acts, this field, which we usually call the Potter's Field, is given the name of Aceldama, which means "the field of blood."

acetylene

Acetylene is the name of a gas that is very important in many ways. You cannot see acetylene, but when it is mixed with oxygen, the life-giving gas that makes up much of the air, the mixture burns with one of the hottest and brightest flames known. It is so hot that it will melt steel and cut through even the walls of a safe. It is important in welding—that is, joining two pieces of metal by melting the edges of both and letting them harden together. (See the article on WELDING.) The flame of this burning mixture, called oxyacetylene gas, is so bright that it would hurt the eyes if one looked at it directly and

The man is using an acetylene torch to weld steel plates together on a ship's hull.

Standard Oil Company of New Jersey

welders must wear dark goggles; these also protect their eyes against flying sparks. Acetylene is also used in the making of synthetic (artificial) rubber.

Achilles

Achilles is a character in one of the greatest stories of all time, a story that may be more than 3,000 years old and was told by the great poet Homer hundreds of years before the birth of Christ, and by hundreds of writers since. It is the story of how the Greeks went to war against the city of Troy.

The greatest of the Greek warriors was Achilles. No one could beat him; he even chased the Trojan champion, Hector, around the walls of Troy. One reason no one could beat Achilles was that he could not be hurt by swords or arrows or spears in any part of his body except one—his heel. But that one vulnerable (which means "woundable") spot finally caused his death.

When Achilles was still a tiny baby, his mother Thetis had a vision that he would be killed in battle. Now, in those days there was a belief that the waters of the river Styx had magic powers that would make anyone safe from death. So Thetis took the tiny Achilles and dipped him in the river Styx. When she dipped him in, she held him by one of his heels, and the waters of the river

Achilles died when an arrow hit his heel.

did not touch that spot. So during the Trojan wars, the vision Thetis had seen finally came true. An arrow struck Achilles in the heel, in his one vulnerable spot, and killed him. Ever since that time, the weakest point of any person has been called his "Achilles' heel."

Achilles' tendon

The Achilles' tendon is a cord, or tendon, in the body. It stretches from the middle of the back of the leg to the heel, and gets its name from the story of Achilles, which you can read about just above this. The Achilles' tendon is very strong, and almost as hard as if it were bone. It is of great importance to our walking, because to walk comfortably we must bend the foot with each step.

acids

The acids we know best are liquids that have a sour taste or a burning effect. In chemistry, acids can be either solids, liquids, or gases, and have many uses. They conduct electricity, and they combine with other chemicals to form useful products.

The liquid acids that we know have some water in them. Some are quite mild, and outside of their sour taste they are either useful or at least harmless to our bodies. Vinegar is water and acetic acid. We digest food because there is hydrochloric acid in our stomachs that dissolves it. It is the citric acid in lemons, grapefruit, and related fruit, that gives them their pleasant sour taste. The lactic acid in milk causes it to curdle and it is useful because it makes cheese. But hydrofluoric acid is so strong that it will burn a hole in glass, as you can read in the article on ETCHING, and if you dropped some sulfuric acid on your skin, it would burn you as badly as fire.

If one of these burning acids should touch your skin, the way to neutralize it is to put an alkali on the burned place. There is a separate article on ALKALIS, which include such common household things as soda. In chemical laboratories, there is usually a pan of soda water around, and if a chemist is touched by an acid, he quickly plunges his hand into this soda water, which stops the acid from burning him. This must be done immediately, because the acid burns very fast.

International Shoe Tannery

The chemist here is preparing the acids used for tanning leather to make shoes.

An interesting experiment can be conducted with litmus paper, which is used in chemistry. Litmus paper comes in two colors, red and blue. If an acid touches blue litmus paper, the paper turns red; if an alkali touches red litmus paper, the paper turns blue. So, if you dip a piece of blue litmus paper into even such a mild acid as orange juice, it will turn red; if you dip a piece of red litmus paper into a glass of plain soda water, it will turn blue. Chemists use this paper to tell quickly whether a chemical is acid or alkali.

acne

Acne is the name of a very unpleasant but usually harmless disease—the breaking out of many pimples and blackheads on the face. This most often happens to boys and girls between the ages of 10 or 12 and 19 or 20. The cause of acne is not definitely known, and any number of different things may cause it, including the changes that take place in the body in the process of growing up. Persons with large pores in their skins are more likely to have it than persons with very closely grained skin in which the pores are small.

Doctors advise the following to those who have acne: The first rule is to keep the face very clean. When the attack is bad, the face should be washed with very hot water which causes the pores to open and makes it easier for the blackheads to come out. Some doctors advise squeezing out the worst blackheads and opening the pimples with a sterilized needle, then squeezing the pus out of them. It is important also to keep clean with frequent baths, to get plenty of sunlight and fresh air, to avoid constipation, and not to eat too many oily or starchy foods. Advertised remedies for acne should be avoided unless they are advised by a doctor, and of course it is best to consult the doctor anyway.

Aconcagua

Mount Aconcagua is the highest mountain peak in the Western Hemisphere. It is in the great Andes chain of mountains that runs all the way down through South America. Aconcagua is in the part of the Andes that lies in Argentina, in the southern part of South America. It is more than 23,000 feet high—nearly four and one-half miles. The highest peak in North America, Mount McKinley in Alaska, is 20,300 feet high, but though Mount Aconcagua is the highest mountain in our hemisphere, it is far from being the highest mountain

Photo by Burton Holmes, from Ewing Galloway

These men are riding burros and horses on the lower slopes of Mt. Aconcagua in South America. It is the highest mountain in the Western Hemisphere.

in the world. Mount Everest is more than a mile higher, and there are more than 200 peaks in the big mountain ranges lying around India that are higher than Aconcagua. Mountain climbers reached the peak of Aconcagua in 1897, and others have climbed it since. It is an extinct volcano.

acoustics

The word acoustics means the whole science of sound—what causes it, how it travels, and its effects. But there is another article on SOUND in a later volume, and here we will consider acoustics only as most people use the word: to mean the "listening qualities" of a theater, an auditorium, a room, and so on. In a theater with "good acoustics" a word spoken from the stage can be heard as clearly in the last row as in

the first. In a theater with "bad acoustics" the sound may be too soft to hear by the time it reaches the last row; or music may make such echoes that it makes the ears ring; or in any number of ways the sound may be unpleasant.

WHAT IS SOUND?

To understand the principles of acoustics, you must first know something about what sound is and how it travels. Sound begins with a vibration, or shaking; in the case of the sound of a voice, it begins with a vibration in the throat. This shakes the air, causing waves to go out through the air. When these waves strike the ear of a listener, his eardrum makes sounds of them that he can understand.

As the sound waves move through the air, if they strike something that will not vibrate the sound will suddenly stop going forward. Something soft like a rug, or heavy velvet draperies, will stop a sound; they are said to "absorb" it. But when the sound waves strike a surface that will vibrate, the sound is bounced back as a new set of sound waves. An echo is an example of a sound that strikes a surface that bounces it back. In a small room, a noise sounds much louder than it does in a large hall, or out of doors, because the four walls, the floor and the ceiling all bounce the sound back—unless they have been "soundproofed" by being covered with a material that absorbs sound. A surface that vibrates and bounces back the sound is said to "reflect" sound.

The famous Whispering Gallery at the Museum of Science and Industry in Chicago has remarkable acoustics. A tiny whisper anywhere in the room can be heard easily at any other point in the room. The walls, ceiling, and floor surfaces are planned so that sound will bounce about evenly. It will reach all of the room without being lost, or "absorbed," and will be clear wherever it is heard.

Museum of Science & Industry, Chicago

A simple illustration will show the workings of these principles. Any toy noisemaker will do for the experiment. Sound it in the bathroom with the door closed, and the noise will be very great; the bathroom floor and walls are hard and sound-reflecting, and even the bathroom fixtures help to reflect the sound. Open the bathroom door and do it again, and it will not sound so loud. Then take it into a large room, and the sound will be still softer.

HOW THE ACOUSTICS EXPERT WORKS

Giving a theater, hall or other room good acoustics is a difficult scientific problem. First, the acoustics expert will want to know exactly what kind of sound is to be used in the room. If he wants the hall to be suitable for piano concerts, he will find out exactly how long it takes the sound of a piano's notes to reach the farthest corner of the hall, and how long it takes that sound to bounce back. He will then choose wall coverings, and sometimes coverings for the ceiling and floor as well, that will bounce back the sound at the right rate of speed to make the piano seem at its very best in all parts of the hall at the same time. If the hall is to be used for a large orchestra, he does the same thing with the sound of the orchestra at full strength. If it is to be used for speakers, or actors, he tests it for keeping the sound clear at the back of the hall even though the speaker uses only a normal tone of voice. It is possible to arrange the acoustics of a large auditorium so that a whisper at one end of the room can be heard clearly at the other end—even several hundred feet away. If the hall is just being built, the problem is one on which the architect and acoustics engineers will work together, and the shape of the walls and height of the ceiling may be planned so as to give the room good acoustics.

There is more information on this subject in the article on SOUND.

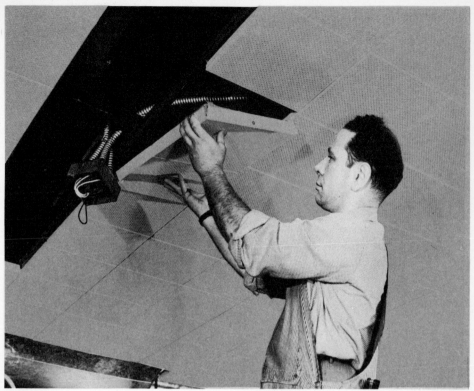

Johns-Manville

Good planning can make a noisy room much quieter. The acoustic ceiling this man is putting up will absorb a great deal of the clattering noise made by typewriters in the office. Those square blocks are made of metal with a lot of little holes, and they are filled inside with a sound-absorbent pad of mineral wool. You can't see the pad inside, but when sound hits the holes in the metal it bounces into the pad. The pad absorbs the noise and softens it.

Westinghouse Electric

When an acoustics expert wants to measure sound, he must have a place where he can be absolutely certain that he will measure only one sound, with no echoes or reflected sounds mixed in. For this, rooms with walls, floors and ceilings like those shown at the right are used. This man wants to find out exactly how noisy the tank vacuum cleaner will be, so he tests it in a room that cannot reflect any sound at all. The box he has gives him an exact measure.

acrobat

Acrobats are men and women who turn handsprings and somersaults, throw each other around, jump, and do other tricks requiring strength and skill. They perform in circuses, on the stage, and on television shows. Years of practice and good teamwork are needed to make a fine acrobat. The tricks done by acrobats are called *acrobatics*.

The chief kinds of acrobat are:

TUMBLERS and LEAPERS. They turn handsprings and somersaults (but all acrobats can do that very well). The tumblers and leapers also train themselves to jump in the air, turn one or more somersaults in midair, and land either on their feet or on their backs. It would seem that when they land on their backs they would be hurt, but they are not because they land at exactly the right point and are rolling as they do so, so that no part of the body hits the floor or the ground too hard.

BALANCERS. These are the acrobats who build themselves into formations with perhaps one of them (called the "understander") standing on the stage;

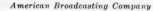

Acrobats have been popular in circuses for years, and are often seen on television.

American Broadcasting Company

two more acrobats standing on his shoulders; and maybe three more acrobats standing on their shoulders. It might seem that men must be very strong to do this, especially the one who holds up all the others, but this kind of acrobatics can be done without great strength. Of course, all acrobats are strong, but skill and training mean much more.

TRAMPOLINE JUMPERS. A trampoline is a sheet of heavy cloth, usually canvas, fastened to a wooden frame by dozens of short, very strong elastic cords. When an acrobat jumps on it, he bounces back, high into the air. Some of the funniest of all acrobatic acts are done by trampoline jumpers, who can make themselves bounce into the air in all kinds of funny positions—on their backs, with their arms and legs stuck out in crazy directions, and in other funny postures. Though a trampoline jumper may sometimes make himself seem clumsy, he really is a very skillful performer who always intends to do exactly what he is doing.

Other acrobats are called aerialists, including the trapeze artists who work high in the air; tightrope walkers who walk on wires, or ride bicycles across them, or do other tricks of balancing; and various acrobats who do their tricks on horses, highstands, or even in the water. These are usually not called acrobats, and more can be read about them in the article CIRCUS.

There have been acrobats since the very earliest times, thousands of years ago. A great deal of science goes into their training. This science was improved through the centuries until it reached its peak during the last century. There were many circuses then, in Europe and America, and the vaudeville show, a show made up of several different acts, was especially popular in the United States. When the movies came along, about fifty years ago, both circuses and vaudeville shows became less popular.

Before, there had been jobs for thousands of acrobats; since then, there have been opportunities for far fewer. The coming of television has given them new opportunities. The Japanese and the Italians have developed many great acrobats.

acropolis

In ancient Greece, where nearly every city was at war with nearly every other city at one time or another, each city would have a walled-in section. This would usually be the highest part of town, and was called an acropolis, in Greek meaning "top of the city." Because the acropolis was the safest part of town, the finest buildings would be built there.

The most famous and most beautiful acropolis was the one at Athens. It was built some 2,500 years ago, and is now in ruins, but even the ruins are beautiful. The finest building was the Parthenon, a temple to the goddess Athena. Many consider it the most beautiful building of all time. It was so well built that much of it still stands. In Nashville,

Tennessee, there is a reproduction of this famous building.

acrostic

An acrostic, in its oldest form, is a poem in which the first letters of the lines, reading down, spell a word or even a whole sentence. Almost as long as men have known how to write, they have written poems like this. Even in the Bible, there are acrostics; the 119th Psalm is so written that the first letters of the lines make up the entire Hebrew alphabet.

Very few acrostic poems have been fine poetry. The poets usually wrote them because it was fun to work out the proper words—somewhat like solving a puzzle. Later, acrostics did become a popular type of puzzle, and developed into the "double acrostic" in which both the first and the last letters of a series of words would be used to spell out words running downwards. For example, a person is given five definitions from which he can find the words sound, lover, elope, extra, and prism. When he writes these out in the proper places, the

On the hill you can see the ruins of the Acropolis of Athens, with the Parthenon in the center.

Trans World Airlines

first and last letters spell sleep and dream, like this:

```
S o u n D
L o v e R
E l o p E
E x t r A
P r i s M
```

Such puzzles were very popular throughout the last century and into the early years of this one. More recently, a puzzle called the Doublecrostic has become popular. This is solved somewhat like a crossword puzzle, and the first letters of the words found will spell out the name of the author of some quotation, and the name of the book from which it is taken.

act

An act is one of the main parts into which a play (on the stage) is divided. When an act ends, the curtain goes down and there is a waiting period or intermission of several minutes at least before the next act begins. A smaller division of the play is called a scene, and there may be two or more scenes in an act, though that has become unusual in the plays of today. The ending of an act may be intended to give time to change scenery on the stage; or it may be intended to show the passing of time in the play; or it may be only because playwrights think their audiences become tired if they watch a play too long without an intermission. The theaters of ancient Rome, a little more than 2,000 years ago, were the first in which plays were divided into acts, and there were always five acts in one of their plays. William Shakespeare, the greatest playwright of the English language, also divided all his plays into five acts. There was no real reason to have exactly five acts, however, and today's plays usually have two or three acts, almost never more. Most short plays, lasting less than one hour, are one-act plays.

actinic rays

Some rays, such as rays of light, can produce actual changes in what they touch. These are called actinic rays. The most common example is found in photography. The film is coated with a chemical that changes when light strikes it; when the light striking it is reflected from a person or object, the film becomes a picture of that person or object. This is an actinic effect.

actinium

Actinium is one of the rare, radioactive chemical elements, found in the same ore as uranium. See the article on ELEMENT.

Actium

Octavian, the grandnephew of Julius Caesar, and Mark Antony, who had previously been allied with Octavian, were fighting for control of Rome, the great empire that ruled all the civilized world. This was about 2,000 years ago, in 31 B.C. Their armies met near the little town of Actium, on the western shore of Greece. Their forces were very large. Octavian had about 100,000 men in his army, and 260 warships. Antony had more than 100,000 men, and 220 warships; and Cleopatra, the queen of Egypt, with whom he was in love, joined him with 60 of her warships. The armies never fought. Antony attacked Octavian's fleet, which was commanded by Marcus Vipsanius Agrippa, a great Roman general. Agrippa handled his fleet so well that Cleopatra ran with her ships, and Antony deserted his army and the rest of his ships and followed her. Antony's army and ships surrendered, and Octavian with his army then chased Antony to Egypt, where Antony committed suicide. Now Octavian ruled the entire Roman world, and made himself its emperor, taking the name Augustus. See the articles AUGUSTUS and ANTONY.

Actors and Actresses

actors and actresses

For hundreds and thousands of years, almost as long as men have known how to write, some men have wanted to write plays and there have been people who wanted to act in them. The desire to be an actor or actress seems to be something a person can be born with. And it seems that if he is born with it, nothing will stop him. All through the "Dark Ages" groups of actors toured through Europe, putting on plays for anyone who would watch them, and often they would run out of money and have to beg for food, or be put in jail; but as soon as they could, they would go back to acting again. In England and America too, such acting groups, called strolling players, would travel from one town to another looking for new audiences to watch their plays, and they too would often find themselves stranded and without money far from home. But when they had another chance, they nearly always went back to acting again.

In writing about actors and actresses of plays written in the English language, we must begin with William Shakespeare, not only because he was the greatest of all playwrights, but also because he was the first to write in what we might call the modern English language, enough like the language we speak to-day so that we can still read and enjoy his plays. No play written before Shakespeare's time, about 350 years ago, is ever produced today. Besides, nearly every great actor or actress of the past is best remembered from a performance in one of Shakespeare's plays.

The first of these was Richard Burbage. He was acting when Shakespeare was actually alive and writing plays, and he played in some of Shakespeare's plays the first time they were performed. Of course, he played Hamlet, which is the most popular play Shakespeare wrote and the part that is considered the greatest an actor can play. When Burbage played Hamlet, there was no scenery as there is in modern plays. Yet he was such a great actor that he could make the audience weep, or go wild with excitement, just by the skill with which he spoke his lines.

In those days it was considered quite respectable for a man to act, but not for a woman; and the parts written for women were usually played by boys, who wore dresses and put on long wigs to make them look like women. The fact is that during much of the past it has not been considered respectable to be an actor or an actress. They were thought to be wicked, and nice people would not have them in their homes. During the time of Shakespeare and Burbage, it was differ-

EDMUND KEAN.

Museum of the City of New York

Edmund Kean was a great actor who played the role of Hamlet over 100 years ago.

as a member of the upper classes, and was called Sir Henry Irving. Since then many English actors have become knights, and many actresses have received the title of Dame, which is the same rank for a woman, while in America and throughout the world actors and actresses have come to be persons to be admired and not looked down upon.

Like Burbage and Garrick and many other of the great actors before him, Sir Henry Irving played Shakespeare's plays and was especially famous for playing Hamlet. John Kemble and Edmund Kean, fifty and more years before Irving, were Shakespeareans who played at about the same time, and so was Edwin Booth, who was the great actor of the entire nineteenth century. All were famous for their performances of Hamlet. The famous actresses won their fame in Shakespeare's plays too. Mrs. Siddons, another great member of the Kemble family, and Charlotte Cushman, the first great American actress—and one of the eight women who have been elected to the Hall of Fame—played Shakespeare's plays. These were usually tragic plays. Very few comedians made reputations as great actors before our century. One well-remembered exception is Joseph Jefferson, who delighted many thousands when he played the part of Rip van Winkle, from Washington Irving's story. In our own time, such famous ac-

ent for men; and again about 150 years later, when David Garrick was the great English actor, people in the big city of London felt differently and acting was considered an honorable profession, but then again, after Garrick's time, it fell into disrepute for a time. All that began to change about a hundred years ago. And in 1893, for the first time, an English actor, whose name was Henry Irving, was knighted. That meant he was recognized officially, by act of Queen Victoria,

Traveling companies of actors in England and Europe used wagons like these to live in, and to take their shows from town to town long ago. They gave their shows outdoors.

Museum of the City of New York

Sir Henry Irving was the first actor ever given the title "Sir" in England. This is how he looked playing Shylock in *The Merchant of Venice*, a play by Shakespeare.

Museum of the City of New York

Notice the difference between this picture of Edwin Booth playing Hamlet and Edmund Kean in the same part, on page 34. Booth was born the same year Kean died, in 1833.

Charlotte Cushman is playing the part of Juliet, in *Romeo and Juliet*.

Joseph Jefferson pretended to sleep for twenty years, playing *Rip Van Winkle*.

tors as John Barrymore, Leslie Howard and Sir Laurence Olivier have played as Hamlet. Of course, every one of these actors and actresses has also played in dozens of other plays, but the famous parts are usually the ones for which they are remembered.

Maybe it is not true that actors are born to act, but most of those we have named have been members of large families of actors.

The Kembles and the Booths were big families in which nearly every member was a fine actor, grandparents and parents and children and sometimes more generations than that. In most recent years, the most famous acting family has been the Barrymore family. There are separate articles on all these acting families, and the individual actors and actresses too, in this encyclopedia.

Two of the greatest and most popular actresses in America were from foreign countries, Eleonora Duse from Italy and Sarah Bernhardt from France. Bernhardt could not even act in English, but spoke French; yet, although most of the audience could not understand what she

The great actors and actresses are associated with fancy costumes and courtly manners.

said, she was so good that they packed the houses to see her.

The movies made a great change in the lives of actors and actresses. Before there were any full-length movies—that was more than forty years ago—there were many jobs for actors because that was the only kind of play that could be seen. Every small town would have a play now and then, and in many of them there were companies that put on one play after another for several months of the year. At first the good actors and actresses scorned the movies, thinking that they were not artistic enough; but finally some of the best, like John Barrymore, began to make movies and after that there were few of the fine players, except the oldest ones, who did not turn to the movies now and then. Meanwhile, the movies were developing their own great acting talent. Notable among them were Charlie Chaplin as a comedian, and Greta Garbo as a dramatic actress, both of whom are ranked with the greatest actors of any age.

But during this period the quality of acting improved so much that there would not possibly be space here to name all the fine actors and actresses who have played in this century and who are actually to be seen today. An exception might be made to mention Katharine Cornell, a great actress who has at times put on plays that seemed unlikely to make money, because she thought they were worthwhile and should be seen by those who wanted to see them.

The opportunities offered to actors and actresses today are many, when one considers the movies and television, but not so many when it comes to acting on a stage before a live audience; and every actor wants, and needs, this kind of experience on the stage. However, there are still opportunities in summer theaters, amateur groups, and organizations whose purpose is to help the acting profession. These are discussed in the article on THEATER.

Eleonora Duse was a famous Italian actress.

All Photos Courtesy Museum of Modern Art

Sarah Bernhardt as Queen Elizabeth I.

John Barrymore was one of the famous actors to go from the stage to motion pictures. This is how he looked playing Hamlet.

Laurence Olivier as Hamlet (left); Leslie Howard (Romeo); Norma Shearer (Juliet).

Actors' Equity

Actors' Equity Association is a union, or workers' association, to which nearly all professional actors and actresses belong. It was formed in 1913 to protect the interests of American actors. Producers had been taking advantage of actors, making them rehearse for long periods without pay, then sometimes not even putting on the show; or taking them to a faraway place to put on a show, then not paying them their salaries and leaving them without money to get back home. Actors' Equity Association, nearly always simply called Equity, makes the would-be producer of a show pay the actors to rehearse, and put up enough money in advance to guarantee them their salaries. It is part of the American Federation of Labor.

actuary, a skillful mathematician in the insurance business. See INSURANCE.

Adam and Eve

The story of Adam and Eve comes from the Bible. Adam was the first man, and Eve was the first woman. The first chapter of the Book of Genesis, known as "The Story of Creation," tells how God made the heavens and earth in six days. On the sixth of these days He made Adam, the first man. In the following chapters, it tells that Adam was made out of the dust of the ground, before God made him come to life; and how God then caused Adam to fall asleep, and took out one of his ribs, and made Eve from this rib. (Nevertheless, men and women have the same number of ribs.)

Adam and Eve lived in a beautiful land called the Garden of Eden. It was full of fine fruit trees, and God told them they might eat the fruit of any tree but one. This was the Tree of Knowledge, and whoever ate the fruit of the Tree of Knowledge would become

New York Public Library Picture Collection

An old picture of Adam and Eve, tempted by the serpent, taking the forbidden fruit.

like gods, and know the difference between right and wrong. There was a serpent in the garden, and he said to Eve, "Why not eat the fruit of the Tree of Knowledge? You will not die, and you will become wise." So Eve picked the fruit of the tree and ate some, and gave it to Adam and he ate some. Before this, they had worn no clothes and were not ashamed; but now they thought it was wrong and put clothes on. God saw this, and knew they had eaten the forbidden fruit. (In most stories, this fruit is supposed to be an apple; but the Bible does not actually say what kind of fruit it is.)

God punished Adam and Eve by making them leave the Garden of Eden, and he punished the serpent by saying it would have to "go on its belly" always. Adam and Eve left the Garden of Eden, but lived a long time after that. They had two sons, Cain and Abel, about whom there are separate stories in this encyclopedia; and another son named Seth, and various other sons and daughters. Adam lived to be 930 years old, which seems remarkable now but was not unusual for the men named in the Book of Genesis; the oldest of these men, Methuselah, lived to be 969 years old.

Adam, Robert and James

Robert Adam was one of the greatest British architects. It is said that he "changed the face of London"; and many of the finest old houses in the big American cities, such as New York, Boston, and Philadelphia, are based on the style he set. Though he did his best work nearly two hundred years ago, it still influences our ideas of good taste in buildings and furniture.

Though most of his work was done in London, Robert Adam was born in Edinburgh, Scotland, in 1728. His brother James Adam, who was also a noted architect, but never as famous as Robert, was born there two years later. Robert Adam went to Italy when he was twenty-six years old, and learned a great deal from the ruins of the buildings of ancient Rome, in its "classic" period that dated back to the time of Christ. When he returned to London, he put into practice the many ideas he had formed in Italy. He was the first English architect to use stucco, the first to build a series of houses in one block so that they look like one imposing building, and the first architect to design the interiors and the furniture of the houses he built. Robert Adam died in 1792 and James Adam, who was two years younger, died two years later, in 1794.

Adams

The name Adams has been borne by many prominent Americans. Foremost among them is the family that gave this country two of its earliest presidents, John Adams and John Quincy Adams, and another of its greatest and earliest patriots, Samuel Adams (who was a cousin of John Adams); there are sep-

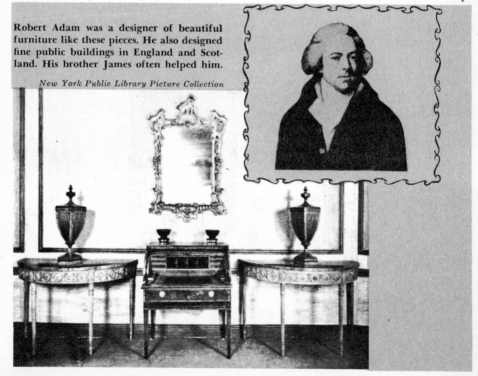

Robert Adam was a designer of beautiful furniture like these pieces. He also designed fine public buildings in England and Scotland. His brother James often helped him.

New York Public Library Picture Collection

Abigail Adams was very helpful to her husband, John Adams, when he was President.

arate articles about these men in the following pages.

Abigail Adams was the wife of John Adams, the founder of this great family. She was the first American First Lady (wife of a president) to live in the White House, which was opened in 1800 while John Adams was still president. She was also the first American woman to have both a husband and a son who became president, but she did not live to see her son president because she died in 1818, and John Quincy Adams was elected president in 1824. There are several biographies of Abigail Adams, some of them for children.

Charles Francis Adams was a son of John Quincy Adams, and was born in 1807. He became a lawyer, studying under Daniel Webster, but instead of practicing law he served in the legislature of Massachusetts, ran for vice-president in 1848 but was defeated, and then served in Congress. During the Civil War he was American minister to Great Britain (a position as important then as that of ambassador is now). This first Charles Francis Adams had three sons who became famous. One of them, also named Charles Francis Adams, was a general in the Union Army in the Civil War, and at one time was president of the Union Pacific Railroad. His brother Henry Adams was a famous professor and teacher who wrote an autobiography, named *The Education of Henry Adams*,

that is considered one of the greatest American books. The third and youngest brother, Brooks Adams, wrote many books of history. Almost all members of this famous Adams family wrote a great deal, both books and letters, and there are many books about them.

In our own century, another Charles Francis Adams (born in 1866) served as Secretary of the Navy under President Herbert Hoover, from 1929 to 1933. The first Charles Francis Adams was his grandfather, so of course President John Adams was his great-great-grandfather. This Charles Francis Adams also won one of the yacht races for the AMERICA'S CUP, about which there is a separate article.

The names of some other prominent Americans who were named Adams, but were not related to the family of President John Adams, are:

Franklin Pierce Adams, better known as F.P.A. (the name under which his best-known writing was done), who edited a daily column called "The Conning Tower" in a famous newspaper, the *New York World,* and also became known to millions by being a member of the panel on a famous radio quiz show, "Information Please." Many of those who became America's best writers had their first writings published, when they were quite young, in "The Conning Tower." F.P.A. was born in Chicago in 1881.

James Truslow Adams was a writer of history, and won the Pulitzer Prize in 1921 for his book *The Founding of New England*. He was born in Brooklyn in 1878 and died in 1949.

Maude Adams was one of the best loved American actresses, especially in the role of Peter Pan, which she was the first to play in the United States. She was born in Salt Lake City, Utah, in 1872, and her real name was Kiskadden, but she used a different name (her mother's maiden name) on the stage, as so many actresses and actors do. She died in 1953.

JOHN ADAMS

No man ever did more to make his native land strong and independent than John Adams, who became the second president of the United States. When John Adams was born, on October 19, 1735, the American states were merely colonies under the rule of the King of England, and no one had dreamed of a nation called the United States. Then the dream was born, and after many struggles and hardships it came true. John Adams played an important part every step of the way. As a young man, he predicted freedom for his country. He was at the first Continental Congress, met to unite the colonies. He helped to write the Declaration of Independence and was one of its signers. Having helped to make the United States possible, he served it first as vice-president —the first man to hold that office—and then as president.

John Adams lived ninety years, the longest life among all presidents of the United States. Late in this long life, he found that his great work had been forgotten by many of the people; he was jeered at by crowds and cursed in newspapers. Sad and bitter, after his term as president he retired to his farm in Massachusetts to live his life out. But in later years he found himself again loved and respected by the American people, and he died a contented man.

Harvard University

HIS EARLY YEARS

John Adams was born at Braintree, Massachusetts, a farming community about twenty miles south of Boston. The Adams family was descended from a Puritan who had come to Massachusetts from England 100 years before that. John Adams' father was a farmer, who made a good living and had gone to college at Harvard; the Adams family were members of the Congregational Church, as were most of the people in that region. In later years, John Adams changed to the Unitarian Church.

As a boy and later as a man, John Adams was small; but he was strong, for boyhood on a farm means hard work and develops a sturdy body. Young John was serious, too, and a good student. He graduated from Harvard when he was 20 years old, taught school for a year at Worcester, Massachusetts, studied law, and in 1758, when he was 23 years old, became a lawyer at Braintree. He was quite successful as a lawyer. When he was 29 years old, he married a girl from nearby Weymouth, Massachusetts, Abigail Smith, who was to become famous as a fitting wife for a great president. In 1768, when he was 33 years old, he moved with his wife and baby son, John Quincy Adams (who also was one day to be president), to the big city of Boston, to practice law there.

THE START OF A GREAT CAREER

While he was still a twenty-year-old school teacher, John Adams had made a remarkable prophecy. America was then an unimportant outpost of a great empire ruled by England. But Adams said, "Mighty states and kingdoms change. A few people came over into this new world for conscience' sake; this apparently trivial incident may transfer the great seat of empire to America. Our people will, in another century, become more numerous than in England itself. The united force of Europe will not be able to subdue us." At the end of the century that he spoke of, the population of the United States was more than double that of England, and not long after it was the most powerful nation on earth.

Then in 1765, while John Adams was still living in Braintree, the English Parliament passed the "Stamp Act." There is a separate article about the Stamp Act in this encyclopedia; briefly, it required that anyone using any sheet of paper as a legal document should buy a stamp to put on the paper, and the price of the stamp went to the British government. This was a tax that Americans would have to pay but from which they would get no benefits—one of the great complaints that led to the American Revolution.

The colonies throughout America argued angrily against the Stamp Act. In Massachusetts John Adams was one of those selected to argue against it before the British Governor in Boston. Addressing the Governor and his Council, Adams declared boldly that the Stamp Act was void, because Parliament had no right to make such a law. It required courage to do this, but Adams was noted for his bravery.

The Boston of 1768, when John Adams took up his profession there, was a city of excited people, most of them unfriendly toward everything British. At one time it seemed that Adams' courage would hurt his popularity with these people. In 1770 the "Boston Massacre" occurred, when a small body of British soldiers led by a Captain Preston fired on a crowd of Bostonians, killing three of them and wounding five more. But Captain Preston had not ordered them to fire, and when he was brought to trial John Adams defended him, and persuaded the jury that Captain Preston was "not guilty." Adams thought his political career was ruined at that point, but he found it was not so. The people respected him just as much—perhaps more—for the courage he had shown. Four years later, in 1774, when the first Continental Congress of the American colonies met in Philadelphia, John Adams was one of the men chosen to represent Massachusetts. It was from this Continental Congress, and the bold decisions it was to make, that the United States of America eventually came into being.

THE STRUGGLE FOR LIBERTY

Eleven of the American colonies sent delegates to the first Continental Congress. They had little idea of full independence for the United States. Most of them wanted only to persuade the King of England to treat them fairly, so that once more they could live happily as British colonies. A few fiery patriots like Patrick Henry of Virginia wanted full independence. John Adams was on their side; he believed that if the British did not change their treatment of the American colonies, the colonies should declare their independence and if necessary go to war to win it.

Little was done at the first Continental Congress, but when the second Continental Congress met in 1775, the spirit was different. Now most of the delegates were willing to take risks in order to have independence. John Adams was there again as a delegate from Massachusetts. Of course he was again on the side that favored independence, and he

When John and Abigail Adams moved into the newly-built White House in 1800, it was a fine suburban mansion, almost out in the country, with just a few near neighbors.

was on the committee that was formed to prepare a Declaration of Independence. This famous declaration was adopted on July 4, 1776, and John Adams was one of the signers.

The Revolutionary War had begun, and the new United States needed help from some powerful European nation. Again John Adams was called upon. Taking along his eleven-year-old son, John Quincy Adams, he went to France and helped Benjamin Franklin to enlist the aid of the French government, which meant so much to the colonies in their fight. Countries at war need a great deal of money, too, and Adams persuaded first the French government and then the Dutch government to lend money to the United States, two million dollars each. Finally, in 1783, John Adams was one of the three Americans (the other two

being Benjamin Franklin and John Jay) who arranged the Treaty of Paris, by which the United States was recognized as a new independent nation. There is a separate article on the TREATY OF PARIS.

HOW HE BECAME PRESIDENT

In 1788, when the people of the United States went to the polls for the first time to choose a president, the manner in which a president was elected was not the same as it is today. Today, each voter votes for a president and a vice-president, two different men. In those days, the vote was cast for one man only, to be president. The person who got the most votes became president; the person who got next to the most votes became vice-president. It was natural that George Washington, the greatest national hero, should be elected president. John Adams got the biggest vote next to Washington's, and was elected the first vice-president of the United States.

At this time, Adams was fifty-three years old. He was a courteous man in his speech, and very polished in his manner. But he was irritable, and was also called "imperious"—that is, he liked to have his own way, and thought his opinion was better than anyone else's. This did not win him a great many friends, though he was admired for his courage and ability.

Washington remained president for two terms, and both times Adams was vice-president. In 1797, when Washington decided he did not want a third term, John Adams got the most votes and was elected president, and Thomas Jefferson got next to the most votes and was elected vice-president.

As president, John Adams had a stormy time. It was a difficult period, and tempers were running high. The French Revolution was under way, and all the kings of Europe were afraid for their crowns, fearing that the revolution would spread to their countries. In the United States, there was argument as to whether the rich people only, or all the people, rich and poor alike, should rule the country. The most tactful of presidents would have had trouble keeping everyone satisfied. John Adams, with his habit of being outspoken and courageous in the face of possible unpopularity, was sure to make enemies—and he did.

Adams had never approved of the French Revolution. He thought it went too far, especially when the revolutionists there killed the French king and queen. The American government, he believed, should have titles of nobility, such as were used in European countries, and it should have a senate made up of "the aristocracy"—that is, the families that were richest and most prominent. This idea was unpopular with the majority of Americans, and Adams was ac-cused even of favoring the establishment of a king in the United States, though this was not so.

Then came the "XYZ Affair." The revolutionary government of France was doing a great many things that seemed unfriendly to the United States. American ships were being captured on the high seas by French privateers (that is, pirates acting with the consent of their government), and the French government would not stop them.

Some private representatives of the French government proposed that the United States should pay a large amount of money, perhaps $250,000, to have the attacks stopped. The French representatives who made this proposal re-fused to sign their names, and used only initials; that is why they were called X, Y and Z, and the whole thing was called the XYZ Affair. The American people were greatly angered by this. Their slogan was, "Millions for defense, but not one cent for tribute." Many of them wanted to go to war against France if necessary. But President Adams was un-willing to risk another war. All this happened in 1797 and 1798, the first year that Adams was president, and it made him very unpopular.

The Alien and Sedition Acts also hurt his popularity. Under these laws, passed by Congress, foreign-born persons, or those who criticized the government, could be arrested and punished. This vio-lated rights that had been guaranteed to the people by the Constitution. The Alien and Sedition Laws were so hated by Americans that they did not last very long, but people did not soon for-get that Adams had been in favor of them.

Thomas Jefferson, who liked the most republican form of government, with no king and no nobility, and who opposed the Alien and Sedition Laws, became the country's most popular man. When John Adams ran for re-election as presi-dent in 1800, Jefferson beat him easily.

Adams was so angry that he would not even stay in Washington to see Jefferson inaugurated as president. He went back to his home in Braintree, Massachusetts, angry at everyone, and particularly at Jefferson. He felt that his great work on behalf of the United States was no longer appreciated.

THE COMING OF PEACE

Now the career of John Adams seemed to be ended. He was 65 years old. He had lost an election, and he considered himself an old man, too old ever to try to seek public office again. He did not know he was to live for twenty-five years more.

In his home at Braintree, he watched everything that happened throughout the world. Often he would express his opinion, and the newspapers would always print it, because the opinion of such a famous man is always news. Soon, the American people had forgotten the things they were angry about, but they remembered John Adams as a great patriot. They eagerly awaited his advice on questions of the times. John Adams and Thomas Jefferson became friends again and wrote each other letters until they died, letters that are intensely interesting and have since been published.

John Adams also watched with great interest and pride the distinguished career of his son, John Quincy Adams, who became president while his father was still alive.

Finally, at the age of 90, John Adams passed away. He died on the Fourth of July, 1826, fifty years to the day after the Declaration of Independence was signed.

It is said that when John Adams was dying, a 90-year-old man propped on his pillows in the Braintree farmhouse, his last words were, "Thomas Jefferson still survives." It would have been better English if he had said only "Thomas Jefferson survives." But he would have been wrong in either case. There was no telegraph in those days, and it took weeks for news to get from Jefferson's house in Virginia to Adams' house in Massachusetts. John Adams could not have known that Thomas Jefferson had died on that same Fourth of July, a few hours earlier. The great men of the American Revolution—George Washington, Benjamin Franklin, Patrick Henry, Samuel Adams, John Hancock, Thomas Jefferson—they were all gone when Adams went. He had been the first to get into the fight. He was the last to leave it.

THE CONSTELLATION'S VICTORY

While John Adams was president, the United States quarreled with France because French warships were capturing American merchant ships. The United States built two great frigates (fast warships). Their names were *Constellation* and *Constitution*. They could outrun and outfight anything on the seas. On February 9, 1799, the *Constellation* was cruising in the West Indies and sighted a French ship, *L'Insurgente*, which had been preying on American shipping. Commodore Truxton, commanding the *Constellation*, chased the French ship, caught it, and in an hour and a quarter defeated it so decisively that the French Captain Barreault surrendered. The *Constellation* carried only 32 guns and 300 men; *L'Insurgente* had 40 guns and 409 men. But the *Constellation* lost only three men and *L'Insurgente* lost seventy. A song was written to celebrate Commodore Truxton's great victory. Both *Constellation* and *Constitution* can still be seen in the Charlestown Navy Yard at Boston, Mass.

John Quincy Adams was the sixth president of the United States, elected in 1824 and serving from 1825 to 1829. He was the son of President John Adams, the only case in which the son of a president has become president. He is also the only former president who returned, after his term of office, as a congressman in the House of Representatives (Andrew Johnson, after having been president, served as a senator). Though John Quincy Adams was recognized as a superior man and a most valuable man to his country, his accomplishments were not spectacular, and the one principally worth remembering—the Monroe Doctrine—bears another man's name.

HIS EARLY YEARS

There was no other boyhood in American history like that of John Quincy Adams; there could not have been, for no other boy ever had the opportunity to be present in person at such an eventful period in the birth of a nation. He was born in the family home at Braintree, in Massachusetts, on July 11, 1767, while his father, John Adams, was still no more than a

Museum of Fine Arts, Boston

successful Massachusetts lawyer. Like his father before him, he was a serious and studious child, but even more so.

When John Quincy Adams was only 11 years old, his father was sent to France as representative of the American colonies, which were engaged in the Revolutionary War for their independence; and John Adams took his 11-year-old son with him. In France, the young John Quincy Adams went to school for two years and learned French, which was to be of value to him in his later work as an American diplomat. Then his father went as American representative to Holland, and again the boy went along, attended school in Amsterdam, and became familiar with the Dutch language. When John Quincy Adams was 14, he accompanied the American minister to Russia, Francis Dana, as his secretary and acquired still more knowledge of the world, its peoples, and its languages. After a return to America, he made still another trip to France with his father, when he was 17. Then he entered Harvard College, and graduated in 1787, when he was 20. After college he studied law and could have been a lawyer, but he preferred politics.

The political genius of John Quincy Adams became apparent when he was still a very young man. The burning issue of the years shortly after 1789 was the French Revolution which had broken out in 1789, and the question of the day was, what should be the attitude of America? John Quincy Adams, without signing his own name, wrote two series of articles for the Boston newspapers. They were so well done that many readers thought his father, the wise and experienced John Adams, had written them. George Washington, as president, considered this young man one of the country's most valuable diplomats, and kept him engaged from 1794 to 1801 as the United States minister in Holland, England, and Prussia. During this period, in

1797, John Quincy Adams married Miss Louisa Johnson, the daughter of the American consul in London.

Nevertheless, as John Quincy Adams approached his fortieth year, he decided that his political career was finished. He accepted a position as a professor at Harvard, and was satisfied to spend the rest of his life there.

HOW HE BECAME PRESIDENT

The year was 1809; James Madison was president of the United States; and it was a troublous time for the world. Napoleon, with his fearsome French army, off and on was at war with the world. The British, his chief enemy, fought back with their powerful navy, capturing any ships at sea that were trading with France or its allies; and often this included American ships. President Madison was having a hard time keeping the country at peace, when some of the most influential American men were pressing him to go to war against England rather than let the country's shipping be swept off the seas. In this unpleasant situation, President Madison would not let one of the country's best diplomats go to waste in a teaching job. He persuaded John Quincy Adams to re-enter public service and become minister to Russia; and Adams, to whom politics was a first love, left Harvard and accepted the appointment. From that time until his death, he was uninterruptedly in public life.

War finally came, the War of 1812, and it was fought and finished. In 1817, James Monroe became president and called John Quincy Adams back from abroad to become Secretary of State. He served in that position throughout the two terms, eight years, of James Monroe's presidency, and it was toward the end of this period, in 1823, that the Monroe Doctrine was pronounced.

The French Revolution was now over. The kings of Europe again felt safe on their thrones. They began to give thought to the smaller revolutions that had succeeded while they were engaged with France—the revolutions that had made the Spanish-speaking countries of South America independent republics. Why, thought the kings, should we not now send our armies across the seas to re-conquer these weak countries of South America and bring them again under European control?

That was the time when John Quincy Adams proposed an American statement that this country would not permit any European power to interfere with the independence of any country in our part of the world. President Monroe stated it in a speech, and it became a policy of the United States that has never been changed or weakened. Since the United States became strong enough to fight any number of foreign enemies, if necessary, the Monroe Doctrine has seemed a simple thing to enforce; but in 1823 the United States was not a strong country, and it took great courage and boldness to defy the powerful nations of Europe.

HIS ELECTION AS PRESIDENT

The presidential election of 1824 was one of the closest the United States ever had. No one got a majority. Andrew Jackson, who later would be elected president twice, got 99 votes in the electoral college; that was the most. John Quincy Adams was second with 84 votes. William H. Crawford of Virginia had 41, and Henry Clay, the great Kentucky senator, had 37. Since no one had more than half the votes, the House of Representatives had the right to decide the presidency—the same system that would be used today if no candidate for president had a majority (more than half) of the votes in the electoral college.

When it came to a vote in the House of Representatives, Henry Clay had enough influence to make his supporters vote for John Quincy Adams, and Adams was elected president over Jackson. When he took office, Adams ap-

The first steam locomotive in the U.S. was bought from England in 1828, when John Quincy Adams was President.

the following of Andrew Jackson, which had been the largest in the United States in the 1824 elections, even though it was not a full majority, became larger and larger until, in 1828, when the next elections were held, Jackson won easily and Adams lost.

John Quincy Adams was not disturbed. He had served well during his life, and he was satisfied to go back to his home in Quincy, Massachusetts, and live quietly. He was a scholar, an excellent writer of both prose and poetry, and a fine speaker. He had nothing to fear of the future.

THE CROWNING OF A GREAT CAREER

So John Quincy Adams went back to his home, rich and famous and admired, and did not dream that he would ever again be a public figure. Then, two years later, his community asked him to be a candidate for Congress. He accepted. He was elected by a big majority, and from then until the end of his life—seventeen more years—he served in the House of Representatives, always speaking for the wise and honorable course in government. He did not live to be 90 years old, as his father had, but he lived to be 81, and they called him "The Old Man Eloquent." He died as he would have wanted to, from a stroke while he was actively serving in Congress, on February 23, 1848. His last words were, "This is the last of earth. I am content."

pointed Clay to be Secretary of State, and there was some talk of a "deal." But actually there had been no arrangement between Adams and Clay. The two men had served together in negotiations in Europe, and Clay had reason to support Adams rather than Andrew Jackson, who was his bitter political opponent. Just as Clay liked Adams enough to elect him president, Adams liked Clay enough to make him Secretary of State.

Very little happened while John Quincy Adams was president. There was peace in Europe, which meant that the United States was not drawn into the arguments of foreign nations. The Erie Canal was opened, and the first railroads were built, and both contributed to the improvement in transportation that was eventually to mean so much in making the country big and prosperous. Slavery was occasionally an issue, and Adams (true to his New England background and sentiments) was always on the side of those who opposed the extension or encouragement of slavery. Meanwhile,

Adams, Samuel

It is sure that no one did more to make the United States a free and independent nation than did Samuel Adams of Boston, one of the great founding fathers. It may be that no one else did so much. Samuel Adams wanted the revolution more than anyone else. He stirred up the spirits and tempers of Americans when otherwise they might have been content to make a bad peace with the English king. He started some of the dramatic events, like the Boston

Tea Party, that "stirred men's souls." He faced danger and dared the fates time after time. From the success of the revolution he gained far less in fame and fortune than any of the others who approached him in stature. Yet he did not seem to care.

A cousin of John Adams, the second president, but a few years older, Samuel Adams was born in Boston in 1722. Like his cousin John, he went to Harvard. Also like his cousin John, he had independent ideas when he was quite young; at the age of 21, he proposed the question, "Is it not lawful to resist the king if you cannot otherwise preserve your country?"

Samuel Adams was in business, but he did not make money; in fact, he lost what little money he had. He was more interested in opposing the harsh acts of the English king and Parliament, which were then trying to collect unfair taxes from the American colonies, not yet a separate nation.

When in 1765 the Stamp Act was passed by Parliament, forcing Americans to buy a tax stamp and put it on every piece of paper used in legal transactions, Samuel Adams opposed it vigorously. The British did not like that, but they were trying to keep the Americans peaceful, and General Thomas Gage, who commanded all the British soldiers in this country, called Samuel Adams to him and said, "You should make your peace with the king." Adams, who was a Puritan and very strict in his religion and behavior, answered, "I have made my peace with the King of kings. I will not abandon the cause of my country."

In 1774 a Continental Congress was called in Philadelphia, with representatives of eleven of the American colonies present. Samuel Adams was a delegate from Massachusetts, and he was one of the few (that included Patrick Henry of Virginia) who were in favor of full independence for America. In fact, he had already been talking about full in-

New York Historical Society

Samuel Adams was known for his humor and witty sayings, as well as for his patriotism.

dependence for five years. In a speech at the Continental Congress, he said, "If only one of a thousand could live and keep his liberty, and the other nine hundred and ninety-nine had to die, I would still favor it. One free man must enjoy more happiness than a thousand slaves."

General Gage did not forget that Samuel Adams had defied him. He sent the British troops out of Boston on April 18, 1775, because he had heard that Samuel Adams and John Hancock were staying in Lexington, Massachusetts, and he wanted to capture them. Paul Revere's famous ride was chiefly to warn Adams and Hancock that the British soldiers were coming to get them. Of course, what happened was that a battle began at Concord and it started the Revolutionary War. But Paul Revere had succeeded in warning the two patriots and they escaped. Later, when General Gage was still trying to make peace with the colonies and bring them back under the rule of the British king, he offered a pardon to everyone except Samuel Adams and

John Hancock, whom he called "arch traitors."

When the Revolutionary War was won, Samuel Adams returned to Boston. He served as governor of Massachusetts, 1794 to 1797, but he never held any national office that might reward him for the good work he had done. He lived and died a poor, hard-working man, but with the satisfaction of knowing he had succeeded in helping a great country to get its start. Samuel Adams died at the age of 81, in 1803.

Addams, Jane

Jane Addams was a woman who spent all her life trying to help people who were not as fortunate as she was, who did not have comfortable houses to live in and warm clothes to wear when it was cold, or enough food to eat. She was born nearly a hundred years ago, in 1860, and she died in 1935, when she was 75 years old. She never married. Because of the work she did, Jane Addams became famous throughout the world, and the place in Chicago where she helped the poor people, a place called Hull House, became famous too. Very few men or women have done as much to help people to better, happier, lives as Jane Addams did. In 1931 she was given the Nobel Peace Prize, because of other work she had done to bring peace to the world.

When Jane Addams was a little girl, most working men in factories did not make enough money to support themselves and families decently. Jane was born a rich girl, but she suffered when she saw how much worse other people lived. Her original home was in Cedarville, Illinois, near Chicago. When she had grown up and graduated from school (Rockford College) she went to Chicago and with a friend, Miss Ellen Starr, rented a building in Chicago that had been built by a man named Hull. In this building she and Miss Starr, and other people who wanted to help the poor, taught the poor people how to take care of their children better, eat better, clothe themselves better, and even earn more money. At the same time, Miss Addams and her helpers at Hull House were working to keep the employers of these people from paying them too little and working them too hard. Working conditions in the United States are now far better than they used to be, and much better than they are on any other continent, and much of the credit for this improvement must be given to Jane Addams.

adder

The name adder is used for several different kinds of snake. It is not really the name of the snake; it is just another name for other snakes, usually snakes that are properly called vipers. For example, the moccasin is often called a *water adder,* and the copperhead is often called a *red adder.* These are very poisonous snakes. Perhaps the best-known snake that is called an adder is a viper found in Africa and called the *puff adder.* Its name comes from the fact that it puffs up its body like a big balloon. It is very poisonous, but will attack only if it is bothered by someone.

The puff adder, a poisonous African snake.

American Museum of Natural History

British Press Service

Few people in Addis Ababa have their own radios. They listen to public newscasts.

Addis Ababa

The capital city of the empire of Ethiopia, in east Africa, is named Addis Ababa. It is quite a big city, with a population of perhaps 400,000, but in other ways it is unlike any big city you might ever dream of. There are only a few paved streets, in one section of the town. There are only a few modern buildings. Most of the large population lives in thatched huts (built of mud and covered with matting made of leaves and straw), and thousands live in tents. Addis Ababa is not very far north of the equator, and it is quite hot there all year around, so the people do not need a lot of shelter.

Though Addis Ababa is less of a city than any other capital in the world, even so it is much better than it was only twenty or so years ago. Now there are some modern buildings, and a few factories; there is a good hospital, and there are roads leading from the city to neighboring Eritrea. There has been a railroad from Addis Ababa to the seaport of Djibouti, since 1917.

All of Addis Ababa lies on a high mountain, about 8,000 feet high, surrounded by even higher mountains. In the highest part of the city, there is the royal palace. It is somewhat like a fort, with walls around it, and it is not a fine building like most royal palaces, except for a few rooms being more like a barracks where soldiers live.

Addison, Joseph

Joseph Addison was an English writer who lived about 250 years ago. He became famous for his essays (short compositions in which the author expresses his personal opinion), and also because he was one of the first men to publish a magazine. Addison was the son of a minister and was born in 1672. He usually had some kind of

Addison

government job, and was able to earn a comfortable living, which was a good thing because in those days it was hard to make much money by writing.

Addison wrote some poetry, and two plays, but he is best known for his essays in *The Tatler* and *The Spectator,* which were called newspapers but were more like today's magazines. *The Tatler* was published three times a week in London, capital of England, by Richard Steele, a friend of Addison's. *The Spectator* was published by Addison and Steele together, daily from March, 1711, to December, 1712.

Adelaide

Adelaide is the name of the capital city of South Australia, one of the seven states into which Australia is divided. Though its population figures make it seem small, Adelaide is really a big and important city, and one of the most modern in the world. Its population is 35,032, but most of its people live in suburbs and the total is nearly 400,000. There are many factories, banks and insurance companies, schools and colleges, and churches. Seven miles away is Port Adelaide, through which the goods of the big state of South Australia are shipped out and goods that it buys are brought in. Port Adelaide was where the first settlers of South Australia landed, and they planned and began to build Adelaide a year after, in 1837. Gold was found in Australia soon after that, and Adelaide became one of the big gold-selling cities of the world. Since then it has become more of a business center. The river Torrens flows through Adelaide, to Port Adelaide and the sea.

Aden

Aden is the name of a large territory on the southern coast of Arabia; it is also the name of the large body of water, called the Gulf of Aden, that forms the sea coast of this territory; it is the name of a small British colony within this territory, and of the city that is the capital of that colony. Most of the territory is a

Adelaide is the capital of South Australia. It is a beautifully planned city, with many parks and fine modern buildings. The Mount Lofty range is just a few miles away.

Australian News Bureau

British protectorate, which means that while it does not belong to the British, and they do not have the right to govern or tax the people who live there, they can use the territory in time of war as a base for troops, airplanes, and ships.

The whole territory of Aden has about 120,000 square miles, which makes it about the size of the state of Arizona, and its population too is about the same as that of Arizona, being 670,-000. Also like Arizona's, the territory is mostly desert, with mountain ranges running through it, and with a very hot, rainless climate. Along the coast of the Gulf of Aden, however, there is much rainfall in the summer. The people of Aden are mostly Arabs, and are Mohammedans. There are no railroads, and very few roads; most travel is by camel caravan.

The British colony of Aden is a tiny peninsula, actually a rocky mountain less than 2,000 feet high, that sticks out into the Gulf of Aden. The mountain was once a volcano, and the city of Aden is built in what was the crater of that volcano. This was called Aden originally because of its wonderful climate; the name Aden is the same as Eden and means "paradise." The sun shines brightly all year, with seldom a cloud and almost never rain.

ADEN (PROTECTORATE). Area, 121,995 square miles. Population (1950 estimate), 650,000. Languages, English, Arabic, and others. Religion, chiefly Mohammedan. Government, self-governing protectorate of Great Britain.

Adenauer, Konrad

Konrad Adenauer was one of the men in Germany who were against Adolf Hitler and the Nazis, and did not want them to start World War II. After the war, Adenauer became the chancellor (head of the government) in West Germany. Adenauer was born in 1876, so he was almost 70 years old when World War II ended in 1945. He had been Mayor of Cologne, one of Germany's biggest cities, before Hitler came to power. The Nazis put him in a concentration camp, a sort of prison where they kept people who disagreed with them. Allied troops freed him and he became leader of the Christian Democratic Union, one of the chief political parties in West Germany.

Adenoids

Between the nose and the throat there are some tiny organs of the body called "lymph glands" which are useful in keeping the body healthy as long as they are healthy themselves, but which often swell up until they nearly block the throat. When this happens, the condition is called adenoids.

Adenoids is a disease of children. It seldom happens to adults. When a child does have adenoids, it may cause earache or eye trouble; and especially it interferes with the breathing because of the way the passage in the throat is narrowed. A child with adenoids has trouble breathing through his nose, and constant breathing through the mouth is not good. Also, adenoids can cause a great deal of snoring, coughing or sneezing, and difficulty in speaking clearly.

Adenoids should almost always be removed. It is a simple operation, and within a few days both the operation and the adenoids are forgotten and the child feels much better. Of course, a doctor should always be consulted.

adhesives

Adhesives stick things together. Glue is an adhesive; so is paste, and so is the gum on the sticky side of a postage stamp. There are different names usually used for different kinds of adhesives, depending on what they are made of: *paste* is made of starch, such as flour; *glue* is made of animal products, for example the bones of animals; *mucilage* is made from gummy parts of plants; and *cement* is a solid substance, ranging from powdered stone to rubber

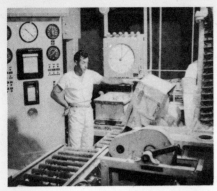

The sticky side of adhesive tape is mixed in a machine such as the one the man is watching here. The different things that go into it are measured and mixed as carefully as the things that go into a cake. Before the sticky substance, or adhesive, is spread over the cloth or ribbon that is the tape, it must be mixed by powerful beaters until there is not a single tiny lump left in it. Otherwise, it would not be a perfect adhesive. Even a very tiny lump would make an air space, and that would be a spot where it could not stick. All of a perfect adhesive should stick.

One kind of adhesive is paper paste, which is made in tanks like this. It is powder at first, and then water is added to turn the powder into paste. It has to be heated, and almost cooked, before the right amount of adhesive quality, or stickiness, will develop. After this man has mixed the paste until it is absolutely smooth, it will be put into large barrels and shipped to other factories where it is put in smaller jars. Millions of tons of paste a year are used in the United States.

and many plastics, that can be dissolved or made soft with a liquid. In the case of nearly all adhesives, the liquid dries in the air and the solid part of the adhesive is left to keep the two things joined together.

Nearly everything is porous, meaning that there are tiny holes in it. While an adhesive is in its liquid or wet form, it can flow into those tiny holes. When it dries out, there are still parts of the adhesive in the tiny holes. This holds them tightly, just as the roots of a tree are held tightly in the earth. If the adhesive is clinging in this way to two different things that are close together, it holds them together and makes it hard to pull them apart.

Even a material that is not porous, for example glass or china, can be held by an adhesive if its surface is rough. The adhesive will flow under the jagged little points that cause the rough surface, and will form a sort of hook there, making it hard to pull away the adhesive (or anything sticking to it).

These are simple ways in which adhesives work. There are other, more complicated ways. Sometimes an adhesive will actually dissolve the surface of the material it is put on, and when the surface dries the adhesive is part of it. Some adhesives are called "heat sealing"—make them hot enough and they become sticky, but after they cool they are hard and no longer sticky.

Hundreds of different kinds of adhesives are used. Paste is the cheapest, but it is seldom used except for paper, because it will not hold heavy things together. Artists use rubber cement, which is rubber dissolved in a liquid like gasoline; the advantage of rubber cement is that it does not wrinkle paper, and it can be rubbed off paper without leaving a trace, when it is no longer wanted for its adhesive effect. Plastic cements are most often used for mending broken dishes, and for making pieces of wood stick together, as on a

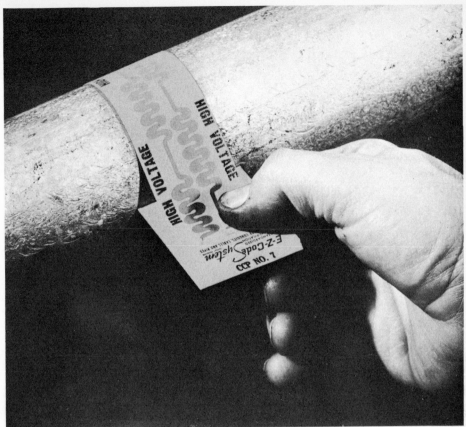

Westline Products Division   *Johnson & Johnson*

Adhesives are used on identification tapes in manufacturing and industry. A tag that is only tied on may fall off and be lost, but the adhesive tag shown here will stay in place. In the picture at the right, a mother is showing another way adhesives are useful. This is surgical adhesive.

chair or table. The invention of cellulose tape opened a large and useful new field for adhesives. The cellulose tape sold as "Scotch tape" and under other trade names is very unusual because the sticky side will stick to almost anything except the smooth side of cellulose tape. That permits the tape to be wound in rolls and handled very easily.

The principle that causes adhesives to join things together is called *adhesion*. You can read more about it in the article on COHESION.

NYSPIX — Commerce

This is one of the beautiful sections of the Adirondacks, with Whiteface Mountain in the distance. Many people visit here in summer, to fish in this river, and enjoy the lovely scenery.

Adirondacks

In the northeast section of New York State are the Adirondack Mountains, the oldest mountains in the United States. They are several million years older than the Rockies. When the center of the earth cooled, many hundreds of millions of years ago, the earth's crust wrinkled and formed mountain ranges in many places. The Adirondacks were among the mountains that pushed up at a time when there were only fish and reptiles living on the earth. Many thousands of years later, a great glacier, or river of ice, moving slowly southward, scraped the Adirondacks as it passed; it cut deep dents that now form many beautiful lakes and make that section of New York State a favorite summer re-sort; it deposited sand and huge boulders along the way, making rocky and sandy slopes in many places.

There are at present about a hundred peaks in the Adirondacks, between 1,200 and 5,000 feet high. Mount Marcy is the highest, 5,344 feet above sea level.

Vacationists go to the Adirondacks for fishing and swimming in the summertime, and, when there is snow on the ground, for skiing and other winter sports. Lake Champlain, Lake George and Lake Placid are perhaps the most famous of the resort lakes.

adjective

A word is called an adjective when it is used to make a noun (that is, the name of a thing) mean more than it would all by itself. If you look out the window and say, "There are men in the garden," anyone who hears you gets a certain idea of what you see. If you said, "There are three men in the garden," he would get a better idea. If you say, "There are three tall young men in the garden," he gets a still better idea. *Three, tall,* and *young* are all adjectives. They are said to "modify" the word *men,* which is a noun, because they give a clearer picture of what the noun means.

A part of speech is a kind of word that has a particular duty when you say it or write it. Noun is a part of speech; the duty of a noun is to tell what a thing is. Verb is a part of speech; the duty of a verb is to tell what something does. Adjective is a part of speech; the duty of an adjective is to tell what a thing is like. An adjective is used to modify a noun, which is, to describe it, to tell how it is different from other things that might be thought of when that particular noun is used.

Sometimes a noun does not mean anything at all unless there is an adjective to describe it or limit it. If you say, "It is a day," it means nothing. If you say, "It is a cold day," the adjective *cold* gives your words meaning.

THE KINDS OF ADJECTIVE

An adjective is said to be *attributive* when it comes before the noun it modifies. If you speak of "a sweet apple," *sweet* is an attributive adjective modifying the noun *apple.* An adjective is said to be *predicative* when it comes after the noun it modifies. If you say, "The apple is sweet," *sweet* is a predicative adjective modifying the noun *apple.*

A predicative adjective can be used only after the verb *to be* in one of its forms (am, is, are, was, were, been); or a word that might be replaced by a form of the verb to be, for example *seem* or *become;* or after a verb that expresses one of our senses: *feel, look, sound,*

taste, smell. You can say, He is healthy, He looks healthy, He seems healthy. Or, The cloth feels smooth, The apple tastes sweet, The music sounds good, The perfume smells good. *Healthy* and *smooth* and *sweet* and *good* are predicative adjectives.

In the English language, adjectives often appear in other kinds of sentence, different from these, because a word or words that would make it clear that they are adjectives have been dropped out— being "understood,". as it is said—because the sentence is perfectly clear without them. Sometimes it is a certain noun that is dropped, as in the sentence, for instance, "The blind read with their fingers." If you put the word "people" after blind, you can see that blind is an adjective. In cases like this, the adjective is always preceded by the word *the,* and its use is called *substantive.* This is only one of many technical terms in grammar. You do not have to know them all to recognize adjectives and use them properly.

COMPARISON OF ADJECTIVES

Often it is desirable for an adjective to show not only what a noun is like, but also to show how it compares with other things of the same kind. Two automobiles may both be fast, but one will go one hundred miles an hour and the other will go only eighty miles an hour. We can use an adjective to show which is which.

When we show this kind of difference between exactly two persons, things, or groups, the word *more* can be used, or *-er* can be added to the adjective, as by saying of the automobile that goes one hundred miles an hour, "It is faster than the other." With short adjectives like *fast, -er* is added. With long adjectives, the word *more* is used because it is easier to say: "Men are stronger than women; John is more athletic than William." This is called the *comparative degree.*

When we compare three or more persons, things, or groups, *-est* is added to short adjectives, and the word *most* is used before long adjectives. This is called the *superlative degree.* "There are three boys, and John is the tallest; but as between the two others, William is taller." "Men are usually heavier than women, but whales are the heaviest animals alive."

Read also the article PART OF SPEECH.

adjutant

The word adjutant means "helper" and is used for an officer in the army who helps the commanding officer by keeping the records of the names and duties of all the men, and by writing letters and issuing orders. The Adjutant General is in charge of the records of the whole army. He must send notifications to the families of soldiers who are missing or lost in battle, and he is in charge of the very complicated machinery by which the millions of soldiers are listed by name and rank and number. In World War I, Peter C. Harris was Adjutant General of the United States Army; in World War II, it was James A. Ulio. In the Navy, the Chief of Naval Personnel has the same kind of duties. The rank of an adjutant general is usually a major general. See also the article ARMY, U.S.

adjutant bird

There is a very big, funny bird called the adjutant, or adjutant bird. It is related to the stork, and is found in India, some of the islands near India, and parts of Africa. It is six or seven feet high, with long legs, a heavy body, and a long bill. It is a dark gray color on its top and wings, and white below. It has a pouch in its neck that it puffs out with air when it flies. The adjutant feeds on small animals and also on carrion—the bodies of dead animals. Feathers from its tail and wings were much used, years ago, in making fans and in decorating women's hats; they are called

N.Y. Zoological Society

This adjutant bird is taller than most men.

marabou because they look like feathers of the real marabou, which is a different bird. The adjutant bird got its name from being seen so often strutting around parade grounds of the British army in India; see the article on ADJUTANT.

administration

In the United States, "the Administration" means the president of the United States and the men and women he appoints to help him as cabinet ministers and other high-ranking officials in the departments of the government. In other words, it is the Executive Branch of the government, which you can read about in the article on UNITED STATES, under the heading Government. In other countries the word is not used in the same way, because they do not have the same system of government as the United States. The Administration is usually made up of persons who belong to the same political party as the President, and it is usually criticized by most of those who favor the political party that lost the last election for the presidency and does not control the government.

The word *administration* is also used to mean management of almost any business, and especially the management of the money and other property left by a person who is dead. When the word is used in this meaning, the person in charge of the management is called administrator.

admiral

In the navy of nearly any country, throughout history, the highest rank an officer could hold was that of admiral. The word originally meant "lord" or "chief." An admiral is an officer who commands all of a fleet of big ships. In the United States Navy, there is now an even higher-ranking title, the Fleet Admiral. Next below an admiral is a vice admiral, and then comes a rear admiral. Any of them is addressed as "Admiral" when you speak to him. The rank of Admiral of the Fleet had been known in the British Navy long before the United States adopted it in 1946.

Admiralty

In the United States, the navy is under the control of the Department of the Navy, which is part of the Department of Defense. There is a Secretary of the Navy who is in charge of the Department of the Navy, and he is usually a man who is not a naval officer; and there is a Chief of Naval Operations who is a naval officer and who advises the Secretary of the Navy.

In Great Britain, the department of the government that does the same thing is called the Admiralty. At the head of the Admiralty are six men. One of them is the head of the whole department, appointed by the Prime Minister, and usually he is not a naval officer. He is called the First Lord of the Admiralty. Winston Churchill was First Lord of the Admiralty during World War I and again during World War II, until he became the Prime Minister. The other five are high-ranking naval officers. The one who ranks highest is called the First Sea Lord. These six men direct the British navy.

Admiralty Islands

Admiralty Island is the name of an island that belongs to the United States, and lies off the coast of Alaska; the Admiralty Islands are a group of small islands in the South Pacific Ocean, thousands of miles away, and they are governed by Australia.

The United States possession, Admiralty Island, is about 90 miles long and about 35 miles wide; its northern tip is only a few miles from the city of Juneau. The island is mountainous, with its highest point 4,639 feet above sea level, or almost a mile. There are many pine trees on Admiralty Island, and they are valuable as timber, while the waters surrounding the island are fine fishing grounds.

The Admiralty Islands in the South Pacific, like so many of the islands in that part of the world, are old volcanoes of which just the tips stick out of the ocean. Coconut trees grow there, and the natives dive for pearls in the clear waters around the islands. In World War II, the Japanese captured the Admiralty Islands and based some airplanes there, but the United States recaptured them in 1944, and they were returned to the control of Australia.

adobe

Adobe houses are found all through Mexico and the Southwest of the United States, western Texas, Arizona, New Mexico, and parts of southern California. The word adobe simply means sun-dried clay in the Spanish language. It has been used for thousands of years in North Africa, and the Spanish learned how to make bricks of clay from the Mohammedan invaders who conquered Spain for a period of a few hundred years, back in the Middle Ages. The Spaniards brought the word to America, and also the best method of making the clay bricks, when they came over four hundred and more years ago.

The adobe bricks are made by wetting clay, mixing it with straw or hay, and packing it into wood frames that make it into the shape of a brick. These frames are put out in the sun, where they dry. After the bricks dry, they are used for building a house. Adobe houses are usually only one story high. They are very comfortable, cool inside in the summer and warm in winter, and also fireproof. Because they are made of clay, which is

This adobe building is a Taos Indian house, in New Mexico. There are no stairways inside, the ladders you see being used instead. A Taos Indian wears different-colored blankets like this one. When he stands in front of the brown walls of an adobe house, the colors make a beautiful picture.

New Mexico State Tourist Bureau

little more than mud, you might think that they would wash away in a heavy rain, but they do not. An adobe house usually lasts 100 years or more, and some are known to have lasted as long as 300 years.

adolescence

Adolescence is the period in which a boy or girl is changing from a child into a man or woman. A boy or girl in this stage of development is said to be *adolescent,* and is called *an adolescent.* There is no definite age at which adolescence begins, and none at which it ends. Some boys and girls become adolescent when they are 10 or 11 years old (or even younger); with some, adolescence does not even begin until they are 14 or 15. Some are out of adolescence by the time they are 18 or 19, while with some it lasts into the twenty-fifth year. However, almost any 16- or 17-year-old is fairly sure to be adolescent.

Some of the signs of adolescence are physical. A boy grows hair on his upper lip and around his chin, and needs to shave; he also grows hair in his pubic region, around his sex organs. His voice begins to change to a deeper level, but is likely to "break" without his being able to control it. In a girl, the physical signs are the beginnings of menstruation, a discharge of blood at regular intervals, which eventually will probably become once each month; she also may begin to grow hair in the pubic region, and her breasts may grow larger and occasionally feel sore.

Changes in tastes and habits are also likely to come during this period. Boys begin to be more interested in girls, and girls in boys. Both boys and girls will have a tendency to take everything too seriously, to feel self-conscious and ashamed whenever they seem to do anything wrong or awkward; to become very particular about the way they dress and what they say and what other people do and say—especially the other people that they love and feel responsible for, like their parents and other members of the family. It is not unusual for an adolescent to feel ashamed of his parents, home, and abilities, in a period like this.

There is no "cure" for adolescence. Everyone has to go through it. The wise adolescent will try to understand what is happening to him, and laugh as others do at the unnecessary worries and fears that are likely to bother him at this time, but that will be forgotten in later years.

Adonis

Adonis was a character in Greek mythology, the stories the ancient Greeks told about their gods and goddesses. Adonis was a very handsome young man. He was so handsome that the most beautiful goddess of all, Aphrodite (whom the Romans called Venus), fell in love with him. Adonis loved to hunt; Aphrodite, who knew it was dangerous, begged him not to. But he hunted anyway, and was killed by a wild boar. As the Greeks believed, this meant that Adonis had to spend the rest of time in the "underworld," which was their version of hell. But Aphrodite persuaded the other gods to let Adonis come up to earth for six months out of every year. She changed his blood into a flower, which we call the anemone, and which blooms every spring. According to the story, when the anemone blooms, it means that Adonis is leaving the underworld and coming to earth to be with Aphrodite. When the cold weather comes again, he must go back to the underworld. Shakespeare wrote a poem about Venus and Adonis.

adrenal glands

The adrenal glands are organs of the body that lie just above the kidneys. What glands are, and what they do, is explained in the article on GLANDS. From the adrenal glands comes a hormone that is called adrenalin. No one knows exactly what makes the adrenal glands

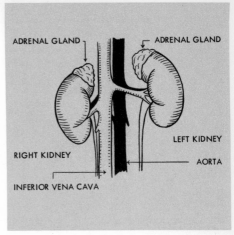

Here you can see how the adrenal glands are placed directly at the top of the kidneys.

work, but when you are threatened with danger, or when your brain tells you that you simply must have extra strength to do something necessary, the adrenal glands pour out more adrenalin, and this flows through the blood to the heart and makes the heart beat faster and your strength increase until you can do what you have to do. It is also the adrenal glands that make you blush when you are embarrassed, and that make your hair stand on end when you are angry or afraid.

There is a drug called adrenalin that strengthens the heart. There are cases in which a person's heart has stopped beating, and he has been thought to be dead, but when adrenalin was injected into his heart it began beating again and he lived.

Adrianople

Adrianople is our name for a city in the part of Turkey that is in Europe. The Turks call it Edirne. It was named for the Roman emperor, Hadrian, about eighteen hundred years ago, and was captured by the Turks six hundred years ago, in the year 1360. It was their capital for nearly a hundred years, and became a great city of 100,000 population, which was large for those times. Then,

Adriatic Sea

The Adriatic Sea is a large body of water, the part of the Mediterranean Sea that runs up between Italy and the coast of Yugoslavia. Many of the principal Italian cities that are famous for their seagoing peoples, such as Venice, are on the Adriatic Sea. So is the city of Trieste, which for many years has been the chief Mediterranean seaport for Central European countries, and after World War II caused trouble between Yugoslavia and Italy. On the Adriatic Sea are many fine harbors, beautiful beaches that are summer resorts for the people of Italy and for visitors to Italy, and a world of cities, buildings, and ruins where one can look into the history of thousands of years ago, when the Roman Empire, on Italy, ruled the world.

Turkish Information Office

This is a mosque in Adrianople. Mohammedan people worship at mosques. The tall steeples are called minarets.

The map shows where the Adriatic Sea lies. The city is Venice, where the sea flows into canals, on which gondolas float about.

Italian State Tourist Office

when they captured Constantinople (now called Istanbul) they made it their capital and Adrianople has never been a very important city since. Its population now is little over 30,000. It is quite a modern city, with fine buildings and some factories.

Advent

The word *advent* means "coming." It is often used to mean the coming of Christ as the savior of the world. In Christian churches, the season of the Advent has been observed for well over one thousand years; it lasts four weeks, beginning with the Sunday that is nearest to Saint Andrew's Day, which is November 30, and lasting until Christmas.

Adventists

Adventists are members of Christian churches in which it is believed that Jesus Christ will again come to earth in person. The Bible says Christ will come again, so this is a part of the belief of every Christian church, but the Adventists have special beliefs as to the time and manner of his coming. There have been several churches of Adventists. The largest in the United States is the Seventh-Day Adventists, who observe the Sabbath on Saturday instead of Sunday. The original Sabbath was Saturday.

adverb

A word is called an adverb when it is used to tell how something is done, or where it is done, or when. An adverb is one of the parts of speech. A part of speech is a kind of word that has a particular duty when you say it or write it. These are the duties of the adverb:

If you say, "The choir sings," you tell what the choir does. If you say, "The choir sings clearly," you tell how the choir does it. The word *clearly* is an adverb that tells how. In the sentence "I saw John yesterday," *yesterday* is an adverb that tells when; in the sentence, "I see him there," *there* is an adverb that tells where.

When a word adds to the meaning of another word, it is said to *modify* it; in the sentence "The choir sings clearly," *clearly* adds to the meaning of *sings*. In this case, the adverb *clearly* modifies the verb *sings*. An adverb may modify a verb, or an adjective, or another adverb. If you say, "It is a very clear day," *very* is an adverb that modifies (adds to the meaning of) the adjective *clear*. If you say, "The choir sings very clearly," the adverb *very* modifies another adverb, *clearly*.

In the English language, most adverbs end with *-ly*. In fact, you can form an adverb from almost any adjective by adding *-ly* to the adjective, as in the case of *clear* and *clearly*. However, there are many adverbs that do not end in *-ly*. The word *there* was one of the examples in the sentences used above.

COMPARISON OF ADVERBS

Often it is desirable for an adverb to show not only how something is done, but also to show how it compares with the way other things are done. Two men may both write well, but one may write better than the other. The word *better* is an adverb that shows how the two men compare in the way they write.

Adverbs are compared in the same way that adjectives are, and this is explained in the article ADJECTIVE. When there are exactly two ways of doing things to be compared, the form of the adverb is said to be *comparative,* and it is formed by adding *-er* to a short adverb, or using the word *more* before a longer adverb. "John came sooner than I did"—*sooner* is the comparative form of *soon*. "John sang more clearly than I did"—*more clearly* is the comparative form of *clearly*.

When there are three or more ways of doing something and you want to compare them, you use the *superlative* form of the adverb, which is formed by adding *-est* to short adverbs, or using the word *most* before longer adverbs. "They all ran fast, but John ran fastest"—*fastest* is the superlative form of *fast*. "They all sang clearly, but John sang most clearly"—*most clearly* is the superlative form of *clearly*.

Read also the article PART OF SPEECH.

Advertising

Advertising

Advertising is telling other people that you have something you want to sell to them. When we say today that a person advertises, we mean he is paying someone else to publish (that is, "to make public") the information that he has something to sell.

There are many ways in which this information may be made public. The different ways are called *media* by advertising men. These may be printed announcements ("ads") in newspapers and magazines; or spoken announcements ("commercials") on radio and television broadcasts; or displays, such as billboards, electric signs, and posters; or direct mail, which means mailing a letter to the person you want to sell to; or souvenirs, such as matchbooks or calendars with the advertiser's name on them; and many other media all the way up to skywriting.

Advertising is a big business in the United States. In a typical year in the 1950s, American businessmen spent more than 7 billion dollars advertising the things they had for sale. The biggest share of this—more than a third—was spent for "space" in newspapers. Another third of the 7 billion dollars was shared about equally by television, radio, and magazines. This means that each of these media received about 10% of all the money that was spent. Direct mail accounted for about 15%. The rest of the advertising money was split up among the many other media.

Advertising is also an art. The best authors and artists combine their skills to write and illustrate the ads. The finest actors appear in commercials on television and radio. It may be a good joke to groan when a commercial comes on, and to skip over advertising pages, but very few persons, fail to notice them. The best brains go into making them attractive and interesting.

Advertising is also a career. Nearly a million people in the United States make their livings from advertising. Nearly every manufacturer or store has an advertising department. There are hundreds of *advertising agencies*, companies whose business is helping other companies to advertise the things they have to sell. Advertising agencies have offices all over the country—all over the world, for that matter. Newspapers, magazines, broadcasting networks and stations, all employ large staffs of men and women in their advertising departments. Advertising work has the reputation of being interesting and giving a bright and ambitious person a chance to make a great deal of money. A large number of boys and girls look forward to advertising as the work they will do when they are out of school.

HOW ADVERTISING BEGAN

It is usual to say that a flower "advertises" to the bees and butterflies, by dressing itself up in bright colors; and that a bird "advertises" when it sings a love song to its mate; and that a man "advertises" every time he makes his wishes known. But that is not the kind of advertising we are talking about here.

It was not really advertising when, in the old days, a peddler used to drive his cart through the streets of a town and shout "Apples for sale!" or whatever words would let the townsfolk know what he had in the cart and was offering for sale. But when a merchant in the Orient would bring his camel caravan to a town, and would spread out his pottery and silks and rugs in the market place, and then would hire someone

Most advertising today depends on pictures for "eye appeal," but illustrated ads were a new idea in 1820, when this pioneer picture was used.

with strong legs and a loud voice to go through all the streets and shout "Abdul the Merchant has arrived at the market place with rugs, silks, spices and other fine things from China!"—that was true advertising, because he was paying someone else to make public the news of what he had for sale.

For many years, even for centuries, that was the chief kind of advertising—the "crier" in the streets. Storekeepers did hang signs out in front of their stores, just as they do today, so that passers-by would know where to buy things. Of course, hundreds of years ago most of the people could not read, so the shoemaker would hang out a big shoe, and the baker a picture of a loaf of bread, and so on; and some of those signs have lasted right down to the present day, for example the barber's pole.

Modern advertising began when printing was invented, about 500 years ago. The first English printer, William Caxton, printed a poster advertising pies; that was in the year 1480, twelve years before America was discovered by Chris-

MEN WANTED for Hazardous Journey. Small wages, bitter cold, long months of complete darkness, constant danger, safe return doubtful. Honor and recognition in case of success — Sir Ernest Shackleton.

100 Greatest Advertisements

Unadorned type was the rule in early advertisements, yet when this one appeared in a London paper thousands of men applied.

topher Columbus. It wasn't long before someone thought of publishing a newspaper, and it wasn't long after that that someone else thought of advertising in a newspaper; it was done in Germany as early as 1591, and in England in 1625. Since that time, or for more than 300 years, nearly every newspaper has published paid advertisements. But until quite a short time ago, these were not much more than printed notices, all looking alike as do classified advertisements in today's newspapers. And in England the advertisements almost always covered the front page of the newspaper. The news began farther back.

The kind of advertising we see today was born and grew entirely in the United States. It was an American invention; and it remains an American specialty.

The first ad in America appeared in the Boston News Letter, a newspaper published in Boston, Massachusetts, in 1704. It was a plain notice, just like the ones in England and European countries. For about 150 years American advertis-

This was one of the earliest series of advertisements to use "jingles."

This is the butcher of Spotless Town. His tools are bright as his renown. To leave them stained were indiscreet. For folks would then abstain from meat. And so he brightens his trade you know By polishing with

SAPOLIO

ing stayed that way. Then it began to change. Ads began to have clever pictures and forceful "copy," written in such a way that people would want to come and buy.

Much of the credit for bringing about this change belongs to the advertising agency. The first agency was opened in 1840, in Philadelphia; others came along in the following years, and by the 1870s there were several. Here for the first time were men whose *only* interest was advertising—planning it, buying it, selling it, and making it pay. In many ways our lives would be much different today if it were not for the revolution in advertising brought about by the advertising agencies.

HOW AN ADVERTISING AGENCY WORKS

An advertising agency is a company, often a very big one, where everyone is an expert on something connected with advertising. There is the layout man, who knows how to fit printing type and pictures together for the greatest "eye appeal." There is the media man, who knows how many people read each magazine, and what kind of people they are, and what kind of merchandise can be sold to them. There is the television man, who knows how to produce a show or a commercial; and the copywriter, who knows how to describe the product well and make people want to buy it; and the "account executive," whose job is to plan the advertising of a particular product or "account." These are only a few examples. There are literally dozens of other specialized jobs in an advertising agency.

The advertising agency's customer is called a *client*. The client is the company that has the product for sale. The agency prepares the advertising, but the client does not pay more than he would have paid if he had gone to the trouble and expense of preparing the advertising himself. Whatever the advertising costs, the agency gets 15% of it—but this is

Lord & Taylor

Every department-store window is an ad—one of the best. This is one of a celebrated group of "Christmas windows" on Fifth Avenue, New York.

paid by the magazine, newspaper, broadcasting company or any of the other media that carries the advertising. The money the client spends for this kind of advertising is called "commissionable" because the agency receives a commission on it. There are some kinds of advertising that are not commissionable; for example, when the agency prepares letters and circulars to go out by mail. In such cases the client pays a fee to the agency for its work, and this is called a "service charge."

Advertising agency business is big business, because so much money is spent on advertising. There are over 200 companies in the United States with a "budget"—for advertising—of more than a million dollars a year. On every million dollars, the advertising agency gets commissions of $150,000.

WHO REALLY PAYS FOR ADVERTISING

Many people have grumbled about the billions of dollars that are spent for advertising. "It comes right out of the cus-

tomers' pockets," they complain. "If the manufacturers didn't spend all that money for advertising, they could sell us the goods that much cheaper."

But could they? It is no accident that people in the United States, where most of the advertising of the world is done, also have most of the desirable goods in the world—automobiles, electric refrigerators and washing machines, good clothes and good food, and all kinds of conveniences in their homes. The United States is a country of mass production. When products are made in great quantities, they cost less and more people can afford to buy them. Manufacturers could not count on selling so many if they could not advertise and let the public know about the product they have for sale. Therefore they would not make so many, and the price of everything would have to go up.

You also hear people complain of the advertisements themselves, especially the commercials on television and radio. "They spoil the show," these people will

All Photos MacMullen Associates

Manufacturers advertise to retailers at "trade shows," also called "industrial exhibits." At these shows, booths are rented to manufacturers who set up displays or exhibits in their booths. These pictures show how the exhibits are designed and finally put together. In the top picture the designers are planning the details. In the center photo the man is fastening samples to a board so they can be seen easily. In the bottom photo you can see a booth that is almost ready to be shipped where the show will be held.

complain. But if it were not for the commercials, no one could afford to put on the shows themselves. It is the advertiser who pays for them. It is also the advertiser that pays for the newspaper and magazine you read. Every newspaper and magazine is sold to you for less than it actually costs. A magazine that you buy for 25 cents may cost the publisher 35 or 40 cents. The publisher sells his magazine at a loss because he wants more circulation—more readers. The greater his circulation, the more he can charge the advertisers. The buyer of the magazine benefits from this.

KEEPING ADVERTISING HONEST

Most advertisers have always been honest, but there have always been some who want to deceive the public. Dishonest advertisers try to make false claims for their products. This could weaken the faith of the public in all kinds of advertising, and everyone would suffer.

Today there are many things that act to prevent an advertiser from being dishonest.

The Federal Trade Commission, called the FTC, is a branch of the United States Government. It checks on the claims made by advertisers. If an advertiser makes claims that are not true, the Federal Trade Commission sues him and forces him to stop. The Department of Health, operating under a law passed by Congress, called the Pure Food and Drug Act, examines foods and medicines to make sure they are as good as their labels say they are. Dishonest claims for patent medicines have become a thing of the past. The selling of products that are poisonous or harmful is rapidly being stopped.

The Better Business Bureaus are private organizations, but like the Federal Trade Commission they expose dishonesty in business and advertising and make it difficult or impossible for a company to fool the public in its advertising.

Honest publishers do not accept advertising unless the manufacturer is substantial and can be depended on, and unless the advertising itself is trustworthy. A would-be dishonest advertiser would have a hard time getting anybody to sell him the advertising space or time nowadays.

There were never many dishonest advertisers, but it takes only a few to hurt all. The advertising business has grown a great deal since the advertisements themselves became more dependable.

HOW AN AD IS MADE

You see an ad in a magazine. How did it happen to be there—that exact ad, in that magazine, on that date?

Here is the way, step by step.

Our story will begin when a manufacturer appoints an advertising agency to handle his advertising for him. Let us suppose that this particular manufacturer makes a brand of soap for washing dishes, doing the laundry, and other kitchen purposes.

First, the account executive of the advertising agency studies the product. He compares it with every other kind of kitchen soap. He will probably send samples to a laboratory, to have it tested by scientists. From the laboratory, he will probably find out what this soap has that makes it different from, and perhaps better than, other soaps.

Next, the account executive wants to know what kind of soap American women want in their kitchens. He may send out a large crew of men and women to go from one house to another and ask the women questions. From the results of this "survey" the agency will make out a list of what is most appealing in a soap.

Suppose they find out that American housewives like soapsuds with fine, small bubbles. And suppose, by coincidence, their client's soap (the laboratory said) happens to make these small, fine bubbles. That will be a "selling point" worth advertising.

Top to bottom: Coopers, Inc., N.Y. Board of Transportation, Outdoor Advertising, Inc.

These pictures show three different kinds of advertising. At the top, photographers are setting up lights and cameras to make an advertising photo. In the middle you can see the posters used to advertise different products in a New York subway station. At the bottom is Times Square at night, showing the huge electric signs called "spectaculars." These are electric billboards. Most of them flash on and off at times, to show different words or make figures seem to move.

The third step is to find the best way to advertise this selling point. They may choose some catchy name, like "pearls," or "beads," to describe the suds made by their soap. Or they may decide to use a certain kind of picture that will surely attract the attention of these women. Or they may decide to pay some famous person to "endorse" the soap, because experience has shown that the name and picture of a famous person will usually attract attention to an ad.

Once they have decided, the production department will take over. The production men will find the best writers, the best artists, the best layout men. They will plan ads that are very appealing in words and appearance.

The next step is to select the media. Suppose the survey has shown that this particular kind of soapsuds appeals most to women whose husbands earn about $4,000 a year and live in medium-sized towns. The media expert will look for any magazine and newspaper that is read by women whose husbands earn about $4,000 and live in medium-sized towns. He will not spend the advertiser's money on magazines and newspapers that sell chiefly to richer women or to poorer women, or in bigger cities, or in smaller towns.

At this point the media department of the agency will present to the client a "schedule." This will be a list of the newspapers and magazines in which the agency thinks the ad ought to appear, with the dates on which the agency thinks the ad should run, and with the price of each ad.

The cost of an ad depends partly on the circulation—number of readers—of the publication. It depends partly on the quality of this circulation. A publication whose readers are rich can charge more than a publication whose readers are poor. Publications with rich readers are called "class" media. Their readers buy more, because they can afford to.

The advertising business is so well organized that all kinds of information are available to every agency and advertiser. An organization known as the Audit Bureau of Circulations (called the "ABC") makes sure that no publication claims a higher circulation than it actually has. Many of the publications themselves make surveys to find out how much money their readers have, and how they spend it. There are independent organizations that make surveys of the same kind. Every magazine and newspaper guarantees that each issue will sell a certain number of copies, or more, and if fewer copies are sold, it has to give some of the advertiser's money back.

The cost of advertising in a newspaper or magazine depends on how much space the ad occupies. The page is always considered to be divided into columns, and each column is measured by the "agate line" or "line." There are fourteen lines to the inch. Each line costs so much, depending on the circulation. If an advertiser takes "a fourteen-line ad," it means his ad is one inch deep and one column wide, and if the price is one dollar per line, he pays fourteen dollars for it.

Advertising in big magazines and newspapers is expensive. A full page in a Sunday comic section in big newspapers throughout the country will cost an advertiser about $30,000, in addition to the thousands of dollars he spends preparing the advertisement itself. Advertising in big magazines, such as Life, costs almost as much. A monthly magazine charges more than a weekly magazine or a daily paper with the same circulation, because the monthly magazine stays around the house longer before the next issue comes, and there is more chance that someone will see the ad. Most magazines are read by the whole family, so when a publication has a circulation of, for example, 3,000,000 copies, they actually have as many as 12,000,000 or 15,000,000 readers. These figures help them to persuade agencies to buy their advertising space instead of space in other magazines and newspapers.

When the schedule, scientifically prepared, has been presented by the agency to the client, the client's advertising manager may make a change or two, here or there, then he signs the schedule. The agency makes out an order to the publication in which the ad is to appear. The agency's production department makes sure that the type is set for the ad, and the art work done, and everything delivered to the publication for its "closing date," which may be from six weeks to three months before the advertisement is actually in the hands of readers. Now there remains only to wait until the ad appears.

CHOOSING A RADIO OR TV SHOW

It may be that women who prefer this kind of soap don't read magazines very much, but do spend a lot of time watching television or listening to the radio. In this case, the agency will probably advise the advertiser to try a radio or television program.

Again, the agency will have all kinds of figures at its disposal. It will know what hours are the best if one wants to reach these particular women, and what kind of show appeals to them best. This may be a play, it may be a comedian, and it may be a quiz, but whatever the survey shows, that is the kind of program this particular client will want to sponsor.

Television is very expensive advertis-ing. Some programs cost four or five million dollars for a single year. But this is not what interests an advertiser most. The advertiser wants to know how many persons will actually see or hear his ad, and how much it costs him for each one. If the advertiser spends a million dollars, and one hundred million persons see his show, it costs him one cent per person to reach them with his advertising. If he can spend two million dollars and reach 500 million people, it costs him less than half a cent a person. This will mean he has spent his advertising money more wisely, even though in actual cash he spent a million dollars more.

DECIDING WHAT TO ADVERTISE

There are many different media for advertising. All have their appeals, because different advertisers have different purposes in advertising.

If a company makes a great many different products, it may want to advertise its company name, rather than any of the products it makes. Its purpose is to persuade people that it is an honest, reliable company, and that any time they see its name on any kind of product, they can feel safe. When a company advertises its own name, instead of the name of one of its products, the advertising is called "institutional advertising."

More often, a company will want to advertise the particular name or trademark it puts on a brand of soap, or canned peas, or chewing gum, or whatever else it makes. In that case, it adver-tises the name of that particular product.

Skywriting is perhaps the latest method of advertising. An airplane, skillfully piloted, trails smoke behind it to make letters. Each letter is about a mile high.

Pepsi-Cola Company

This is called "product advertising."

Another advertiser may want its customers to remember it at all times, not merely from time to time. A taxicab company, for example, may want its name and telephone number to be handy whenever a person anywhere wants a taxi. A company like that might advertise with calendars to hang on the wall, or desk pads, or matches. It would not be likely to advertise in a newspaper, because a person would probably not be looking at a newspaper at exactly the time that he is thinking about calling a taxi.

A company may make machinery and sell to other manufacturers, not to the general public. This kind of company would advertise in trade journals—magazines that are published only for people in a certain line of work. The advertiser would pick a trade journal read by the manufacturers who are most likely to be customers for his machines.

The advertising business has become so huge that you could name almost anything a person might want to advertise, and any way he might want to advertise it, and there would be a well-known place and way for him to do it.

A.E.F., the initials of the American Expeditionary Force, which went to Europe from the United States to fight in World War I.

Aegean Sea

The Aegean Sea is a part of the Mediterranean Sea that runs up between the countries of Greece and Turkey. It

is dotted with hundreds of islands. The most interesting thing about the Aegean Sea is that the earliest great civilization of man was born in the lands around it and on the islands in it. In this region, men were building beautiful buildings, carving beautiful statues, and writing books, three thousand and more years ago. This part of the history of man was known as the Aegean Civilization.

In all parts of the region of the Aegean Sea, the climate is pleasant and mild and the water is clear and beautiful. On many of the islands, there is fine land for farming. These islands have been much fought over, through the ages and right up to recent times. Almost all of them now belong to Greece.

Aeneas

Aeneas was a character in the legends of ancient Rome. He may have been a real person, though surely the many things that have been written about him are stories, not history, and hardly any part of them can be considered true. Aeneas was the hero of one of the greatest long poems ever written, called the Aeneid, by the Roman poet Virgil, who wrote nearly two thousand years ago.

According to the story, Aeneas was a prince of Troy and fought in the Trojan Wars, about which there is a separate article. He was the son of King Anchises and the goddess Aphrodite (called Venus by the Romans). When the Greeks won the Trojan War, Aeneas escaped from the city of Troy and wandered for years until he finally arrived on the land that we now call Italy.

In his wanderings, Aeneas reached Carthage, an ancient great city on the northern coast of Africa. Carthage was ruled by a queen named Dido, and she fell so in love with Aeneas that when he left to put to sea again, she killed herself in her grief.

Next Aeneas landed in the country of Latium, in Italy. This country was ruled by King Latinus. From the country and

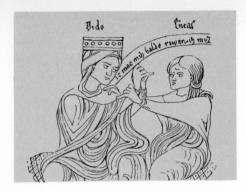

An old picture showing Dido's grief when Aeneas tells her he is leaving.

the king, we get the word Latin, the language of the ancient Romans. Aeneas married Lavinia, the daughter of the king, and founded a city that he called Lavinium. A rival king, named Turnus, had wanted to marry Lavinia, and now he made war on King Latinus. Both kings were killed in battle. The story told in the Aeneid ends here, but later stories say that Aeneas became king of Latium, and that his grandsons, Romulus and Remus, founded the city of Rome, which was later to rule nearly all the world.

aeolian harp

An aeolian harp is a musical instrument, made of strings stretched over a wooden frame. The strings are not plucked, as they are on most stringed instruments of this kind. Instead, the player blows air across them or between them, and the air makes the strings vibrate and produce music. (See the article on SOUND to understand how this happens.) Serious musicians seldom play the aeolian harp, considering it more of a toy than a musical instrument. It was given the name "aeolian" because Aeolus was the god of the winds in Greek mythology.

Aeolus

Aeolus was the god of the winds, in Greek mythology. His home was

thought to be in a group of islands in the Mediterranean Sea, between Italy and Sicily, now called the Aeolian Islands. According to the legend, he kept the winds in caves, and let them out to blow around only when he wished to.

Aerodynamics is the study of how air and other gases move and why they behave as they do; it is very important in understanding why an airplane flies. It will be explained in the article on FLIGHT.

Aeschylus

Aeschylus was a writer of plays, one of the greatest of all time, who lived 2,400 years ago in the city of Athens, in ancient Greece. It was Aeschylus who invented the tragedy, a sad play in which the hero is usually doomed to die.

Aeschylus was born in 525 B.C. Before his time, a serious Greek play would have a big chorus, of perhaps fifty persons, and just one actor. The actor and the chorus talked to each other but did not really act out the story. Aeschylus introduced scenery backgrounds, masks to be worn by the actors, and costumes; he added a second actor and had the actors move around on the stage and really act out the story instead of just reciting their lines. Because of the changes he introduced, Aeschylus is known as the Father of Greek Tragedy. He is thought to have written about ninety plays, of which seven are still known and read. He died in 456 B.C.

Aesculapius

In the stories of the ancient Greeks, Aesculapius was a great physician or healer. Later they called him the god of medicine, and built a temple to him. The priests of this temple were called Asclepiads and they were the doctors of ancient Greece and Rome. There are many stories about Aesculapius, and in some of them it is said that he could bring the dead back to life. One unusual thing about the temples of Aesculapius was that the priests raised snakes in them, and each snake was supposed to hold the spirit of a god.

Aesop

Aesop was a writer who lived 2,600 years ago in ancient Greece. His stories, called *fables,* were so clever and amusing that they are still read today. A fable is a story with a "moral"—that is, a lesson that can be learned from it.

Although Aesop was really writing about the foolish things that people do, the characters in his stories are always animals—foxes, crows, frogs, and so on—who talk and behave like human beings. Here is one of Aesop's fables:

THE ANT AND THE GRASSHOPPER

On a cold frosty day an Ant was dragging out some of the corn which he had laid up in summer time, to dry it. A Grasshopper, half-perished with hunger, besought the Ant to give him a morsel of it to preserve his life. "What were you doing," said the Ant, "this last summer?" "Oh," said the Grasshopper, "I was not idle. I kept singing all summer long." Said the Ant, laughing and shutting up his granary, "Since you could sing all summer, you may dance all winter."

Winter finds out what Summer lays by.

Aesop lived on Samos, a Greek island in the Aegean Sea. He is said to have been a slave who was freed by his master. The exact time or reason for his death is not known, but some writers of history say that he angered a mob of people in the Greek city of Delphi and they threw him over the edge of a cliff.

THE "SOUR GRAPES" STORY

The famous story from which we get the saying "sour grapes" is illustrated at the left. Here is the story the way it was originally told:

A hungry fox stole one day into a vineyard where many bunches of grapes hung ripe and ready for eating. But as luck would have it, they were fastened upon a tall trellis, just too high for Reynard to reach. He jumped, and paused, and jumped again, in the attempt to get at them. But it was all in vain. At last he was fairly tired out, and thereupon, "Take them who will," he cried, *"the grapes are sour!"*

Afghan hound

The Afghan hound is long-legged and slender, like other hounds, but in other ways it does not look a bit like any other kind of dog. It has such long, thick hair on its chest and legs that it almost seems to be wearing fur leggings and chest protector. Its ears are so long they hang down all the way to its shoulder. The tail is unusual, too. The Afghan hound's tail is quite short, and it curls high up over the dog's back like the top of a question-mark, ending in a thin little point.

In Afghanistan, the country where Afghan hounds came from, they are used to hunt leopards and gazelles because they can run so fast, even over land where there are many rocks and high bushes. Afghan hounds are very good jumpers.

Many people keep them as pets, and they are very gentle, quiet dogs, but they are too large for a city apartment, and they need a great deal of care as well as plenty of space for exercise. Their long, silky hair has to be brushed all the time, to keep it from getting tangled and dirty.

The Afghan hound's color can be white, gray, black, tan, or brown. It is about 2½ feet high at the shoulder and weighs about 50 pounds.

Afghan Hound Club of America

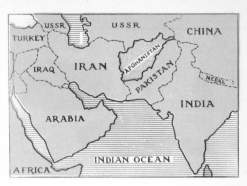

Afghanistan

Afghanistan is a small country in Asia, about halfway around the world from the United States. It is about the size of Texas, having an area of 250,000 square miles, and about 12 million people live there, which is twice as many as there are in Texas. It takes about four days by the fastest airlines to get to Afghanistan, and it would take several weeks by boat and over land. Living in Afghanistan is not at all like living in the United States, or in any country in what we call the Western World. It is only beginning to be a modern country.

THE PEOPLE WHO LIVE THERE

Most of the people of Afghanistan follow the Mohammedan religion, but they belong to several different tribes who came from different places and speak different languages. Through the ages one conquering army after another passed through Afghanistan and always some of the soldiers have stayed there, and married, and formed new tribes.

More of the people belong to the Durani tribe than to any other. The Durani say they are descended from the Jews who were slaves of King Nebuchadnezzar in Babylon, thousands of years ago, as told in the Book of Daniel in the Bible. They call themselves Beni-Israel, which means "sons of Israel." But actually the Durani came to Afghanistan from Persia (the country now called Iran), and they speak a Persian

An Afghan farmer stands before his house; a mounted soldier from a nomad tribe is at the left.

language called Pushtu, which is the official language of the country.

Another big tribe, the Pathans, came originally from India, and still another, the Ghilzais, were once Turks. With the Durani, these tribes make up about half the people of Afghanistan, and together they are called Afghans. (The "-istan" in the name means "held by," so Afghanistan means "land held by the Afghans.")

Among the smaller tribes, there are the Hazars, who once were Mongol people and were brought to Afghanistan by the cruel conqueror Genghis Khan. These are the Kaffirs, who once were Greeks, and whose name means "unbelievers"—that is, people who are not Mohammedans. There are the Tafirs, who may have been the earliest of all the people to live in Afghanistan.

The men of Afghanistan are athletic and handsome. They have dark hair and eyes, and fair complexions. Many have flowing beards. Many of them are great horsemen and marksmen with their rifles, for their people have been warlike for many generations, though they now live at peace with their neighbors. The men can take great hardship, are very stern, and can be very cruel. They are hospitable and kind to visitors, but sometimes two of the smaller tribes, or families, have private fights or feuds, and then they kill one another on sight.

They wear turbans on their heads, and long robes called caftans.

The women still follow some old Mohammedan customs that have been given up in several more modern Mohammedan countries. They cover themselves with long robes that reach to the feet, and wear veils over their faces. They do not eat with the men, or join in men's conversations. A man may have more than one wife—as many as four wives are permitted—though it is more customary for a man to have only one wife, as in Christian countries.

The children first learn to read and write from the Mohammedan priest. He teaches them from the Koran, the Holy Book or Bible of their religion. It is only since 1931 that Afghanistan has had a law requiring all children to go to school.

HOW THE PEOPLE LIVE

Most of the people of Afghanistan are either farmers or shepherds. They are quite poor. The average Afghan makes only $50 a year, not much more than the average American makes in a week.

The farmers live in houses in villages. They have to work very hard, because there is no modern farm machinery and there is not enough rainfall to make the land very fertile. The farmers raise enough food for their families. Their biggest crop is wheat. They also raise cotton, tobacco, sugar beets, and other plants and vegetables, which they sell. The women are famous for weaving rugs and making handmade jewelry, and the children used to help, working all day from the time they were five or six years old. Now they go to school, but they still work during other hours.

About half the people are nomads ("wanderers"). They live in tents and move from place to place. Many of these nomads are the shepherds. Among the sheep they raise is the karakul, from which is made a black, curly fur that is used for women's fur coats.

The government of Afghanistan sends its young, college-trained men to teach the natives how to avoid many diseases, and to explain how inoculation works.

There are several big cities, and Kabul, the capital of the country, has a population of 300,000, with a university, and a college of arts. But only one family out of twelve lives in a city. (In the United States, more than half the people live in cities.) It is only the people in the cities who ever see books or newspapers, but somehow any important news soon spreads all over the country, through the chiefs of the tribes.

Though Afghanistan has laws that apply to all the people, the farmers in the villages and the nomads wandering through the country are ruled in most matters by the chiefs of their tribes.

There isn't much "fun," as the American would think of fun, for either grown-ups or children. No television, no movies; and radio broadcasts are for the few people in the cities, because the farmers and shepherds don't have radio sets. But children love to hear the village "story-teller" read or tell stories, often playing on a stringed instrument like a guitar as he does so.

WHAT KIND OF PLACE IT IS

Most of the people of Afghanistan live in the central part of the country, on level plains with rivers running through them and high mountains rising on all sides. Some of these mountains, the Hindu Kush range on the eastern border, are among the highest in the world.

On the plains, where the farming is done, there is a "rainy season" from December to April, but even during this season there is very little rain. At other times there is no rain at all and the temperature often goes as high as 120°, which is higher than it ever gets in the United States, except in desert regions like Death Valley. The farmers have to depend on the melting snows running down from the mountains in three important rivers, the Amu Darya, the Kabul, and the Helmand. From these the farmers get enough water for their fields.

On the slopes of the mountains, the shepherds tend their flocks of sheep. Here it is sometimes very hot, often

100°, as it is in the valleys, and sometimes it is very cold, 12° below zero—both hotter and colder than it ever is in most parts of the United States.

The people might be rich if they could make use of the valuable minerals in these mountains. It is believed that there are iron, gold, copper, and other metals, and oil, too, in the southern part of the country. But the Afghans lack two things needed for mining. They do not have the machinery and they do not have the transportation. There are no railroads at all in Afghanistan. There are some roads, from the capital city of Kabul to the other cities, but there are very few automobiles. Most of the traveling is done by caravans of camels, or riding a camel or on horseback.

There are many animals, both wild and tame. The tame ones include the Afghan hound, about which you can read in the article just before this one. One of the unusual wild animals is the jerboa, a little jumping rat with long hind legs; it looks like a tiny kangaroo. Many of the wild animals seen in zoos are native to Afghanistan—tigers, leopards, bears, and others.

HOW THE PEOPLE ARE GOVERNED

Afghanistan is a constitutional monarchy, which means that it has a king, a parliament that makes the laws, and a written constitution that protects the rights of the people.

The king's name is Mohammed Zahir Shah ("shah" means king). He has been king since 1933, and he has done much to make the country more modern, by building roads and factories and schools.

All men who are 20 years old or more may vote. They elect members of the National Assembly, which is one of the two branches of the parliament. The other branch of the parliament is the Senate. It has fifty members, who are appointed by the king.

Afghanistan is divided into provinces. There are ten provinces, and each one has a governor appointed by the parliament.

Every man from 22 to 42 years old must serve in the army. There are only

The capital of Afghanistan at Kabul is a widely spread-out city on a flat plain. Look closely and you will see that all the buildings are adobe, though only the white walls show clearly.

Ambassade Royal d'Afghanistan

90,000 men in the army, but the others can be called if they are needed. The army is not a strong one, and its air force has only a few planes and 300 men.

AFGHANISTAN IN THE PAST

For thousands of years, Afghanistan has been used as a battleground. Some armies have come to conquer the country itself. Others have passed through on their way to fight other countries. One reason for this is the Khyber Pass.

The Khyber Pass is a fairly low and level gap in the giant Hindu Kush mountains, whose highest peaks are almost five miles high. That has made the Khyber Pass the only way to reach India from the west.

Alexander the Great, the king who almost conquered the world more than 2,000 years ago, marched his armies through Afghanistan, and he was only one of the great conquerors who have ruled the land. The Mongols led by Genghis Khan did so much damage, burning villages and towns and killing the people, that Afghanistan did not recover for hundreds of years. Its people became wild and warlike. Raiding parties of fierce Afghans used to ride through the Khyber Pass and swoop down on the British settlements in India, killing and robbing. Finally the British, in 1878, sent armies into Afghanistan. There were several bloody battles, but the British won them and took charge of Afghanistan's affairs.

Afghanistan became fully independent again in 1907. A few years after World War I, a very modern king named Amanullah came to the throne. He was too modern for the people, who did not want to change their old way of living. They made King Amanullah abdicate. After him came Nadir Shah, who had been a great warrior. He became king in 1931 but was assassinated two years later because he was just as modern as Amanullah was. The present king,

Unations

This cow in Afghanistan has just been inoculated against a contagious disease of cattle.

Mohammed Zahir Shah, was Nadir Shah's son. He is a modern ruler too, but the people have finally come to like modern ways and he has not had trouble with them.

Today, Afghanistan lives at peace with its neighbors and is respected as a country that is rapidly improving itself. In 1946 it joined the United Nations. The United States has lent it some money ($21,000,000 in 1949) to use for improvements such as irrigation of the farms and machines for the factories. One measure of advancement in Afghanistan is that thirty years ago four out of five Afghans could not read or write; today four out of five can read and write.

AFGHANISTAN. Area, 253,250 square miles. Population (1953 estimate), 12,000,000. Language, Pushtu. Religion, Mohammedan. Government, constitutional monarchy. Monetary unit, the afghani, worth 6 cents (U.S.). Flag, three bars, black, red, green; in the center (red) bar, two ears of wheat around a mosque (church).

Africa

Africa

Africa is a continent, one of the seven big masses of land that make up the Earth. It is the second-biggest continent, with 11,500,000 square miles; North America has only 9,300,000 square miles, and the United States only 3,000,000.

There are about 200 million people living in Africa, not very many more than live in the United States. That is because in large parts of Africa there are very few people, or none at all.

Africa is shaped somewhat like a pear, with the wide part "on top"—that is, in the north—and closest to the Americas. During World War II, American airplanes flew to the nearest places in Africa in a day's time, and it could be done faster now. But most of Africa is thousands of miles from the United States and it takes weeks to get there.

For hundreds of years Africa was called "the Dark Continent." No one in Europe and America knew much about it. It had not been explored, the way America was, until less than 100 years ago. In the last hundred years much has been learned about Africa and its people, and now it is not the Dark Continent any more.

Some parts of Africa are as modern and up-to-date as the United States, but millions of square miles are still wild jungle and desert, with no signs of civilization as we know it.

THE COUNTRIES OF AFRICA

Like other continents, Africa has a number of different countries and territories under different governments.

There is a separate article about each of the independent countries. Here they are, briefly:

EGYPT, which lies along the rich valley of the great river Nile, on the northern coast of Africa. It is one of the oldest civilized countries on earth, and has figured in our history longer than any other.

ETHIOPIA, a kingdom in the northeastern part of Africa. It too is very old, going back to Biblical times, but it is just beginning to become a modern country.

LIBYA, on the northern coast of Africa (that is, on the Mediterranean Sea). Until after World War II, Libya was a territory controlled by Italy. Now it is independent. Libya is big but it is mostly desert and so there are not many people living there.

LIBERIA, a small republic on the western coast (that is, on the Atlantic

Ocean). Liberia was settled about a hundred years ago by Negroes who had been slaves in America.

UNION OF SOUTH AFRICA, a big, modern country at the southern tip of Africa. It was settled by Dutch and British peoples, and it is now one of the British Commonwealth of Nations, but governs itself.

THE TERRITORIES

The rest of Africa is divided into territories. They are governed by various European nations, or by United Nations Trusteeships, but many of them hope to become independent.

The territories controlled by Great Britain are Sierra Leone, Bechuanaland, the Gold Coast, Nigeria, both North and South Rhodesia, Kenya, the Anglo-Egyptian Sudan, and British Somaliland.

The territories controlled by France are Algeria, Tunisia, French Morocco, French West Africa, French Equatorial Africa, and French Somaliland.

Italy's territory is Somaliland, and Portugal's is Angola. Belgium has the Belgian Congo. The United Nations Trusts are Togoland, Tanganyika, Cameroons, and Southwest Africa.

The earliest peoples of North Africa were related to the Arabs, Jews, and others who spoke languages called Semitic. Along the western part of the Mediterranean coast, the largest group of these people were the Berbers; along the eastern part, they were the Egyptians. The descendants of these earliest North Africans still live there, but their ancestors married so many of the Arabs and Turks and other races that invaded their countries that today they are a mixture of several bloods.

Nearly all of these North Africans follow the Mohammedan religion. They speak languages that are much like Arabic, because that is the language in which the Koran, the Mohammedan Holy Book, is written. In the western part of North Africa, the men wear turbans on their heads, and long flowing robes, just as the Arabs do. Some of them live in big cities and follow the ways of Europeans and Americans. Others are nomads, or wandering tribes, who move from one place to another to do their farming or to raise sheep and cattle. Still others are farmers who raise wheat and other useful crops. These are the people of Morocco, Algeria, Tunisia, and Libya. There is a special article about each of these lands.

In Egypt, the people live more as the people of Turkey do, because for a long time Egypt had Turkish rulers. Most of the Egyptians are farmers, but there are big, modern cities, especially Cairo and Alexandria.

The Ethiopians are a Semitic people too, but they are chiefly Christians. They are very dark-skinned, and many of them still paint their faces and wear little more than loincloths, as many Negroes of Africa do, but it is a mistake to call Ethiopians Negroes, or to call Negroes Ethiopians, though the mistake is often made. They are of different origins.

Except for the northern edges of the vast African continent, nearly all the natives are of the Negro race. These will be described next.

THE NEGRO PEOPLES

The section that runs across Africa from the Nile to the Atlantic Ocean was once all called the Sudan, which means the African Negro Land. The Negroes who live in this territory are called the Sudanese. They were the most advanced of the original Negroes of Africa, and at one time they had big empires of their own. They adopted the religion of the invading Arabs years ago, and the Arab costume. Most of the people who are called Sudanese today are still Mohammedans, and still dress in Arab style. Even the Sudanese, however, are not all alike. The tribes living on the west coast are more advanced than those in the central part of the continent.

Negroes related to the Sudanese live throughout Africa, all the way down to the Cape of Good Hope at the southern tip. They are called Bantus. But neither the Sudanese nor the Bantus are all alike. They are of many tribes, religions, and customs. Some are nearly giants in size; among the Watussi, for example, the men are seven feet or more tall. Some tribes are of average size, like Europeans.

Nearly all of the African Negroes are good farmers, and hardworking people. There are many things that only the women do, however. It is not considered a man's work to do anything but hunt for the family's meat. The African Negroes love meat, and they eat all kinds. By some of the tribes, snakes, crocodile meat and monkey meat are considered delicious.

The women make pots and pans out of a plant called the bottle gourd, and their system of making them is very unusual. While the gourd is growing, they tie strings around it wherever they want it to stay slim and narrow, and it will grow only where it isn't tied. The cord makes little necks here and there, wherever it is tied, and then when the big gourd is ripe, the women take it off the vine and put it in the sun to dry. When it is completely dry and hard, it is painted and decorated. It is called a calabash, and it is used for pots and pans, or water jugs, or sometimes for drums.

Some gourds make a fine booming noise when they are beaten with the hands, and that is the sound of jungle drums that can be heard for miles across the wild sections of Africa. The natives have drumbeats that mean very definite things. There is one kind of beat, for instance, that might mean, "We have just seen a caravan of white men approaching across the desert." Another kind of beat might mean, "There's a herd of elephants stampeding to the south." Each kind of beat means something different, and in a very short space of time, news travels for hundreds of miles. One tribe starts it, the next picks it up, and the next, and the next, until all the native tribes for miles and miles know the story.

In most of the settlements, the natives have strange little round huts for houses. They drive poles into the ground in a circle, and pull the tops together in a point. Then they weave straw in and out between the poles, or pack the spaces with mud, to form walls and a roof. Sometimes they build separate roofs, by making a second ring of poles outside the first, and setting a roof on top of the outside ring, so that the roof isn't attached to the house walls at all, but just forms a sort of shed over the house. In some parts of Africa the natives build their house on long poles, like stilts, or high up between the trunks of trees, and climb to them on ladders. This protects them against crawling insects and snakes, and against wild animals.

SOME STRANGE CUSTOMS

The African Negroes have many customs that seem strange to people in Europe and America. For example, they have very fancy hair styles. Sometimes their hair is wound up on sticks into such long, complicated shapes that they can't lie down flat at night. They rest the back of their necks on a wooden block, to hold their hair off the ground, so that the carefully twisted sticks of stiffly arranged hair won't be mussed up.

There are other kinds of ornamentation that seem beautiful to African Negroes, and which would seem very ugly and strange to us. Two of them in particular are worth mentioning. The Ubangi pierce holes in the lips of girls when they are very young, and slip a peg into the hole. After the flesh has healed, they take out the peg, and put in a larger one. The peg gets larger all the time, until finally the woman's lips are stretched out so far that they look like a pair of small shovels. It is very hard to talk, and

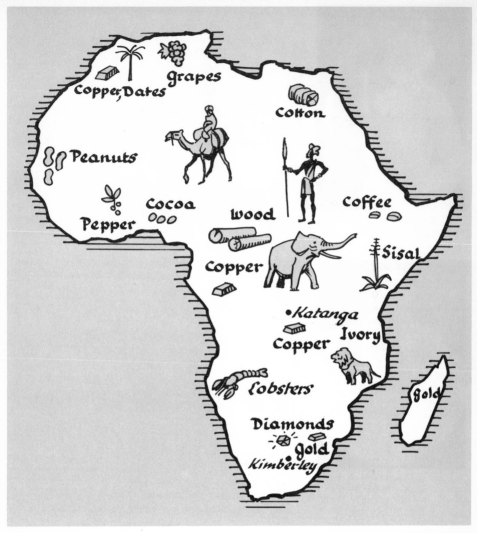

Africa offers every kind of climate and much of the natural wealth of the earth—no one knows, as yet, how much. Even the animals are a form of natural wealth. This map shows you a few of the things that come from Africa, and the section each comes from. Diamonds, gold and copper are mined at the places shown on the map. The ivory comes from the wild elephants in the jungle. Camels are used to cross the Sahara Desert, and for milk.

hard to eat, when the lips are stretched out like that on stiff wooden pegs, but the people of some tribes think it a sign of great beauty. Another strange form of decoration is scarring. They scratch their skin, and keep it from healing until great scars develop all over the body. Each tribe has its own patterns for scars, and a native can tell what tribe a stranger belongs to by the shape of the scars

scratched into his skin. They think this also is very attractive.

One of the customs that nearly all tribes have is the great ceremonial war dance on the evening before a hunt. For this they dress up in fancy costumes, and dance to the rhythm of their drums, while they pray to the gods of the hunt to send plenty of game to shoot the next day when the hunters go out.

S. African Tourist Corp.

Pan American World Airways

This Swazi warrior in Africa has bleached hair.

South African natives dress in elaborate costumes of fur and feathers for their ceremonial dances.

S. African Tourist Corp.

Unations

A baby of the Ndebele tribe.
↓ Native African sculpture.

Above: Modern education has reached the Cameroons.
↓ Hairdressing styles in Africa can be very fancy.

British Information Service

S. African Tourist Corp.

S. African Tourist Corp.

Aero Service Corp.

The natives of South Rhodesia in Africa call **Victoria Falls,** shown in this picture, "the Smoke that Thunders."

Natives of Mozambique examine an airborne magnetometer.

Pan American World Airways

Native-style houses and outdoor cooking in a South African park. Below: The beach near Capetown is sandy and beautiful.

Pan American World Airways

S. African Tourist Corp.

A baby ostrich is hatched.
↓A Gold Coast bull calf.

British Information Serv.

The fanciest and weirdest costumes are reserved for the witch doctors, who are the priests of the natives' religions. Many of the Negro tribes still worship gods or spirits of their own. There have been Christian missionaries in Africa for years, but many tribes live in sections that are very hard to reach. There are not many Christians among the backward natives.

THE RECORD OF SLAVERY

Throughout the ages, Negroes have been taken from Africa and enslaved in other countries. Many were slaves in ancient Egypt and in Rome, more than two thousand years ago. In later centuries, Arabs and other Mohammedans had Negroes as slaves. One of the blots on American history is the large numbers of Negroes who were brought overseas from Africa and turned into slaves.

One reason why Negroes were often enslaved is that many of them were less advanced than other peoples, so warlike countries like Rome had little trouble capturing them. But another big reason is that the African Negroes practiced slavery themselves—and many of them still do. Parents would sell their children into slavery. Native kings or chiefs would sell young men and women by the hundreds, to slave traders. Slavery has been made unlawful everywhere else in the world, except in Africa. Even today, you will find it practiced among native tribes there. The United Nations is trying to stop the practice of slavery everywhere.

Most of the African tribes have their own kings. Even when a European government controls a territory, the native rulers are allowed to continue their control of matters inside the tribe.

THE BACKWARD PEOPLES

In the central parts of Africa, where the Congo River runs through thick jungles, there are some very wild tribes of African Negroes who are among the most uncivilized people on earth. Some of them used to be cannibals, before modern governments put a stop to it.

There is one group called the Pygmies. These are very small men. They live in the dense jungle sections of the Congo basin. Pygmy men are no taller than a 12-year-old child in the United States—about four and a half feet tall. They are very shy, and will hide when strangers come near, but they are very brave hunters, and hunt the elephant. For hunting,

The lion (left), rhinoceros (right), and wild ox called the zebu are native to Africa. Big game hunters killed so many of them that laws were passed to protect the wildlife. It is still possible to hunt in Africa, but no one is allowed to kill too many animals.

and to protect themselves they have poison-tipped arrows. They also gather wild berries and fruits to eat. They would starve otherwise, because the land where they live is very poor, and there is almost no food available.

Pygmies are quite peaceable if no one bothers them. They never start trouble themselves with other tribes. They do not have any cities or churches or schools. In fact, they don't even have houses. They sometimes make rough shelters of branches, but quite often they just sleep on the ground, or crawl in among the roots of an old tree. None of them can read or write, but they speak a form of the Bantu language that many other natives of Africa speak. (There is a separate article about the BANTU language.)

The Pygmies don't have much reason to use a lot of words, but get along without any particular conversation.

Another of the strange wild tribes in South Africa are the Bushmen. They are no better off than the Pygmies. They don't build huts for shelter, either, but merely go to sleep under bushes when they are tired. They live in a miserable desert section of country, and there is very little food, because sometimes it doesn't rain for years. This is the western section of South Africa. Bushmen are very poor, and very ugly to look at. The women especially are strange looking. There is a fold of fat in the middle of a Bushman woman s back, so that she sticks out in back, below the waist, like a flat shelf. To make themselves look even stranger, the women tie on tails made of grass, so they really look more like monkeys than people.

Bushmen make a sort of clicking sound when they talk. They have no schools or churches. All they do is look for food, and then eat all they can at one time when they find it. After they have eaten, they go to sleep, and when they get hungry again, the hunger wakes them up, and off they go on another hunt for food. Food is very scarce in Bushman country, though, and they often go hungry for days, which makes them a very weak and unhealthy people.

Another kind of African Negro is the Hottentot. There are not as many Hottentots as there once were, because so many of them have died of smallpox and other diseases.

WHAT AFRICA IS LIKE

The equator runs through the middle

This group of African antelopes will travel for miles in search of good grazing land. They have to be ready at all times to run swiftly away from any sign of danger. Danger might be a native hunting party looking for food, and it might be a hungry lion.

In South Africa's Kruger National Park drivers wait patiently until the lions go past.

of Africa. Here it is always hot, and there is much rain, so that every kind of plant grows so fast and so big that you can hardly control it. This is the famous jungle. The leaves are so thick that the sun never reaches the ground except when a tree falls over. Monkeys and snakes and insects by the million live in the jungles. Millions of men live there too, even though the climate is not very healthful and the danger from animals and insects is very great.

When you look at a map of Africa, you'll see a big section marked Sahara Desert. This is the biggest desert in the world. It covers 3,000,000 square miles in the northern part of the continent, as much territory as the entire United States covers. The desert is all sand. It never rains, and there are few places where plants will grow. It gets as hot as 120 degrees, which is hotter than any place in the United States ever is, except Death Valley in California, which is also a desert.

But though it is so hot during the day, nights on the Sahara are always cold. You would need a thick blanket every night. That is because the air is so dry there is nothing to hold the heat, once the sun has gone down, and the sand has cooled off after dark.

Apart from the Sahara, the northern part of Africa is very much like the southern part of France and Spain. It is warm and fertile along the coast, and then becomes dry where it joins the Sahara.

Think of any kind of country, any kind of climate, you ever knew or heard of, or even dreamed about—and Africa has it. There is warm weather and cold weather; dry weather and rainy weather. There are deserts, mountains, wide stretches of grassy plains, big rivers with fertile valleys, jungles where you would have to cut a path for yourself to get anywhere because the plants are so thick, big lakes and waterfalls—one of them, the Victoria Falls, is as big and as beautiful as Niagara.

Farther to the south, Africa is in the temperate zone, as the United States is. The climate is quite pleasant. In the southeast section, there are mountains with peaks that are so high there is snow on them all year around. These are Mt. Kilimanjaro, 19,565 feet high, and Mt. Kenya, 17,040 feet high. These mountains are in a section with many rivers and lakes. Lake Victoria, which was named for Queen Victoria of England, is especially famous, and it is very beautiful. It is on the western border of British Kenya.

In the plains of South Africa, there is plenty of rainfall for rich and productive farming. The winters never get very cold, and even in the very coolest sections there is very little snow.

Throughout Africa there are millions of wild animals. There is a separate article on this; see HUNTING. The natives in some sections go on lion hunts, and even the Pygmies are fond of elephant hunting. Besides the elephants and lions, there are enormous herds of zebras running wild; gorillas live in the jungles (though no one is permitted to hunt them now); and there are thousands of smaller varieties of ape, and many monkeys. The crocodile, rhinoceros, hippopotamus, and wild boar all live in Africa. There are herds of giraffes and many kinds of deer, many different snakes, and birds with beautiful plumage. Wild beasts live in Africa just as they have for hundreds of thousands of years.

THE RICHNESS OF AFRICA

The natives lived in Africa for tens of thousands of years without knowing or caring that they had one of the richest continents on earth. But the countries of Europe knew it—though even they did not know how much wealth was hidden in the mountains and mining lands of Africa. Anyway, the European nations managed to split up most of Africa among themselves, often with such quarrels that they almost led to warfare. Now the natives have learned enough to want their own country back, but the European countries are not so willing to let go.

Most of the world's diamonds come from Africa, and much of the world's gold has come from there; African gold and diamonds are still worth hundreds of millions of dollars every year.

In the Belgian Congo and in Northern Rhodesia there are huge deposits of copper, and many experts think that they are the world's richest. As late as 1952, great iron mines were opened for the first time in Liberia, and Africa also has a lot of coal in some parts. There are other minerals, too, that are used all the time in modern manufacture, though their names are not familiar to most people.

But the most valuable property Africa holds was not even thought about until very recent years. It is uranium, from which atomic energy is obtained for the

Mancala is the national game of Africa. It is played even by the blind, as in this picture from the Gold Coast. There the game is called oware.

British Information Office

South African Government Information Service

African Bushmen are among the most primitive people on earth. Their paintings on the walls of caves are very much like those made by European cavemen thousands of years ago.

A-bomb and for peaceful purposes too. The Belgian Congo, and other parts of the Congo region, may turn out to be the place from which most of the world's uranium is obtained.

Africa could easily feed much of the world, if its fertile lands could be farmed and its other lands cleared and irrigated as land in the United States has been. For many years North Africa has produced wheat and cotton and other valuable crops for Europe, but the greatest part of Africa is still undeveloped. Some fine and beautiful woods, mahogany and ebony and others, come from Africa.

Electric power is unknown in most parts of Africa, because the people are so backward that most of them have never even heard of electricity. When they learn what can be done with electric power, there are rivers that could supply enough electricity to run factories and supply big cities beyond anything Europe has. The power in African rivers had never been used, except for a few places on the Nile and in South Africa, until the last twenty years or so. Since then, the rivers have been developed rapidly.

THE EXPLORATION OF AFRICA

For thousands of years no part of Africa was known except North Africa. There, the Egyptians had the earliest civilization known to modern man. The people of Carthage (which is now Tunisia) fought for years against the powerful Romans, whom they almost defeated with their great generals Hamilcar and Hannibal. (There are separate articles about HAMILCAR and HANNIBAL.) Ethiopia, in northeast Africa, was a civilized country hundreds of years before the time of Christ, and some of the Negro peoples—especially the Hausa —had thriving cities. But the rest of Africa was not known at all.

Then the great explorers, especially those from Portugal, began to sail from Europe to India and China, to bring back silks and spices and other fine things

These are schoolchildren in the British Cameroons. They go to school at Gwoza, a town there. Though they receive modern education, they dress in native style and like ornaments better than clothes.

The Watussi tribe of the Belgian Congo are probably the tallest people on earth. A man seven feet tall is not unusual. The Watussi have been shown in several motion pictures filmed in Africa.

that Europe did not have. Their voyages took them southward around Africa. As much as seven hundred years ago they had sailed down the west coast of Africa and they built little towns near harbors where they could stop to rest and take on fresh water and food. Bartholomew Diaz sailed all the way to the Cape of Good Hope in the year 1488. Vasco da Gama sailed all the way around Africa a few years later. Dutch, British and French sailors followed him.

It was only a few years after Columbus discovered America that Europeans began taking African slaves to the New World; the first were landed in Haiti in 1510. The slave trade continued for three hundred years. But the slavers landed only on the coast. The Dutch started their Cape Colony in 1652, and the first British colony dates from 1807, but these too stayed near the coast. The rest of Africa remained "the Dark Continent," unknown and unexplored.

A Scottish missionary, Dr. David Livingstone, was the first white man to learn much about the unexplored part of Africa. He went where no man had ever gone before. Among his discoveries was the Victoria Falls. One of the most interesting stories of Africa is how Dr. Livingstone became sick somewhere in the unexplored interior and was thought to be lost. James Gordon Bennett, a famous New York newspaper publisher, sent a reporter named Henry Morton Stanley to find him, and Stanley not only found Dr. Livingstone but became the greatest of all African explorers. There are special stories about these famous men and their adventures in Africa.

There was still to be much trouble in Africa. The British and the Boers (descendants of the first Dutch settlers in South Africa) fought the Boer War; the Italians twice went to war to gain control of Ethiopia; the Germans under Hitler threatened war if they could not

A Swazi blacksmith sharpens the blade of an African spear called an assegai.

S. African Tourist Corp.

Pan American World Airways

Girls in Pretoria, South Africa, wear fancy decorations as girls do all over the world, even though their "haircuts" are very boyish.

get back Tanganyika and the other African colonies they had lost in World War I. Men will probably continue to quarrel over Africa for a long time. But it is no longer the unknown continent. As surely as America was developed and became great, so, some day, will Africa.

EUROPEANS IN AFRICA

Since the Dutch and British first started colonies in Africa, things have changed a great deal. From just a few handfuls of people from England and Holland, many settlements have grown up and become great modern cities. In fact, if you were to walk through the streets of any large African city, the only thing that would look really different from the cities of the United States would be the great numbers of black-skinned people you would see. The buildings and streets look very western and modern.

In the Union of South Africa alone there are about 2,700,000 people of European descent. Rhodesia has a large European population, too. So does the Belgian Congo, and Kenya, on the west side of the continent. About half a million Indians have settled in South Africa and British East Africa. Many people from all over the world have made Africa their home.

The Europeans in the larger cities have tried to make their African home as much like Europe as possible. They have built schools, churches, theaters, and shops. They have comfortable homes, and their children go to school just as if they were living in England or Holland or France.

There is one thing, however, that is very different about living in Europe or the United States, and living in Africa. On all the great continent, there are fewer railroads than on any other continent in the world. It's a good thing there are lots of big rivers, because if it weren't for those rivers, and the boats that travel on them, people would simply have to ride camels to get from one place to another. It would be very hard to carry tools and equipment for modern construction work in camel caravans. Most of the transportation in Africa has to be done by way of the rivers, but still camels are used to cross the Sahara Desert. People traveling through some of the sections near the equator have to hire men called bearers to carry their camping supplies, guns, cameras, and cooking equipment, because of course there are no such things as hotels or tourist camps in the middle of Africa. There are very few good roads, so it is not practical to drive a car except in and around the cities and larger towns. In many cases, it is easier to fly from one place to another. An airplane can fly right over the jungle, while it would take weeks or months of very difficult travel for a party to push through that same jungle, with all the dangers it would meet along the way.

For years, but especially since World War II, the native and white races have clashed in parts of Africa. The white settler had already treated the natives as an inferior race who could be nothing but laborers or servants. In the Union of South Africa, the system of separation of races (called *apartheid,* which means "apartness" or, as it is called in the United States, "segregation") caused constant trouble. In the British state of Kenya, open fighting resulted from the natives' resentful feeling toward the white settlers. Savage people of a secret society called the Mau-Mau killed many of the British landowners and businessmen.

In each case the natives wanted opportunities equal to those of the white people. Most people in other countries believed that fighting would continue, and the development of Africa would be slower than it should be, until these opportunities were granted. However, in spite of all these difficulties, Africa is gradually becoming a completely civilized continent, and with its great natural wealth may some day become a great modern power, with all its different peoples living together peaceably, and working together to help themselves and each other.

Johannesburg is the biggest city in South Africa, because it is the center of a gold-mining district. Here the city is seen in the background, near the hilly "reefs" or veins where gold has been mined.

BOAC

Pan American World Airways

French Gov't. Tourist Office

1. Above left: A Zulu sits before his hut,
modeling the faces of others who live in his
village. Many Zulus are very talented.
2. Upper right: In French Morocco, there
are many beautiful structures made of pure
white, to reflect the heat and keep the interiors cool.
3. Right center: In the streets of Morocco
you would see many people in robes like
these. The man is in official uniform.
4. Below: This new mosque is in the city of
Kano, in Nigeria, where there are many Mohammedans. They go to a mosque as Christians go to a church.

Unations   *French Gov't. Tourist Office*

African campaign

During World War II it was very important to both sides to have control of Africa, and especially North Africa along the Mediterranean Sea. Important British and other Allied ships had to pass through the Mediterranean Sea and the Suez Canal to reach India and other Oriental countries in the quickest way. If the enemy controlled the coast of North Africa, it could send out bombing planes to destroy so much of this shipping that the cost would be great both in ships and in lost time. So for three years the warring countries, especially Britain and Germany, fought for the control of Africa.

It was one of the most seesaw fights in history. First one side and then the other would seem to win a complete victory, and chase the enemy back for hundreds of miles. Then the enemy would make a stand somewhere, prepare a campaign of its own, and pretty soon it would seem to be winning. United States troops saw their first fighting in North Africa; so did Australian troops, who were very important in the North African campaign, as were Canadian troops. Some great generals won their reputations in North African fighting, including Marshal Montgomery of the British, Marshal Rommel of the Germans, and General Eisenhower himself.

When World War II began, in 1939, Italy controlled Libya, stretching hundreds of miles along the southern coast of the Mediterranean, and Eritrea, which lies on the Red Sea on the eastern side of Africa. The British had forces in Egypt and also on the Red Sea.

Italy was not then in the war. When Italy did enter the war, in May, 1940, fighting between the British and the Italians soon began. In this fighting, the British were soon successful. Their commander was Sir Archibald Wavell. They drove the Italians back five hundred miles through Libya, while in east Africa they captured Eritrea and liberated Ethiopia, the country that Italy had attacked and conquered several years before. Much of the African fighting was in the endless expanses of the Sahara Desert, and was ideal for tank warfare. The Italians did not have enough tanks to match the British. More than 300,000 of them surrendered.

Then Marshal Rommel and his famous German Afrika Corps entered the fighting. Early in 1941 he attacked in Libya, drove the British back those hundreds of miles again to the border of Egypt, and left them holding a small North African town called Tobruk. The seesaw fighting had begun. Sir Claude Auchinleck had become the British General in command, and in the fall of 1941 he attacked, drove the Germans back, and captured many of them. In the spring of 1942, it changed again and Rommel scored a great victory, almost capturing Alexandria; the British finally stopped the German advance at the village of El Alamein, which was to become famous for that reason.

The British changed generals again, Sir Harold Alexander becoming the commander and Sir Bernard Montgomery taking over the British Eighth Army, which was to become even more famous than the Afrika Corps. General Montgomery began planning and preparing for a big attack. For the time being, fighting was at a standstill in the summer of 1942.

But this was the point at which the United States started active fighting in World War II. The United States had sent General Eisenhower to England to take command of American forces there, with General Alfred M. Gruenther as his chief of staff. They prepared the great "Operation Torch," at its time the most ambitious landing operation known. In the fall of 1942, the expedition sailed from Britain and the United States— more than eight hundred ships, nearly 300,000 British and American troops.

British Information Service

When British troops went into Benghazi in World War II, the Arabs of North Africa were very much interested in their equipment. The German campaign there failed.

On October 23, General Montgomery started a great attack from Egypt in the east; on November 8, these American and British forces landed in the western part of North Africa. General Rommel was caught between the two forces. Montgomery drove him nearly 1500 miles to the west, and there the Americans attacked. For a while, the Germans still made a battle of it, but on May 13, 1943, the last of them surrendered and the North African Campaign was over.

It was during the North African Campaign that President Franklin D. Roosevelt and Prime Minister Winston Churchill had the first of the great conferences among the Allied chiefs of state. They met at Casablanca, in January, 1943, a few months before the African fighting ended.

Afrikaans

More than three hundred years ago Dutch-speaking settlers from the Netherlands first went to South Africa, and more and more followed until the larg-

So many ships were bombed in Benghazi harbor in Libya, North Africa, that the waters are still filled with wreckage.

est group of Europeans in South Africa were of Dutch origin. Just as the American language developed from English, so did Afrikaans develop from Dutch, and it is still very much like Dutch, but there are distinct differences, partly because all languages change over the course of hundreds of years, and partly because settlers in a new country pick up many native words—the Americans did from the American Indians, and the Dutch did from the native Africans. Afrikaans is one of the two official languages of the Union of South Africa, the other being English.

Aga Khan

Aga Khan is the title of the leader of the Ismaili sect, in the Mohammedan religion. His full name is Sultan Sir Mohammed Shah, and the title Aga Khan means "Lord Chief." He is a descendant of Fatima, who was the daughter of Mohammed. Most of the Ismaili live in India. In 1936 when the Aga Khan had been their leader fifty years, they gave him his weight in gold, and ten years later they gave him his weight in diamonds. He weighs 246 pounds. He gave the gold and diamonds back to the people, to use for education. The Aga Khan was born in 1877.

Agamemnon

One of the greatest stories of all time tells how the Greeks went to war against the Trojans because Paris, a Trojan prince, had run away with the wife of a Greek prince named Menelaus, whose wife we now call Helen of Troy. Agamemnon was the brother of Menelaus, and the king of Mycenae in ancient Greece. He was the commander-in-chief of the Greek forces throughout the Trojan Wars. He is one of the leading characters in Homer's great poem, the *Iliad*, in which the story of the Trojan Wars is told. Agamemnon's wife was Clytemnestra, who was a sister of Helen. While he was away commanding the Greek armies, Clytemnestra fell in love with a Greek prince named Aegisthus. When Agamemnon came back from Troy, Clytemnestra and Aegisthus murdered him. Later, Agamemnon's son, Orestes, avenged the murder by killing both Clytemnestra and Aegisthus.

agar-agar or agar

Agar-agar is a gummy or gelatin-like substance that is made from a red seaweed. When it is dissolved in water it swells up to great size, and because of this it is used as a laxative, because bulk helps in digestion of food. Agar-agar is also used in cooking, especially in China and other Oriental countries, and in laboratory experiments it is used as a base in which to grow bacteria and study them.

agate

Agate is a hard stone, a kind of quartz, that is formed in streaks or layers of different colors. It is translucent, which means that the light shines through it, and it is very hard and can be polished to a shining surface. All this makes agate very beautiful, and it is used in many ornaments, the very finest agate being made into settings for rings and pins and brooches, and being classed as a semiprecious stone.

There is no limit to the number of different patterns formed by the many colors in agate, but the principal kinds are called banded agate, which has wavy layers of different colors; clouded agate, which has patches of color; and moss agate, which has dark marks that look like moss or ferns. In some pieces of agate the layers of color form rings that look like an eye, and people in Oriental countries sometimes used to cut this into the shape of an eye and wear it on a chain around the neck, calling it "the evil eye"; they thought it would drive away evil spirits that might attack them.

There is a great deal of agate in the world, and as a stone it is not very expensive. That is the reason children's marbles can be made out of it and sold for quite low prices (though of course they do cost much more than glass marbles). The cost of fine agate is mostly in the cutting of it.

Agate is found in Brazil and Uruguay in South America, in India, and in the United States around Lake Superior. Most of it is sent to the Idar-Oberstein section in West Germany, where fine craftsmen have made a specialty of cutting agate jewelry for many generations. It is an important industry of that district.

agave

This is a plant that grows in very dry regions of America. It will even grow in deserts. Many people call it the century plant, because of an old legend that it blooms only once in a hundred years. Though there is no truth in this, the agave does not bloom every year as most plants do; nor does it bloom at any regular time. When it does bloom, a stem or spike shoots up from the center of the stiff, spiny leaves at the base. This spike may grow to a height of twenty feet or even more, and the flower is on top of it. The agave is related to the amaryllis. Some kinds of agave are used in Mexico to make liquors called pulque and mescal, and rope is made out of the stringy fibers of the leaves, called sisal.

The agave grows in very dry places. It may bloom only once in several years, but when it does it reaches 20 feet or more in height.

Netherlands West Indies Tourist Service

age

The word age can have several different meanings. You probably think of it first as indicating how old a person is. It can also be used to mean the lifespan, or number of years of living, of a human being or animal. The next article, on AGE OF MAN, will cover part of this subject. Here we will think of the word age only as meaning a period in history.

An age is a number of years in which something takes place that makes it different from any other years. An age can last only a few years, or it can last hundreds of years, or it can last thousands of years. We speak of the Elizabethan Age, the time when Queen Elizabeth I was queen of England, about four hundred years ago. During her reign, the English wrote great plays and poetry; they sailed the seas bravely and won great territory and wealth for their country; and at home they were rich and gay and happy. It is convenient to say that a man lived in the Elizabethan Age, because those two words can give a picture of exactly what life was like in England when he was alive. In the same way we speak of a "golden age" as one in which the wealth and cultivation and literature and art of a particular country, such as ancient Rome or Greece, were at their peak.

The progress that mankind has made is usually divided into ages. The earliest of these ages is called the Old Stone Age; that was the time many thousands of years ago, when men were just beginning to learn to act like human beings, and the only tools or weapons they had were chipped out of pieces of flint. After that, men entered the New Stone Age, in which they made better tools out of flint and other stones, and also built houses and made pottery and learned to farm land and raise animals. The Bronze Age came next, when they discovered how to use metals; at first, they could use only copper or other metals made from it, such as bronze, and that

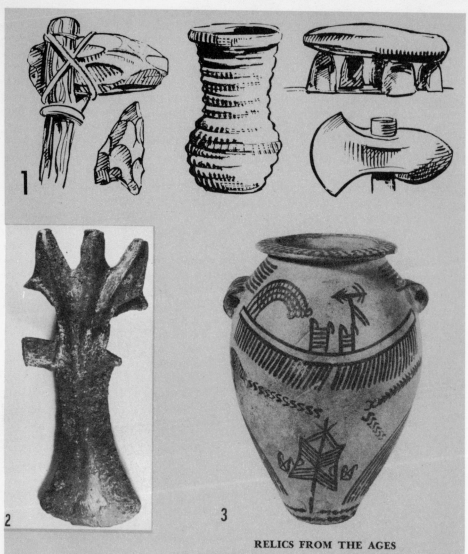

RELICS FROM THE AGES

1. The crude-looking ax and arrowhead at the left of the top picture are from the Old Stone Age of man, also called the Paleolithic Age (which means the same thing). In the center and at the right, are a jug, ax and dolmen (big stone monument) of the Neolithic (New Stone) Age.

2. This ax head from the Bronze Age was a farming implement as well as a tool for many tasks.

3. In the Bronze Age, man had learned to make pottery vases like this one. The decorations on the side are examples of very early art work, and each symbol meant something different. It might be called writing in pictures instead of words.

4. The Iron Age brought cutting implements that had been impossible with the soft metals man had used before. This is an example of his first crude scissors.

All Photos by Margot L. Wolf

is how this age got its name. Next came the Iron Age, when men learned to use iron and then steel and other metals. The Modern Age, in which we are living now, will probably come to be called the Atomic Age. You have probably heard it called that already.

age of man

How long does a human being live? The Bible says "threescore years and ten" are the allotted life of man, and that means seventy years, because a score is twenty. The Bible also tells of men who lived nine hundred years or more (and the oldest of them, Methuselah, lived 969 years), but there is no record that men ever lived to ages like that or anything near it at any other time. The average age to which men live has been going up steadily for years, as medical science has developed new ways of treating disease and preventing illness from killing people at early ages. The average age to which people live in the United States is now 65 years; only forty or fifty years ago it was from 45 to 48 years. That is a decided increase, but it does not mean the oldest people today are any older than were the oldest people of a hundred or five hundred or a thousand years ago. The average goes up because fewer people die young. If a baby of a few months dies, and a man of almost seventy dies, you get the average by adding their ages together and dividing by two, so the two of them have died at an average age of 35. Far fewer babies and children and young men and women die now than they used to, and that has sent the average up. A man who lives to be 100 years old or more is just as rare today as he ever was.

Women live longer than men. For some reason, their bodies seem better able to resist diseases, and not so many women wear themselves out with worry and overwork as do men in the frantic life of this century. The average life of women is more than 67 years, and the average age of men is only 63 years, and that is what makes the average age of all human beings, men and women together, 65 years.

In most other countries of the world, the average age is not as high as it is in the United States. For example, in India, where there is not enough food to keep everyone healthy and in good condition, and not enough doctors and drugs to keep diseases from spreading, the average age is not much more than half of what it is in the United States—31 years. The low average is partly caused by the fact that so many babies die. Many more mothers die in childbirth too, as they used to in all countries until ways were found to prevent infection.

Very careful records are kept on how long everyone lives. In the article on LIFE EXPECTANCY, you can find out how many years you can expect to live, and also everyone else whose age you know.

Agincourt

Agincourt is a tiny village in the north of France. Only 114 people live there. But the name is well remembered in history because of a great battle that was fought there more than five hundred years ago, in the year 1415. This battle took place in a war between England and France, which was part of a long series of wars, the Hundred Years' War.

Before the Battle of Agincourt, the best fighters had been knights wearing heavy armor, mounted on horses that also were protected by armor, and fighting with swords and lances and battle-axes. When the Battle of Agincourt was fought, the French army still depended on knights. But the English army, under King Henry V, had developed a new weapon. It was the longbow, of the type that Robin Hood used, and it had been made so strong, and the archers in the English army had been trained so well, that they could shoot an arrow hard enough to pierce the steel armor of the knights. The longbowmen did not need to wear armor, because they could shoot the knights down before the knights could get close enough to attack them with their swords and lances. This was a double advantage, because a man can get around much faster when he is not weighted down with heavy armor. The English longbowmen won the fight so easily, and killed so many of their French enemy, that no country ever again tried to win a war with armored knights. The Battle of Agincourt, for that reason, was called the "death of knighthood." Shakespeare wrote about it in his play *Henry V*.

agnostics

An agnostic is a person who is not religious and does not believe in God, but neither does he say there is no God. He simply says he does not know whether God exists or not. In fact, the word agnostic is taken from Greek words that mean "not knowing." The agnostic is different from the atheist. The atheist says he is sure there is no God. The word agnostic was first used by Thomas Huxley, a great English scientist, in 1869. Many Americans have been agnostics, but many more—in fact, nearly everyone—believes in God and is a member of some church.

agouti

The agouti is a small animal, about the size of a hare or rabbit (two feet long), that lives in the forests of the West Indies islands and parts of South America. Its flesh is white and tender and it once was the chief food of the Indians on the islands. The agouti is a rodent, or gnawing animal. Its hind legs are longer than its front legs, and it has strong claws. It sits erect on its haunches while eating, holding food in its forepaws, and sits the same way when looking or listening.

Agricola

Nearly two thousand years ago the people of Britain were wild and savage and lived in tribes like American Indians; the people of Rome were civilized, living in fine houses, with books and arts and many conveniences. Gnaeus Julius Agricola was a Roman general who was sent to Britain to turn it into a civilized Roman colony. This was in the year 77. His army defeated the wild tribes in battle, and Agricola became the governor of the southern part of England. He was a good governor and helped the people learn civilized Roman ways without trying to destroy native customs. He was the first to discover that Britain was an island, by sailing around it in his fleet. After governing peacefully for seven years, he returned to Rome. Agricola died in the year 93, when he was 56 years old.

The agouti lives in a hole it burrows in the ground. Like the rabbit, it can run very fast.
New York Zoölogical Society

Agriculture

agriculture

The word agriculture means "taking care of the fields"—in other words, what we are used to thinking of as farming. And, in fact, agriculture and farming mean just about the same thing. But usually we would say "agriculture" when we mean the entire work and science of using the earth to produce food and other plants that are valuable to us; and we would use the word "farming" to mean some particular branch of this, for example dairy farming, or chicken farming.

You will note that the word "science" was used in the paragraph above. Agriculture is as much of a science as engineering, medicine, or any other scientific fields to which men and women turn for their life's work. Many different sciences go to make up the whole work of agriculture. Many different sciences have helped in making agriculture the respected and profitable work it is today.

This has not always been so. Farming used to be laborious, poorly paid work. A farmer had to work hard in his fields all day long, just to raise enough food for his own family. Usually his wife had to help, and had no time for comfortable living; his children had to help, and had no time to get good educations. Today the young man or woman of a family in the field of agriculture will go to one of the hundreds of agricultural colleges and universities in the United States and will learn to make the family's farm even better in the future.

In this encyclopedia there are separate articles on DAIRY FARMING and CATTLE FARMING and FARM MACHINERY and other branches of agriculture. In this article we will tell about what agriculture used to be, how it has changed, and what it is today.

HOW AGRICULTURE HAS CHANGED

There have been farmers as long as there has been history and for tens of thousands of years before that. Agriculture is probably the oldest work done by man. In the Bible, the first man born on earth—Cain, the son of Adam and Eve—was "a tiller of the soil," in other words a farmer. Through most of these thousands of years, nearly everyone had to be a farmer because a farmer could not raise much more food than was needed to feed him and his family. Even in the days of the American Revolution, less than two hundred years ago, eight out of every ten Americans were farmers. Today, only one American out of seventeen is a farmer. But that one American working on a farm today can raise twice as much food as eight farmers could in those days.

But if you could have spent even a day with one of those ancient farmers, and could compare it with what you would see today on a modern farm of the United States with its bags of scientifically created seed, and its tractors to prepare the soil for planting, and its seeders to plant the seed at mathematically proper spots, and its other machines to cultivate the soil and kill the pests that destroy crops, and reap the crop when it is grown and transport it to the barn and then to the market, you would think you were in two different worlds—and so you would be. It took man a long time to learn how to raise his food in the ground.

First, man had to learn that plants would give him food. Then he learned that the plants would grow better if the soil around them were loosened, and he would hack away at the soil with tools that he had made by chipping off pieces of stone until a piece with sharp edges for digging would remain. One season it would not rain, and the plants would die, and from this he learned that plants need water, so in dry seasons he would carry water from a nearby pond or stream and throw it on the soil. He learned that plants grow from seeds, and that freed him to move to places where plants were not already growing, because he could take the seed with him, and plant it, and make his food grow where it had not grown before. Even later than this, he learned that some plants that were dry and hard and not worth eating could be made into good food if they were made hot enough for long enough, and out of this new knowledge came the art of cooking. Bit by bit, slowly at first but with ever-increasing rapidity, he added to this earliest knowledge until agriculture became what it is today.

THE CROPS WE RAISE

About eight acres out of every ten that are used for growing plants in agriculture in the United States are used to grow food. Some of this food is for us to eat. Some of it is to feed livestock, which will eventually become meat or will give milk or will lay eggs.

The other two acres are used for crops like cotton, from which our clothes are made; or tobacco, or trees for fruit and nuts, or for other plants besides vegetables.

Almost none of these crops is anything like the crops that our prehistoric ancestors raised. In their day, most plants grew wild on earth. For example the biggest crop of our western world, wheat, was simply tall wild grasses waving on the hillsides. The ancient Egyptians, probably at least ten thousand years ago, discovered that the kernels of wheat would make bread. They noticed which plants would grow best and saved the seeds from those plants and gradually improved the quality of the wheat they grew. The Chinese, and other Orientals, did the same thing with rice. The American Indians did the same thing with maize, the plant that we call corn. In the course of hundreds of years, the food plants that came to be raised were almost entirely different from the original plant that had been eaten by the earliest men. We are still doing the same things, but now the experiments are made by scientists in laboratories, and they take years instead of hundreds of years.

The same kind of development has spread different plants all over the world when once they grew in only a few parts of the world. There was a time when no one outside of Asia had ever heard of oranges. But explorers, visiting Asia, ate the oranges and liked them, and took the seeds back home to

Standard Oil Company of New Jersey

1. In the time of ancient Rome, farmers used wooden plows pulled by teams of oxen. The oxen's yoke is shown separately.

2. The ancient Egyptians' yoke and plow were hardly more crude than the Romans'.

3. In Saudi Arabia even today, the natives level their land by a method hundreds of years old. A pair of bullocks draw a big wooden slab along the ground to smooth out lumps in the dirt. The men in the background are digging irrigation ditches by hand.

4. These Mexican farmers are at work preparing their fields for planting, and they are using old-fashioned wooden plows drawn by oxen.

5. These farm tools are thousands of years old.

be planted. Today more oranges are grown in California and Florida than anywhere else in the world, and they are better oranges—bigger, sweeter, juicier—but they never grew in this country until the seeds were brought in from abroad.

America has made its gift of new food plants to the world. Corn was mentioned above. Potatoes were not known before America was discovered, but the plants were taken to Europe and became so much better known over there that we call one of these native American plants by the name of another country—Irish potatoes—because the Irish people raised so many of them at one time. In Mexico and South America, there was a plant that was completely strange to anyone who had never been there before. We now call this plant the tomato. It was so unusual that it took many years to persuade people from other countries that it was even safe to eat. Men not only learned how to improve the plants they knew, they learned also to create new plants.

Scientists learned that plants mate and have offspring very much as animals do. A male plant and a female plant are both needed to produce a seed from which a new plant will grow. This suggested taking one kind of male plant and another kind of female plant and trying to produce new foods that would combine the qualities of two other foods. Luther Burbank, an American who made a lifelong study of this, created many new plants. He created new, better-tasting fruits by mixing the pollens of two different plants (a process called cross-pollination) and his creations included such things as the honeydew melon and the grapefruit we see most often on our table today. The same kind of work produced string beans without strings (and most people today have forgotten the time when string beans had such strong, tough and unpleasant strings in them that you could hardly bite through

them), and oranges that give much more juice than other oranges, a development that led to the habit of drinking orange juice for breakfast today. Before then, oranges did not have enough juice to make it worthwhile to squeeze them.

The science of chemistry was a great help to agriculture. Farmers would discover that certain insects were ruining their plants. The insects would eat the leaves, or bore into the vegetables or fruits, or even attack the roots and keep the plants from growing. There were poisons that would kill the insects, but those same poisons might kill the plants —or else make the fruit of those plants poisonous to the people who ate them. The problem was to find chemicals that would kill insects without hurting the plant. Chemists have discovered liquids that you can spray or powders that you can dust on many plants that will keep the insects from eating them but will not keep the plants from growing and will not be dangerous to people who eat the vegetables or fruits. Not all the problems have been solved, so the work goes on and every year new ways are found to combat the pests and the diseases of our food plants and so to make the crops bigger and healthier.

THE TOOLS MEN FARM WITH

Plants must have minerals from the soil if they are to grow. They take in these minerals through their roots. But the minerals must be dissolved in water before the plants can take them in. Water does not flow easily through soil that is hard and caked, any more than it can flow through a brick, which was originally the same kind of earth but has been pressed and baked until it is dry and solid. Therefore, to make plants grow best, the farmer must loosen the soil and make it soft and crumbly.

It was told above how man learned to loosen the soil by breaking it up with crude pieces of stones sharpened to cut-

1. A meeting of science writers and chemists, held in a New York skyscraper, discusses new methods of scientific farming. The farmer today uses science more than ever before.

2. Scientific contour plowing, as in this potato field, keeps the water in the ground where it can be used by the growing plants. Old-fashioned methods let it run off.

Monsanto Chemical Co.

U.S. Dept. of Agriculture

In pictures 3 and 4, the two at the lower left, two different systems of crop irrigation are shown. In number 3, you can see how an irrigation ditch carries water to the roots of crops in a planted field, and how the small curved pipes pour that water on the plants. Picture 4 shows a sprinkler system. Some farmers prefer one method of irrigation, some the other. Picture 5 shows a big combine, harvesting wheat in Saskatchewan, Canada. It does as much work in one day as twenty men used to do in a week.

Nat'l. Film Board of Canada

U.S. Dept. of Agriculture

ting points. Not too long after that, man learned to make the rake and hoe, implements with which he could cut into the soil and loosen it without bending over or kneeling. When he learned to tame and domesticate animals, man invented the plow, a heavy tool that would turn over and loosen more of the soil, and that could be pulled with the strength of a horse or an ox. All these implements go back to prehistoric times. All of them remained almost unchanged until not much more than 100 years ago.

A man with a hand tool, such as a hoe, could hardly loosen the soil in an acre in a full day's work. And a man with a plow, and a strong animal to pull it, could do several acres. But even that was not enough of an advancement. To do that well, a man had to work hard every day from sunrise to sunset. No free man was willing to do that if he could help it. So the rule of life was that countries went to war, captured slaves from other countries, and set the slaves to work in their fields. For thousands of years, farming was done by slaves or by men who were little better than slaves. Captured slaves did the farming in ancient Rome. Men called serfs, who were about the same as slaves, did the farming in Europe from the time that Rome fell until modern times. In the United States, the entire wealth of the southern states was based on its Negro slaves that worked in the cotton fields, until the Civil War ended slavery. Slaves cannot advance a science because they have no reason to care whether the science advances or not. Agriculture became a respectable occupation and a scientific study when it became the work of free men and not slaves.

The first farm machinery was not advanced enough to change the old order of things. An Englishman, Jethro Tull, invented a "drill" (a machine for planting seed) more than two hundred years ago, but men still had to loosen the soil by hoeing all day, and then had to reap the crop by hand. When Eli Whitney invented the cotton gin, a machine for separating the usable fluffy fibers of the cotton plant from its unusable pod, he greatly stimulated the raising of cotton because it was now much easier to convert it to a usable condition, for making thread and after that cloth, but this did not actually advance the science of agriculture. Cotton still had to be cultivated and raised by the old-fashioned way.

The first great advancement was when Cyrus McCormick invented the reaper in 1831. This machine was designed for cutting grain, and even the first crude machine would cut as much grain in a day as five men had been able to cut before. The biggest thing the reaper did, however, was to show people that many of the old jobs of farming could be done by machine when formerly they had been done by hand. It was an easy step from there to the cultivators, the harrows, the haying machines, and all the other farm machinery that followed in quick succession. The coming of the Motor Age brought the tractor, which could do the work of twenty or thirty horses. Soon the giant "cats" were dragging over the acreage of the United States machines that could do everything that man had ever done, do it fifty or a hundred times as fast, and do it better. The farmer who once would have had to struggle to feed his own family could now almost literally "feed the world."

By the 1950s, the problem in the United States was not how to get enough food for the people but what to do with all the food that was left over after the people had been well-fed. For thousands of years, periods of famine in China and India and even in Europe could cause millions to die of starvation. As the twentieth century entered its second half, the means were there for feeding all these millions, and the only problem—how to get it to them—was the job not of agriculture but of transportation and international money relations.

When modern equipment is not available, man does the best he can. In the photo at the right, the man and woman in their rice field in Asia are operating a machine that removes the kernels of rice from the stalks. This is an old-fashioned method of rice-threshing, but the government of India is trying to develop better kinds of rice, and the rice in this field is part of that project. In the picture below, a team of oxen pulls a modern farm machine, in Arkansas.

Unations

U.S. Dept. of Agriculture Photo

The man at the left, with his old-fashioned ox-drawn plow, uses the most modern farm practices. The Department of Agriculture helps by telling him what he needs to keep his soil in good condition, and how to practice crop rotation for the best possible harvests each year. If he had more modern equipment, he could do even better. In the picture at the very bottom of the page, the Mexican farmer with his primitive equipment faces a very big problem. His oxen have been taken from him for another job, and he can do nothing about his planting till he gets another team.

THE SOIL IN WHICH THINGS GROW

Plants grow by a very complex process. The leaves, which are above the ground, take in some of the nourishment that the plant needs by absorbing sunlight and turning it into chemicals. The roots, which are below the ground, soak up minerals dissolved in water, these minerals coming from the soil in which the roots grow.

A plant never runs out of sunlight, but the soil does run out of chemicals. When this happens, healthy plants will no longer grow in it. There must be a waiting period in which the soil can enrich itself with more minerals of the kind the plant needs.

So long ago that history does not go back so far, men learned that they must let the ground rest between crops. The ancient Egyptians, nearly ten thousand years ago, let a field "lie fallow" every few years, which meant that they planted nothing in it or else planted a crop (such as alfalfa or another hay) that could grow without taking any important minerals out of the soil, and in fact would cause the soil to acquire new minerals to replenish the ones it had lost. Not long after that, farmers learned that various fertilizers (which were then generally called manure) would supply minerals to the soil and make it grow better plants.

Finally, scientists began to apply their knowledge of chemistry to the problem and to analyze the soil to see what chemicals and minerals it needed and did not have. These missing chemicals and minerals, especially nitrates, carbon, iron, and others, they could feed to the soil so that the soil in turn could feed them into the roots of the plants.

One of the ways of preventing the soil from wearing out, and one that has been known for thousands of years but is still practiced, is called crop rotation. First a certain field is used to raise a crop that takes from the soil some of the minerals but not all. Then a crop is raised that does not take those same minerals, but does use the ones that were left from the year before, and that restores to the soil the minerals that were taken out by the previous crop. These missing minerals are restored because they are in the roots and stems of the plants that die, and rot, and become part of the soil. Rotation means "turning around," and the rotation of crops is a changing from one crop to another, then going back to the first one, so that the whole process goes around as though in a circle.

The farmer learned all these things, and he bought the best seed and the best fertilizer, and he worked very hard, and he still found his farm becoming less and less valuable. The reason, very often, was "erosion," which means "wearing away"; in spite of everything he did, the topsoil, which is the most important soil, was wearing or washing away from his farm.

The topsoil is the layer of soft, black earth that lies on top of the harder, poor level of clay or packed sand that is called subsoil. The topsoil is rich in the stuff that life is made of. It is the level of soil that is soaked when it rains. Through this topsoil worms and insects burrow, both loosening it while they live and enriching it when they die. Just because it is on top, the topsoil is most likely to wash away in a heavy rain or blow away when it is dry and the winds are high, leaving for the farmer only the barren subsoil in which he cannot grow anything of value.

The problem of soil erosion became so severe that even in the rich United States, not more than thirty years ago, many farmers were unable to make a decent living because their soil was no good. It was one of the great problems of the country. The problem has now been solved to a very large extent. One way has been to cut level fields or terraces into hilly country, so that when the water pours down from the hills

Metropolitan Museum of Art

U.S. Dept. of Agriculture

U.S. Dept. of Agriculture

The picture above shows how a prosperous American farm looked in 1787. On this farm could be raised everything the family needed, including their Thanksgiving turkey. It was later that soil erosion spoiled many farms. In the picture at the upper right you can see how modern methods correct the erosion caused by winds that blow away dry, dusty soil. This is a field covered with a crop called weeping lovegrass. It is never cut, but animals graze on it. It holds the soil down and never lets it get dry enough to become dust and blow away. In Nebraska, in the picture at the center right, trees have been planted all around the level fields, to protect them from winds.

U.S. Forest Service, Dept. of Agriculture

U.S. Dept. of Agriculture

U.S. Dept. of Agriculture

Dust storms are one of the results of wind erosion. The clouds of dust you can see in the background of the picture above were caused by garden soil that was so dry it blew away. This ruins good farmland for a period of many years, and it is what caused the so-called Dust Bowl in the midwestern United States. Wind erosion can even cut away rocks. The picture at the bottom of the page shows some interesting peaks in Oregon, near Crater Lake. They are entirely due to the action of wind. These peaks are made of pumice stone, which is fairly soft, and when sand blew against and around them, it wore them into the shapes you see here.

it will stay on the level terraces and soak in instead of washing the soil down into streams, and from there into rivers, and from there into the ocean, where it is lost forever. Ditches are dug to trap topsoil that would otherwise be washed into the streams, and good supplies of water make it possible to keep the soil damp enough so that it will not blow like dust into a high wind.

THE PROBLEM OF WATER

No matter how well the soil is cared for, with crop rotation and good fertilizers and protection against soil erosion, it still must have water or plants will not grow. Land without water is desert. Land with water is fertile. Even the Sahara Desert would be a rich farming country if enough water could be supplied to it.

Many parts of the world do not have enough rainfall during the year to grow the food the people need. Where there is plenty of rain, the climate is likely to be tropical and too hot for men's comfort or health. Even where there is normally water enough for farming, a dry year, or drought, will come along now and then. This used to cause famine in big countries like China and India, where at best people hardly have enough to eat.

Where nature does not supply enough water for farming, the problem can often be solved by irrigation. This is the bringing of water to farmlands from rivers or wells nearby. The oldest way of irrigating land is to dig ditches or trenches to carry water from a river or stream. They were doing this thousands of years ago in Egypt. The great rice fields of China and other countries in the Orient are formed by irrigation.

There are other ways of irrigating fields. Sometimes big pipes are laid on the ground, with holes punched in them every few inches. Water is pumped through the pipes, and as it flows through it sprays out of the holes and waters the fields. Another way is to drive a tank truck between the rows of plants, spraying them much as trucks sprinkle city streets—or the way you would water a garden with a watering can, except on a much larger scale.

Many things we love to eat depend on a large supply of water. Tomatoes and oranges and lemons must be juicy to be good, and this means there has to be plenty of water for the plants to suck up. The government is constantly building dams and aqueducts to store the water of rivers and carry it to the farms when it is needed.

OPPORTUNITIES FOR THE FARMER

Many boys and girls see agriculture as one of the finest careers they could choose. Population is growing all over the world, and in most places there is not yet enough food to feed everyone. The United States and Canada already raise far more food than they need. With scientific advancements coming more and more rapidly all the time, they will raise still more; and some way will be found to get the food to the people who are hungry.

The person who is educated to be a scientific farmer lives a healthful, outdoor life. He can pick his own place and climate—farming is done in every state of the United States, every province of Canada, every country on earth. Even in New York City, the most densely populated place on earth, there are large sections devoted to farming.

See also the separate articles on the different branches of agriculture mentioned in this article.

Agriculture, Department of

The Department of Agriculture is one of the main divisions of the United States Government. Agriculture, or farming, is one of the most important parts of American life, and the purpose of the Department of Agriculture is to help the farmer in every way. It was

Strip planting does two things to preserve farmland. It provides a constant ground cover crop, in strips that hold back the water in the soil; and also it gives farmers a simple way of changing crops from year to year so that the soil never wears out.

U.S. Dept. of Agriculture

This stretch of level land between Kansas City and Lawrence, Kansas, is beautiful to see from an airplane. The patterns formed by the different shades of green make it look like a great artist's arrangement of colors.

Standard Oil Company of New Jersey

U.S. Dept. of Agriculture

To get full use of the rain that falls in a dry section, everyone must cooperate. The Department of Agriculture Soil Conservation Section helps farmers save valuable rainfall. Water in one farmer's land will soak into the soil and seep through to the next field.

established almost a hundred years ago, in 1862, the eighth United States Department to be formed. The head of it is the Secretary of Agriculture, one of the government's most important officials and a member of the President's cabinet.

Altogether, 78,000 people work for the Department of Agriculture. There are 62,601 full-time workers and 14,101 part-time workers in the United States, 941 people in United States territories and possessions, and 545 in foreign countries to keep us up to date on what other governments are doing for farmers.

The Department of Agriculture is divided into fifteen big sections. One section takes care of preparing "literature," or booklets, to teach farmers all that is known about farming, and to help the farmers' wives. Some of these booklets tell mothers how to care for their babies and children, and give instructions and recipes for cooking, canning, and preserving, and tell how to plan nourishing, well-balanced meals for the family. Other booklets explain the best and most modern methods of bee-keeping, poultry-farming, cattle-raising, and nearly every other kind of farming. There are booklets to explain how leather is made out of animal hides, and how skins of wild animals are made into fur. There is a Department of Agriculture booklet to tell how to do almost everything that is done around a home or on a farm, even how to knit and crochet. Many of these booklets cost only 5 cents or 10 cents apiece.

The Forest Service is part of the Department of Agriculture. It has scientists who check constantly for plant diseases that might attack our trees. It plants trees to replace those that are cut for timber, so we will not run out of wood.

Another division of the Department of Agriculture lends money to farmers, so that they can improve their farms, or form coöperative organizations and make more profit when selling their crops. This is the Farm Credit Administration.

The Commodity Credits Corporation pays money to farmers each year to make sure they get enough money for the things they grow. If the market price is too low, the Commodity Credits Corporation pays the difference necessary to make up what seems a fair price. This is called a subsidy.

The Agricultural Research Administration, another branch of the main department, makes scientific studies of all farming methods.

Aguinaldo, Emilio

Emilio Aguinaldo became a leader of his people in the Philippine Islands when he was quite a young man. He was born in 1870 on the largest island of the Philippines, Luzon. At that time the Philippine Islands were colonies of Spain. They were ruled by Spanish governors and subject to unfair Spanish laws, much as the Americans had been ruled by British governors and British laws before they fought the Revolutionary War. When patriotic Filipinos revolted against Spanish rule, Aguinaldo joined them. He was then 25 years old. The Spanish put down the revolution, and they exiled Aguinaldo—they sent him out of the country and forbade him to come back.

But in 1898, the United States went to war against Spain. This was the Spanish-American War, and the principal purpose of the United States was to free the people of Cuba, who had been under Spanish rule just as the Filipinos had been. However, when Spain became engaged in a war with the United States, the Philippine Islands revolted again. Aguinaldo went back to help lead the revolt, and was made a general. He fought bravely with the United States troops.

The United States won the war easily.

Spain was forced to give up its control over Cuba and the Philippine Islands. The United States thought Cuba was now ready to govern itself, and Cuba became an independent country. But the United States Government thought that the Philippine people were not quite ready to govern themselves, and that the United States should remain in control for some years. General Aguinaldo disagreed. He thought the Philippine Islands should have full independence immediately. So in June 1898 he set up an independent Philippine government and became its first president. He formed an army and began to fight to chase the Americans out of the islands. The United States won that fight, too, and in 1901 captured General Aguinaldo. He said he believed he had been wrong, and took an oath of allegiance to the United States.

HIS LATER YEARS

The Philippine people still admired and respected General Aguinaldo, but he did not appear very much in public life. More than thirty years later, he did become a candidate for president of the Philippine Islands, but he was defeated by President Manuel Quezon. However, when the Japanese went to war against the United States in World War II and occupied the Philippine Islands, he let them make him head of the controlled Philippine government they set up there, although he did say he disapproved of their attack on Pearl Harbor. The Filipinos, who were fighting so bravely against the Japanese, considered this treason on the part of their old leader, but because he had been such a great patriot long ago they did not take any steps to punish him.

As you can read in the article on the PHILIPPINE ISLANDS, the United States did keep its word, and the Philippine Islands became an independent country, the Republic of the Philippines, in 1946.

Metropolitan Opera—Le Blang

A scene from the famous ballet in Aida, set in the royal Egyptian palace.

Aida

Aida is the name of a grand opera, which is a play in which all the conversation is sung, not spoken, and the music is classical, intended to be played by a symphony orchestra and sung by the greatest singers. The music for Aida was written by Giuseppe Verdi, a great Italian composer, and many people consider it the most popular of the many grand operas he wrote. The story of Aida is set in Egypt, because Verdi wrote it for the khedive (that is, the king) of Egypt, to be performed at the opening of the Cairo Opera House in 1869. Actually it was not performed until two years after that, in 1871. It was a great success from the start. Aida is still performed in the United States many times each year by the largest and the smallest opera companies.

THE STORY OF THE OPERA

Aida is the name of a princess of Ethiopia. She has been captured by the Egyptian army and is now the slave of Amneris, daughter of the king of Egypt. Aida is in love with Rhadames, even though he led the Egyptian army that defeated Ethiopia and captured her.

The Princess Amneris is in love with Rhadames too, and is very jealous of Rhadames because he loves Aida and not her. Because of her jealousy, she has Rhadames accused of betraying his country. He is not guilty, but they condemn him to death anyway. They bury him alive in a large tomb. Aida, because she loves him, has hidden herself in the tomb and is buried alive with him. The opera ends with them waiting together to die, while Amneris mourns for Rhadames, sorry for what she has done.

This opera has some very beautiful music that is often played and sung in concerts. In the first act there is a famous aria, Celeste Aida, which was one of the great tenor Enrico Caruso's most famous solos. In the second act, there is a great triumphal march of the Egyptian armies returning victorious from Ethiopia. There is also a magnificent ballet. The costumes and scenery recall the times of ancient Egypt in the days of the Pharaohs.

ailanthus

The ailanthus is a tree that is grown because its big leaves look beautiful and give such fine shade. It comes from the Orient, China and Japan, and is often called the "Tree of Heaven" because of its beauty. Some ailanthus trees have been brought over from China and grow well in the northern states of the United States. The leaves of the ailanthus are one or two feet, or even more, in length. When the tree flowers each year, it has upright spikes of greenish blossoms. In China and Japan, silkworms are grown on this tree, feeding on its leaves.

Ainu

The people we call the Japanese have not always lived in Japan. They invaded the Japanese Islands from Asia, about a thousand years ago and perhaps even longer ago than that. At that time

This is an Ainu, one of the original people of Japan. They are white-skinned, and the men like to wear heavy beards.

there were already people living in Japan, and some of their descendants are still there. They are called the Ainus. They belong to the Caucasian race, as Europeans and Americans do. They are short, like the Japanese, but their skin is quite white. About 25,000 of them are left now. The Ainu religion includes the worship of bears; in their religious rites they give gifts to the bears, then kill them as a sacrifice, and then eat them. The Ainu women tattoo their mouths, arms, and foreheads. The men never shave, and their beards grow thick and long; the Ainus are among the hairiest of all people. The Japanese have let the Ainu people follow nearly all their own customs, but during this century the Ainus have been attending Japanese schools and many of them have married Japanese men and women. People of races related to the Ainus live in Siberia and on the island of Sakhalin, the island at the north of the Japanese Islands that is controlled by Russia.

air

The air around us is actually a gas. It does not kill you as the gas in the stove does, or put you to sleep the way ether does, and in fact it gives life to both animals and plants, but it is a gas just the same, just as much as they are. Rather, it is a mixture of gases. Nearly four-fifths of it, to be exact 78%, is the gas called nitrogen. About one-fifth, or more exactly 21%, is the gas called oxygen, which is so important to the lives of all living things. The rest of air is made up of other gases, in tiny quantities.

Much of the fascinating story of air is told in the article on ATMOSPHERE. Some other interesting facts will be found in the article on AIR COMPRESSION. Here you will be told some of the facts about air itself, considered as a gas.

The air we breathe in is not the same as the air we breathe out. Our bodies take some of the oxygen from the air, combine it with carbon (an important element of which our bodies are made) and breathe out a mixture of carbon and oxygen which is called carbon dioxide, in addition to the nitrogen and other gases that we do not use in our bodies. The air we breathe in, if it is fresh, pure air, has very little carbon dioxide in it; the air we breathe out is more than 5% carbon dioxide. In return, we keep about 5% oxygen (that is, about a fourth of all the oxygen we breathe in) to keep our bodies going. The plants take the carbon dioxide out of the air we breathe out, and also take much of the nitrogen out of the air. Plants need both nitrogen and carbon dioxide to live. Animals need oxygen.

Air has weight. Although gases do not weigh much, the air reaches so far up into the sky that the weight of it puts a pressure of fifteen pounds on every square inch of the earth. That explains why you can suck things up through a straw. When you suck the air out of the straw, the weight of air pressing down on your drink or other liquid forces it into the empty straw and so into your mouth.

The oxygen in the air is what makes it possible for things to burn, and without that oxygen we could have no heat when it is cold, or to cook our food with. If you put a burning match down on a saucer and cover it with an upside-down glass, it will almost immediately go out. That is because it soon burns up the oxygen that is in the air inside the glass, and then there is no more oxygen and it can no longer burn.

Air is a very fine insulating material, because it is a poor conductor of heat. This fact makes it harder to get a room warm, because the air will not carry the heat from a fire or stove. But the same fact makes it possible to seal heat or coldness out of a room or refrigerator or other place by having two panes of glass or metal with dead air in between them. On a hot day, the room inside will be cooler because the heat cannot get through the air from the outside; on a cold day the room will stay warmer because the heat from the inside cannot get out.

airbrake

An airbrake is a brake that uses the power of compressed air to stop a wheel from turning. There is a separate article on BRAKES that explains how a clamp or "shoe" grips a turning wheel and makes it stop turning. In a light automobile, or on a bicycle, a man has enough strength to work a brake. When you take a truck or bus weighing dozens of tons, or a train weighing many hundreds of tons, the strength of a man is not enough. The tremendous power of compressed air, which is explained in the article on AIR COMPRESSION, is needed.

Back in the last century, about a hundred years ago, the brakes on trains

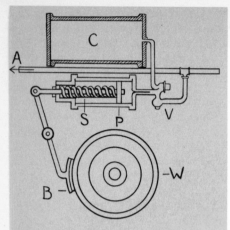

The air brakes on a railroad train work very simply. An air compressor keeps the tank ("C") full of compressed air. The tube ("A") is also full of compressed air, and this compressed air keeps a valve ("V") shut so that air cannot get from the tank to the piston ("P"). The spring ("S") pushes the piston far back in the cylinder, so that the brake ("B") does not press against the wheel ("W"), and the wheels can turn. The tube "A" runs from the locomotive along all the cars. To apply the brakes, the engineer lets air escape from this tube. Now the valve can open. This lets air from the compressor press against the piston. Since the air pressure is much stronger than the spring, the piston is pushed forward, the brake presses against the wheel, and the train stops. The safety in this arrangement is that if the tube "A" should ever break or open (as, for instance, if two cars come apart), the valves will automatically open and the brakes will be applied. The drawings below show why heavy, fast vehicles like trains and trucks need more powerful brakes than automobiles.

Bendix-Westinghouse

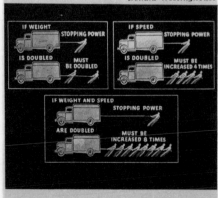

worked slowly and not very well. They depended on man power. On each railroad car, there was a big wheel on top, which turned a long screw reaching down to the wheels, where long rods joined it with a block of iron or wood that was the brake shoe. There was a railroad employee called a brakeman on each car. When the engineer wanted to stop the train, he blew a signal on his whistle. Each brakeman would then turn the wheel to apply the brakes and stop the train. This took so long that many trains were wrecked because they could not stop in time, and many people were killed. Another trouble with these hand brakes was that the different brakemen turned their wheels at different times, so that one of the cars would slow down quicker or faster than others, and passengers inside would be bumped even when the train did stop smoothly.

An American inventor named George Westinghouse thought he could solve this problem by using the power of compressed air to apply all the brakes on the train at the same time, and much better than men could do it. He went to work on the problem, and in the year 1869 he had developed an airbrake that would stop a train. There were still many things wrong with his first invention, and it took many years before it was perfected, but it made railroad travel smooth and comfortable, and airbrakes based on George Westinghouse's invention (with many improvements that have been added since) are used today not only on trains but on every heavy vehicle that needs to stop quickly and safely when its driver wants it to.

The Westinghouse airbrake began with an air compressor. You can read in the article on AIR COMPRESSION how much power a small stream of compressed air can exert. The air compressor in a railroad train, or bus, or truck, or streetcar, is driven by the same power that drives the wheels forward. It stores up tanks full of compressed air, to be ready for use when they are needed. A line, which is a thin pipe, leads this compressed air to the brakes. The air pressure applies the brakes with far greater power than human strength could exert.

EARLY TROUBLES WITH AIRBRAKES

With the first airbrakes, when the engineer wanted to stop the train he opened a valve that let compressed air from the tank force a brake shoe against the rim of each wheel. This would prevent the wheel from turning. When the engineer wanted to start the train again he would close the valve. With the air pressure removed, the wheels could turn freely again. The trouble was that if the air pressure fell too low, or the line broke, the brakes could not be applied and there would be danger of accidents.

So a few years later—in 1872—Westinghouse replaced his first airbrake with an automatic one. In the automatic airbrake, the normal condition of the brake is "on," so that the train cannot move. The engineer has to open his valve and apply air pressure to take the brakes *off*. If anything goes wrong, the brakes must automatically stop the train.

THE DEAD MAN'S PEDAL

The "dead man's pedal" was one of the big changes that were made in the original Westinghouse airbrake. There were some bad wrecks because the engineer of the train would faint or even die, and be unable to apply the brakes. Then the train would keep going at full speed, crash into something, and cause a lot of damage. When an airbrake is used with the dead man's pedal, if the engineer relaxes and takes his foot off the pedal for any reason, the brakes go on and the train stops automatically. This same device has been used on subway trains and on streetcars.

The airbrakes on big trucks and buses work on the same principle as those on trains, but they do not use the dead man's pedal and the brakes are worked by two small brake shoes that are placed inside the rim of a brake drum in each wheel, and that press this rim outward against the wheel when they want to stop it. The driver of a bus or truck has a brake pedal at his right foot, very much like those in automobiles. When he steps even lightly on this brake pedal, it brings the enormous power of compressed air to bear on the brakes, and even a giant twenty-ton trailer truck stops quickly.

air brush

An air brush is like an atomizer with which perfume is sprayed, or a spray gun with which houses and automobiles and other things are painted. It is not like a brush at all. It is more like a pistol, except that the operator works it by pressing down a lever instead of by pulling a trigger. A stream of air is brought to it from compressed air in a tank. The air brush is attached to a little can full of paint. The air sprays the paint out through a nozzle. If just a little bit of air is let through the nozzle, the paint comes out in a fine spray; this creates a light color like the blush on the cheeks of a little girl's doll (which was painted with an air brush, as all dolls are). If a lot of air is let into the air brush, a solid thin

An artist uses an air brush to color an advertising poster. The paint is in the bottle.

Paasche Airbrush Co.

stream of paint comes out, such as to make the eyebrows on a doll (and those were painted with an air brush too).

The animated cartoons in colors, that you see in the movies, were all colored with air brushes. That is how they get such beautiful shadings of color. Working with an air brush is not easy, but it is possible to study it and learn to do it very well, as thousands of people have done. Then it is possible to make very attractive pictures with the air brush.

air compression

Take a sponge in your hand and squeeze it as tightly as you can. It will become much smaller—as small as a marble if you squeeze it tightly enough.

Now open your hand and release the pressure on the sponge. It will quickly spring out to the large size it was originally.

Although most people never stop to think of it this way, the air around you is a gas, a substance just like a piece of iron except that it is thinner. Air is so thin that you can press it into a smaller space, exactly as you can a sponge. You could easily press (or a better word is *compress*) all the air in the room you are sitting in so that it would occupy no more space than your fingernail. In fact, air can be compressed into such a small space that it becomes a liquid. But the minute you take away the pressure that has forced the air into such a small space, it wants to fly back to its original size, exactly as the sponge does. It puts forth so much force in trying to return to its original size that this force can be put to use to drive many machines and serve many useful purposes.

You can measure this force for yourself, in a small way. Blow up a rubber balloon. As you blow, the air has to fit itself into a smaller space and become compressed. The more you compress it, the more power it exerts in trying to

get out of that rubber balloon. Blow long enough and this power will be so much that it will break the rubber balloon with a loud pop. Even if you have strong lungs and good wind, you probably have not succeeded in putting more than a few pounds of pressure into that rubber balloon. You can imagine how much force air can apply when so much air is forced into a tank or other space that it exerts hundreds of pounds of pressure in its effort to get out. It can drive many machines and do many jobs that a man is not strong enough to do.

The compression of air is accomplished by quite a simple device. Any pump for a bicycle tire is an example of it. There is a "cylinder"—the round, hollow tube of the bicycle pump. There is a piston, the wadding that moves up and down in the tube when it is worked by a rod and handle attached to it. There are two valves. One valve opens into the small tube that leads to the bicycle tire. The other valve opens on the outside air. When you press the piston down, it closes the valve that leads to the outside air and opens the valve that leads to the tire. The piston forces all the air that is in the cylinder into the bicycle tire. At this point, you pull the handle back and move the piston to the top of the cylinder again. This closes the valve that leads to the tire, and at the same time opens the tube that leads to the outside air. Air rushes in from the outside and fills the cylinder again. Now you press down again; you again close the valve to the outside and open the valve to the tire, and you press more air into the tire. As you pump away at the handle, it takes more and more of your strength to move that piston down. That is because the compressed air that is already in the tire is pressing back on the piston with almost as much strength as you have to press the handle down. If you keep on long enough, either the tire will burst from the force of the

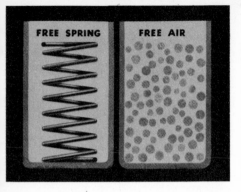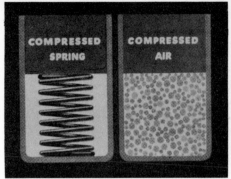

Bendix Westinghouse

These diagrams show how air compressors work. At the left is a picture of two cylinders. In one is a spring, in the other air. If you put a round, tight disc in each and press down, as in the picture at the right, you compress them. Let go, and pressure pops them out.

compressed air inside it, or the power of that air will be so great that you will no longer have the strength to push the piston down.

An air compressor for use in factories and in other big ways works on the same principles as the bicycle pump, but it is run by an electric motor or gasoline engine that can exert more strength than you can and so can force more compressed air into a tank. Once you have filled a tank with air under high pressure, you can use it for many purposes. One of them is the AIRBRAKE about which there is a special article in this encyclopedia.

The many tools that are operated or driven by compressed air include: rock drills, which can bore deep holes in the hardest rock; spray guns, which spray paint on wood or metal much faster and much more evenly than anybody can paint with a brush; rivet guns, which fasten big pieces of metal together with rivets (short, thick, round-headed nails); and giant hammers used in factories to hammer heavy pieces of metal into any desired shape. While the tool is being used, the compressor keeps working all the time to keep the tank full of compressed air. A strong rubber hose carries the compressed air from the tank to the handle of the tool. By pressing a little trigger or button in the handle, the operator opens a little valve that lets air into the tool. Compressed air tools are much more powerful and much faster than ordinary hand tools.

air conditioning

Anything that is done to make the air cleaner or more comfortable or whatever way you want it, that is air conditioning. It is air conditioning when you open a window to let in fresh air. It is air conditioning when a window is built into a house so that you can open it if you want to. It is just as much air conditioning when you heat air so as to be comfortable in cold weather as when you cool air so as to be comfortable in warm weather. But people are so used to having the air heated in cold weather that they take it for granted. When they speak of air conditioning they usually mean air cooling.

In this article, we will speak of air conditioning mostly in the sense of the cooling of air. The heating of air will be left for the article on HEATING. But even when air conditioning is mostly the cooling of air, there is much more to it than that. The air-conditioning machine that brings cool air into a house or store or theater, to reduce the discomfort of the summer's heat, also filters the air, which means that it cleans it of dust and other impurities; it dries the air,

Frigidaire-General Motors

A window air conditioner like this keeps a room comfortably cool and much less dusty.

which means that it removes some of the moisture or water that is in the hot outside air and makes it so uncomfortable; and it freshens the air by taking out of the room the stale used air that has already been breathed in and out.

AIR CONDITIONING IS IMPORTANT

It is very nice to be cool in the summer time, and anyone who can sit in an air-cooled house or theater and escape the summer heat is lucky, but that is not the biggest job done by air conditioning. Air conditioning is important in many other ways.

It is important in manufacturing. Some factories make parts out of metal, and they must fit very tightly. Metal becomes larger when it is hot and smaller when it is cold. This is the process of EXPANSION AND CONTRACTION, about which there is a special article in this encyclopedia. Factories cannot make metal parts to exactly the size they want them if they must make them in hot factories and then send them out into colder temperatures when they will shrink down to a smaller size than they are supposed to be. This is only one of hundreds of examples of ways in which air conditioning has helped factories.

Air conditioning is important to business. Motion picture theaters used to have very bad business in the summer-

time, because it was so hot and uncomfortable inside. Stores used to sell less merchandise in the summertime, because people did not want to go into a hot store to buy. Now the theaters and the stores are air-conditioned, and many people go in just because it is cooler inside than outside. This has helped business for these and many others.

Air conditioning is important in offices. People do not work as well when they are hot and uncomfortable as when they are cool and comfortable. By air-conditioning their offices, many companies have made money in the long run because their employees work better. Many new buildings in New York, Chicago, and other big cities are now being built with no windows that open. Instead they have glass walls that let in enough light but keep out dust, dirt, and street noises. The fresh air is supplied by an air-conditioning system that runs pipes, called ducts, to every office. The air-conditioning system sucks in fresh air from the outside, cleans and dries and cools it, and then pumps it into the offices. At the same time, it sucks out all the stale air. Some of these air-conditioning systems also heat the offices in the winter by pumping in warm air instead of cold.

Air conditioning is important in other ways. People who suffer from hay fever often have air conditioning because it filters out from the air all the dust and pollen that make them sneeze.

These are only a few of the ways in which air conditioning can be important. It does not matter much how many different ways there are. People would still want air conditioning because above all else people like to be comfortable.

WHY HOT WEATHER IS UNCOMFORTABLE

When you wash a dish but don't dry it with a towel, it will soon dry itself in the air. The moisture on that dish will evaporate. That means it will be sucked up by the air. The air has room in it for a great deal of moisture, which is water in such tiny drops that they cannot be seen.

Every human being must get rid of some of the waste matter in his body by perspiring. When he perspires, moisture comes out of the pores in his skin and lies there. He usually does not feel it, because the air soaks it up, just as it soaks up the water from that dish. But the air can hold only so much moisture. When it already has as much moisture in it as it can hold, it is said to be saturated, and it will take in no more. The dish would not dry. The perspiration would not be taken into the air.

That is what often happens in very hot weather. The air has soaked up as much moisture as it will hold. When you perspire, the perspiration does not immediately dry off your skin, but lies there, wet and clammy. You feel very uncomfortable.

When the air is saturated with moisture and will not soak up the perspiration from the skin, we call it "sticky" or "muggy" weather. We say, "The humidity is terrible," meaning that the air is very humid, or full of moisture. It already holds as much as it is able to. That is a case in which air conditioning is helpful. One of its jobs is to take the extra moisture out of the air. Then, when the air reaches us inside, it can again take on more moisture, and it soaks up the perspiration. We no longer drip and feel uncomfortable.

HOW AIR CONDITIONING WORKS

How does an air conditioner work? There are different kinds of air conditioner. The big ones that are put into theaters and stores and office buildings and hotels you are likely never to see. They are hidden away in the basement, and all you see are the grills out of which the conditioned air comes and into which the stale air goes. But you

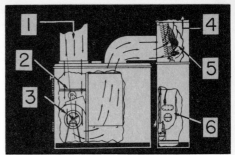

Minneapolis-Honeywell

Air conditioners are very important in summer. If summer air is not cooled and dried in large buildings where many people are at work, the people are very uncomfortable and do not work as well. Such a building needs an air conditioner as big as a furnace, and bigger. It has two large tubes (1) & (4). In one tube (1) stale air from the building is mixed with fresh but warm outside air and sent through a filter (2) to remove bits of dust and pollen. Then it is blown through a fan (3) and sent over a cooling coil (5) that is run by a motor and pump (6). Here the air is cooled and dried and is blown through the second tube (4) into various parts of the building.

will also often see the "room air conditioner," the window box that fits into the window and serves only one room, usually in a house. We will describe what goes on inside that box.

A room air conditioner looks like a long metal box about 12 to 15 inches high and anywhere from 24 to 30 inches wide—the width of the window. It is made to rest on the window sill with part of it inside the room and the rest of it outside in the open air. The window sash in the lower part of the window is brought down till it rests on the top of the air conditioner.

Air from the outside is drawn into the box by a powerful fan. It passes through a filter which removes dust, dirt, and pollen. The filter is a flat, square metal frame holding a woolly sort of material made of closely packed fine glass threads known as Fiberglas. Dust and dirt cannot pass through this filter. Only clean air gets through.

The clean air is then blown over a group of little copper pipes called a cooling coil. The pipes are cold, so they chill or cool the air. Cold air cannot hold as much moisture as warm air, so the moisture in the warm air turns to drops of water which drip down through the cooling coil to the back of the box, where they are carried away by a pipe. A fan called an exhaust blower then blows this moisture out into the outside air. The exhaust blower also sucks stale air out of the room through an opening in the front of the box. While this is going on, the clean cool air passes from the cooling coil to another opening in the front of the box and out into the room.

The most important part of the air conditioner is the cooling coil. Inside the cooling coil is a liquid called *freon*. This liquid will turn to vapor (that is, boil) at the temperature of 35 degrees (Fahrenheit).

When a liquid vaporizes it turns into a gas. The freon, which enters the cooling coil as a liquid, vaporizes inside the pipes of the coil and leaves as a gas.

During political conventions and other big gatherings in hot weather, the air-conditioning expert uses a device to measure the temperature and dampness of the air, to be sure his huge machines are properly adjusted.

Carrier Corporation

Just as water in a kettle turns to steam by drawing into itself the heat of the fire below the kettle, the liquid freon vaporizes by drawing heat from the warm air around the cooling coil. This makes the air cool, and in this cool state it enters the room.

The freon, which is now a gas, leaves the cooling coil and travels through a pipe to a machine called a compressor. This machine has a cylinder and a piston. The cylinder is a short steel tube and the piston is a round piece of metal with a flat end that fits closely inside the cylinder and moves freely up and down. The piston is connected by a rod to an electric motor that makes it move up and down. The freon is sucked into the cylinder through a small opening called a valve, and compressed or squeezed together by the fast-moving piston. This makes the freon hot, because compressing a gas always makes it hot.

The warm freon now moves through a pipe to a condensing coil. This is simply a metal box in which the pipe goes around and around in spiral turns. In larger air conditioners the condensing coil is cooled by cold water, which flows in and out of the box. In a room air conditioner, the coil is cooled by a stream of cold air from an electric fan called an exhaust blower. The warm freon gas condenses or becomes liquid when it strikes the cold copper tubes of the condensing coil. This liquid freon is then carried by a pipe to the cooling coil, where it again begins to vaporize and turn to gas, and the whole process starts all over again.

The power needed to drive the compressor and the two fans in the room air conditioner is obtained from the house current by simply plugging a wire into an outlet.

aircraft, any machine that flies. See the articles on AIRPLANE, BALLOON, BLIMP, and DIRIGIBLE.

Aircraft Carrier

USS *Franklin D. Roosevelt,* a carrier of the largest class, with its planes—wings folded—on deck.

aircraft carrier

An aircraft carrier is a warship capable of landing and launching planes, and equipped to service these planes and their crews. The planes take off from and land on a floating runway, or flight deck, that causes the ship to be called a "flattop." It is this flight deck that makes the ship an aircraft carrier. The United States Navy was the pioneer in the creation of the aircraft carrier. The first time an airplane ever took off from a warship was on November 14, 1910, when a plane of the United States Navy took off from a platform on the bow of the cruiser *Birmingham.* On January 18, 1911, the battleship *Pennsylvania* built on its stern a platform so large that it was able not only to launch a plane but also to land one. In 1922, the United States built its first warship exclusively for the purpose of carrying and flying aircraft—the first real aircraft carrier, in basic design not much different from the aircraft carriers of today. It was the United States Ship *Langley.*

By 1944 the aircraft carrier had become the first-line ship of every navy, for both offensive and defensive purposes. The Navy had been reorganized around the carrier. After five hundred years and more, the battleship was no longer the most important warship of the fleet.

THE CLASSES OF AIRCRAFT CARRIER

In 1952, there were four general classes of aircraft carrier in operation, and two new carriers of a super-class were being built. Of the aircraft carriers already afloat, the classes were:

CVBs, the largest class, such as the *Midway* and the *Franklin Delano Roosevelt.* These have a displacement of about 60,000 tons, or about the same as a large battleship. The flight deck is about 900 feet long and 113 feet wide. The top speed is 34 knots.

CVs, the next largest class, such as the *Boxer* and the *Valley Forge.* These have a displacement of about 40,000 tons, and are almost as long as the largest carriers, but the flight deck is narrower, about 800 feet by 93 feet. The speed is about the same, 34 knots.

The CVLs, with a flight deck 620 feet by 76 feet, a speed of about 33 knots, and a displacement of 10,000 to 15,000 tons.

The CVEs, the smallest of the carriers, known as the "jeep" carriers. On the jeep, the flight deck is 580 feet by

Official Navy Photos

1. These bombing planes are warming up for take-off on the flight deck of the carrier USS *Leyte*.

2. The Panther Jets in this picture are on their way back to the carrier USS *Princeton*. They had been on a mission over Korea, striking at the Communist forces there. Another carrier is shown in the background.

3. A scout bomber cracked up in trying to land on the deck of its carrier after a mission over Korea. It was half on and half off the deck when this picture was taken. No one was hurt in the accident.

4. The crews of an aircraft carrier have regular exercise. This is the crew of the aircraft carrier USS *Randolph* doing calisthenics on the flight deck.

5. Men being ferried from San Francisco to Pacific bases sleep on cots on the hangar deck of an aircraft carrier. You can get an idea of how large the deck is by noticing how many cots there are without crowding.

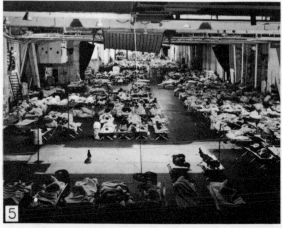

75 feet. The speed is about 18 knots, and the displacement 8,000 to 12,000 tons, about the same as the CVLs.

The big carriers can carry large planes for offensive as well as defensive purposes. Their length, approaching 900 feet, is about as much as six 14-story buildings placed end to end—higher than any building in the United States except the Empire State Building. Their flight decks are 60 to 70 feet above water.

The smaller carriers, the CVLs and the CVEs, are used mostly in submarine hunting and patrol. They can carry about 50 single-engine planes, whereas the bigger carriers, the CVBs and CVs, can carry about 90 single-engine planes. In the middle of any of these aircraft carriers, along the right side is a structure called the *island*, where the smokestacks are, and from where the ship is steered. In every other way, except for its flat top where the planes land and take off, the carrier is like any other ship.

FLIGHT OPERATIONS

Before a flight all the planes that are going to fly are spotted (arranged or parked) on the back half of the flight deck. They are brought up from the hangar deck, where they have been stored (and repaired when necessary). This hangar deck is one story below the flight deck, down in the hull, and is a little smaller than the flight deck. The carrier has three very large elevators, one toward the front of the deck, one to the rear, and one (called the deck-edge elevator) on the left side in the middle, to bring them up. If there are jets, they are spotted in front.

The pilots are "briefed"—told what to do on the flight—in "ready rooms" located just below the hangar deck. When the call comes over their loudspeaker from the bridge, "Pilots, man your planes!" they run up to the flight deck and get into their planes. On a

signal they all start their engines together, and a short time later the carrier turns into the wind and adjusts her speed so that there will be 30 knots of wind blowing down the deck. (If the wind is 20 knots, the carrier goes 10 knots.) The jets are catapulted off first, and then others are catapulted off until the remaining parked planes occupy only half the deck. Then they can take off under their own power.

There are two catapults, one on each side of the front of the ship. Jets have to be catapulted because they cannot accelerate fast enough to get flying speed.

THE PLANES IN ACTION

While the planes are on their mission, the carrier watches them on its radar scopes and keeps in constant contact with them by radio. It directs them to the enemy planes, which can also be seen on the screen, and directs them back to the carrier when they are ready to return. This is done in CIC, the Combat Information Center, a room in the center of the ship, where all the radar scopes are.

When the planes come back from their mission they circle over the carrier in formation, breaking off from the formation one by one to land in turn. In the final approach to the landing they fly a 180° (half a circle) left turn at a level altitude just a little above the flight deck. When about 500 feet from the ship they begin to see the L.S.O. (landing signal officer), who stands in the back left corner of the ship. He has two paddles, one in each hand, with which he signals to the pilot, telling him whether he is too low or high, or too slow or fast; whether to come on in and land, or to go around and try again. When the planes are landing at night, the L.S.O. wears fluorescent clothing— clothing that gleams in the dark—so the pilots can always see him.

Every plane has a tail hook that the

The new U.S. carrier *Antietam* has a canted deck—that is, a deck that slants outward to make a separate runway on which some planes can land at the same time that others are taking off. All of the new carriers are being built with canted decks. Before this type of deck was used, a plane often could not land until the runway was cleared.

pilot can lower from the cockpit. This hook, when it lands on the deck, will catch one of nine arresting (stopping) wires, which are one-inch cables stretched across the deck about 8 inches above it.

As soon as the plane catches onto a wire, men called *hookmen* run out from the side of the ship, take the wire out of the hook, and make sure that the hook goes back up into the plane.

If a pilot forgets to put his hook down—and he does sometimes forget, since a pilot more often lands on land than on a carrier—he is given a wave-off—that is, he is told to go around and try again, and this time to get the hook down. When this happens it is a custom for him to buy the L.S.O. and his hook-spotter "geedunks"—carrier talk for ice cream cones.

If a plane misses all nine wires, which are set up over about half of the deck, there is a barrier of more wires strung across the deck at the middle of the ship to stop him. This barrier is made of cables like the arresting wires. They are strung across the deck, 4 to 8 feet above the deck, and can be lowered. After his plane is stopped, the pilot

taxis forward over the lowered barrier, to get out of the way of the other planes. Finally, when all the planes have landed, the deck is respotted, the planes are pulled back with tractors to the rear again, and all is ready for the next flight.

FLUSH-DECK CARRIERS

Before the canted deck was developed, there was a plan to build "flush-deck" carriers on which there would be only a small island that could be lowered into the ship. Then a giant bomber with its big wingspread (such as the latest "super-carriers" carry) could land without danger that its wings would hit the island. The no-island idea was abandoned, because the canted deck makes it unnecessary, and such super-carriers as the U.S.S. *Forrestal* are designed with the usual fixed island.

Always following a carrier is a destroyer, to pick up aviators who for some reason miss the carrier and land in the water. Too, there is usually a helicopter that hovers near the destroyer during flight operations to pick up, or assist the destroyer to pick up, the downed pilots.

Since the flight deck is a lot smaller than the runway at an airport, there is never much margin for error and mistakes are very dangerous. But most carrier pilots feel that it isn't much more difficult to land on a carrier than it is to drive a car into a garage. In fact, some carrier pilots, upon approaching the large CVB-type flight deck after having flown off a jeep, have called the carrier to ask "Which runway is being used?"

By 1953, several two-engine patrol planes had taken off from CVBs by means of JATO (jet- or rocket-assisted take-off), but these are too big to land safely on the small deck, and so return to land bases.

The carrier is usually guarded by cruisers and destroyers, and also by its own guns and planes. Four large carriers of the U. S. Navy have been sunk, but after the Battle of Midway in June, 1942, the Navy perfected the carriers' defenses so well that no more large carriers were lost for the rest of World War II, although some were slightly damaged.

AS A CITY

A carrier is a city in itself. It has a crew of 3,000 men, consisting of sailors, aviators, and plane crews. Of course, it has room to sleep and feed them. It carries enough fuel and gasoline for the ship and the planes to stay at sea for months at a time. It also supplies the destroyer with all its needs. Carriers have movies, soda fountains, shoeshine shops, tailors, every kind of store, and even basketball courts on the hangar deck, which can be used when the planes aren't parked there. One of the new carriers has an escalator to take the men up and down the various levels of the ship.

The machine and repair shops are factories in themselves, with complete facilities for repair and maintenance of planes.

aircraft engine, see AIRPLANE ENGINE.

Airedale

The Airedale is one of the most popular dogs among American and English people. It is the largest of the terriers. In appearance it is wiry-haired, with a heavy tan body that has dark markings on it. Its tail is always cut short or docked. Its ears are never cut, but it is bred to have short ears.

It is one of the best fighting dogs known, and has been used in big-game hunting in Africa, India, Canada, and the United States, and in police work in Germany and Great Britain. During World Wars I and II it was used to carry messages, even though this meant crossing the battlefronts where firing was going on. When some dogs might have been scared and run away, the Airedale was so faithful that it kept on going until it delivered the message.

The Airedale was first bred in Great Britain, and got its name because it was used for hunting small game in the valley of the River Aire. This was less than 100 years ago. It is a very affectionate dog and is a fine pet even for small children. The Airedale is about 22 inches high at the shoulder, and weighs 25 to 30 pounds.

An Airedale terrier is about two feet tall.

Harham Kennels

Air Force

All Photos U.S. Air Force

The famous U.S. Air Force song and its composer, Captain Robert Crawford.

Air Force, U. S.

The Air Force is one of the three armed forces that have the duty of defending the United States against any enemy that might attack. The other two armed forces are the Army and the Navy. The Air Force is the youngest of the three. Through World War II it was a branch of the Army and was called the Army Air Corps. On September 18, 1947, the Air Force became independent. Because air power is absolutely necessary in modern warfare, many people consider the Air Force the most important branch of the defenses of the United States.

There are four ways in which the Air Force must be prepared to defend the United States and fight for the country in time of war.

1. If the enemy sends bombing planes to attack the United States or any of its possessions or bases, the job of the Air

Force is to fight them in the air and destroy them or chase them off. For this it uses "fighter planes," especially of the type called interceptors.

2. In time of war the Air Force must bomb enemy territory, to destroy the factories in which they make war materials, and the bases from which they might attack the United States, and sometimes for the purpose called retaliation—that is, to punish the enemy for its attacks on the United States. For these purposes the Air Force uses bombing planes of various types.

3. When United States soldiers are fighting in the field, or when an amphibious attack is made, the Air Force has the job of supporting the ground forces. It does this by attacking the enemy troops and installations against which the United States ground forces are fighting. The Air Force must also try to win "control of the skies" where the

fighting is going on. That is, it must fight the enemy planes that try to attack the United States ground forces. For these purposes the Air Force uses light bombing planes and fighters.

4. The Air Force transports both men and supplies for the Army and other services. For this it has huge fleets of transport planes. The Air Force also has planes for observation of enemy positions, for scouting, for aerial photography, for training, and for several other purposes that are different from actual bombing or fighting.

For the carrying out of these duties, Congress authorized the U. S. Air Force to have, as of July 1, 1954, nearly a million men—955,000, including Aviation Cadets who are undergoing training. The Air Force had 30,000 aircraft of all types, and 21,000 of these were in active service.

THE PLANES OF THE AIR FORCE

The warplanes of the Air Force are either bombardment planes (bombers) or fighters. The bombardment planes are of three main types. The fighter planes are of five main types.

The three types of bombardment plane are:

1. Light bombers. These are high-speed planes usually based 400 to 500 miles from the enemy. Their speed may exceed 600 miles per hour. Their primary mission is to support ground troops by destroying enemy supplies, trucks, and so on. They are also used for spotting enemy positions and photographing them (Photo-Recon).

North American B-45 "Tornado"

Martin B-57 "Night Intruder"

Douglas B-66

2. Medium bombers. These operate from bases 2,000 to 3,000 miles from their targets, but they can be refueled in midair, giving them even longer range. They are the "workhorses" of the Air Force. They may have speeds of over 600 miles per hour.

Boeing B-29 "Superfortress"

Boeing B-50

Boeing B-47 "Stratojet"; world's fastest operational bomber

3. Heavy bombers. These giant "intercontinental" planes can bomb an enemy in his own backyard, destroying his ability to fight. They may have speeds of over 600 miles per hour.

Convair B-36

Boeing B-52 "Stratofortress"

The five types of fighters are:

1. Strategic fighter. This plane may accompany medium or heavy bombers to protect them on missions deep in enemy territory. It can be refueled in air.

Republic F-84-G "Thunderjet"

Republic F-84-F "Thunderstreak"

2. Interceptor (all-weather and day fighter-interceptors).

All the interceptors are jets, stressing firepower, fast climb, and speed instead of range. The all-weather interceptor is equipped to fly by night and in bad weather. It uses radio and radar to find the enemy bombers or guided missiles. It fires rockets instead of machine guns or cannon, and has automatic electronic equipment for tracking, aiming and firing.

Northrop F-89 "Scorpion"; carries 104 high-explosive rockets

Convair F-102; first supersonic delta-wing interceptor

Lockheed F-94-C "Starfire"

North American F-86-D

3. Superiority fighter. Designed to sweep

A separate "command" or department does each job required for the air defense of the U.S. The chart shows how this works.

the air clear of enemy fighters. It emphasizes fast climb, speed, and ability to maneuver.

North American F-100 "Supersabre"; set world speed record of 754.98 m.p.h.

Lockheed F-104

North American F-86 "Sabre"

4. Fighter-bomber. Used for concentrated close support of friendly ground troops. Can launch destructive attacks against enemy armies and equipment, both in rear areas and in front lines.

Republic F-84 "Thunderjet"; can carry small atomic bomb

Republic F-84-F "Thunderstreak"

5. Reconnaissance fighter. Designed for high-speed, high or low altitude, day or night flights into enemy territory to spot installations and photograph them. It is armed and can fight its way in and out if necessary. It can also be slung under the belly of the giant RB-36 bomber for extra-long missions deep in enemy territory.

Republic F-84-F "Thunderflash"

Among these eight basic types of plane, the three types of bomber and the five types of fighter, will be found many different designs. Most of the new planes are jet-powered. Many of the new fighters are supersonic, flying faster than the speed of sound, and some combine speeds of more than 700 miles per hour with ranges approaching 2,000 miles. The "robot" planes that so much was written about for twenty years became a reality after World War II. In March, 1954, the Air Force sent to Europe a squadron of pilotless bombers, the B-61 "Matadors," capable of carrying atomic warheads with a speed of 600 miles per hour and a range of 300 miles. At the same time the Air Force released news of a "heliplane," which can take off and land nearly straight up and down, as a helicopter does, but which in level flight is an airplane. Many helicopters are used by the Air Force, and progress in designing improved helicopters was very great during the late 1940s and the 1950s.

Supersonic speeds came to be taken for granted in the 1950s, and before 1954 an experimental plane, the rocket-powered Bell X-1A, had been flown at a speed two and a half times the speed of sound.

WINGS, GROUPS, AND SQUADRONS

The Air Force makes a distinction between "strategic" and "tactical" operations. A strategic operation is intended to increase the general power of the United States or to decrease the general power of the enemy, without thought of any single battle. Bombing an enemy factory is strategic warfare, because in the long run it will make the enemy weaker. A tactical operation is intended to win some immediate objective. Bombing enemy artillery in the course of a battle is tactical warfare, because it aids the ground troops in winning that particular battle.

Whether the purpose of the operation is strategic or tactical, the Air Force assigns its planes to the job in units that are known as wings, groups, and squadrons.

A wing is the basic unit. It is made up of a number or group of planes, the men who fly them, the men who service and supply them, and all the other men who do work that is necessary to keep the planes flying.

Suppose there are forty-five B-47 medium bombers at an Air Force base. The actual crews of these bombers number about 275 men; they are the men who are in the planes when they take off on a mission. Behind them are 942 other men who service the planes, supply them with fuel, load them with bombs, guide them to their targets and keep in radio contact with them, and do other work connected with the flying and operation of the planes. Behind all these are 1,783 more men who must maintain and supply the airbase, run the medical units, do the "paper work" of keeping records and issuing orders, and perform numerous other duties. Altogether, these 3,000 men make a "wing."

Each wing is composed of a combat group, three supporting groups, and a

45 YEARS OF AIR FORCE PLANES
1. Wright Biplane of 1909.
2. Airplane of U.S. Army Signal Corps, 1916.
3. Boeing low-wing bomber, the YIB-9, of 1931. One of the first modern designs.
4. B-17G, the Flying Fortress.
5. C-97's can carry over 34 tons of cargo.
6. This jet bomber is the B-47B.
7. The F-100 "Super Sabre" jet of 1953.
8. The B-61 Matador pilotless bomber, 1953.

The F-102 delta-winged, supersonic jet interceptor streaking over an Air Force base in California in February, 1954. It is designed to fly in any kind of weather.

recruiting officers often have to discourage young men who are in too much of a hurry to get into the Air Force. "Finish your education," they say, "then fly." A good education is especially important in the Air Force, because so many duties of the airman fall into scientific fields.

For the young man who wants a good career, however, the Air Force offers exceptional opportunities. There are forty-two "career fields" in all—Air Force positions in which the airman gets training that will be of value to him when he leaves the Air Force and returns to civilian life. A few of these are: Communications (radio, etc.); metal-working; mechanic on internal-combustion and other engines; parachute repair; rocket propulsion; teaching; office work; meteorology. There are many others. All Air Force men can take correspondence courses from the United States Armed Forces Institute, which is at Madison, Wisconsin.

An *aviation cadet* in the Air Force may take training either as a pilot or as an aircraft observer. For either field he needs the same qualifications, which are: Age, 19 to 26½ years old. High-school education. He may not be married, and must agree not to marry during his training period. The physical examination is very thorough, with high requirements for eyes, ears, heart, height, and weight. Each applicant is interviewed by a board of Air Force officers, who rule on his moral and personal qualifications.

headquarters unit. The combat group is the striking force. This is the outfit that flies the planes. In peacetime, a group has three squadrons; in wartime, it has four. A squadron is simply a number of planes commanded by the ranking officer in one of its planes. When planes can be refueled in the air, there may be another squadron, the refueling squadron. Such a squadron has about 20 planes.

The Air Force has 150 bases in the United States, and about 100 bases overseas. Its personnel is stationed in 25 foreign lands. Of the 150 home bases, 42 are used for training.

THE MEN IN THE AIR FORCE

The million men in the United States Air Force are not all flying men. Not more than one in fifty of them even knows how to pilot a plane (unless he has learned, as so many do, outside the Air Force). But all have important jobs, and the Air Force has usually been able to get as many recruits as it needs without having to draft them. In fact, the

PILOT TRAINING

Aviation cadets in training to be pilots first take a pre-flight course that lasts three months. Then they receive about six months of flying training. When a cadet has soloed, he has more to learn, in classroom work, about the scientific phases of flying. After this, there are five months more of flying training and three months of advanced training. The whole process takes at least fourteen months. Only when he has completed it satisfactorily does the cadet receive his "wings."

During training, the cadet gets his living and a monthly allowance of $109.20, plus a free $10,000 life insurance policy. When he finishes he is commissioned as a second lieutenant.

AIRCRAFT OBSERVER TRAINING

The aviation cadet in training as an aircraft observer finishes a pre-flight course lasting three months, then has primary training lasting thirty weeks (about seven months). The further training is different for different kinds of work, but all successful candidates receive their commissions after fourteen months of training. Some of them become crew members of planes, for example navigators; some become ground officers in engineering, electronic, or other fields; some specialize in photography, meteorology, and so on.

WOMEN IN THE AIR FORCE

Women can be full members of the Air Force. They are known as the WAF ("Women in the Air Force"). They take their basic training at San Antonio, Texas, then a large number of them go to Air Force Technical Schools.

The WAF have many different occupations. The Air Force has found that women can handle four out of five of all its job classifications (446 out of 556). Some of the career fields open to women are: photomapping, parachute rigging, air traffic control and warning, phases of radio, radar and aircraft maintenance, and instructing in technical schools.

HISTORY OF THE AIR FORCE

Other countries, notably Great Britain with its Royal Air Force, Germany with its *Luftwaffe,* Canada, and Australia, had independent air forces long before the United States did. The use of air power in the United States began on August 1, 1907, when the United States Army set up an "aeronautical division" consisting of one officer and two enlisted men to study the "flying machine," but it took more than forty years for this to become the proud United States Air Force that exists today.

A B-47 Stratojet bomber refuels in mid-air.

Northrop F-89D Scorpion Interceptor.

Martin B-57 Night Intruder Bomber.

Lockheed F-94C Starfire Interceptor.

At first, airplanes were considered useful only for observing where the shells fired by the artillery were falling, so that the aim could be corrected. Then airplanes were thought to be useful for scouting out enemy positions. When World War I came along in 1914, the European countries found that aviation was a real fighting arm of the military services, and the United States ordered several thousand planes, but not all of them were delivered before the end of the war. Colonel William ("Billy") Mitchell was in charge of the planes used by the United States Army in World War I, but he had little to work with.

After World War I, the Army and Navy both experimented with airships, especially dirigibles, but there were many accidents. Mitchell, now a General, insisted that air power would decide all future wars, and that airplanes would destroy battleships. Although he proved this in actual tests, most of the higher-ranking officers in both the Army and Navy disagreed with him and he was forced to retire. Not until years later was it known that he had been right all the time, and that the United States

This great C-124 cargo plane can carry a 17-ton giant bulldozer. The nose of the plane opens and the bulldozer drives in.

U.S. Air Force

could have been far ahead of other countries, instead of far behind them, if it had taken his advice.

During the 1930s, Italy and Germany especially showed how important air power would be in the next war. The Air Force, which was then the Army Air Corps, designed and tested some of the finest fighting planes in the world, but Congress had not given it enough money to build up a good fighting force. Not until France fell before the German armies in 1940, in the first year of World War II, and President Franklin D. Roosevelt called upon the United States to arm the free world, did the Air Force receive the go-ahead it needed. When President Roosevelt said United States industry must produce 50,000 planes a year—more than any other country had ever produced—most people said it was impossible; but before World War II ended, that production rate had been almost doubled.

Under General Henry H. Arnold, the Army Air Corps during World War II became the greatest in the world, though it was much weaker at the start of the war than the Government was able to admit. Though the air forces had 275,-000 enlisted men and 23,000 officers, and 12,000 planes on Pearl Harbor Day in 1941, most of the planes were old and the enemy and allied countries alike had greater air power than the United States. In rapid succession the United States proved that planes could be built faster than anyone had ever supposed, that modern science could make it possible to bomb the enemy around the clock (in daylight as well as at night), and that a war could be decided by destruction of the enemy from the air. The final proof of American leadership came when the atomic bomb was developed and its use against Japan ended the war in a matter of weeks and may have saved several hundred thousand American lives that would have been lost if it had been necessary to invade Japan.

The men on the ground are especially important to the Air Force in bad weather. These Air Force sergeants, highly trained technically, are guiding in F-86 Sabrejets and F-94 All-Weather jets that protect the Atlantic Coast cities.

During World War II, the Army Air Force dropped nearly three million tons of bombs on the enemy and destroyed more than fifteen thousand enemy planes. The air forces grew to almost two and a half million men and eighty thousand planes.

All during World War II there had been argument about making the Air Force a separate branch of the armed services. When the war was over, this was done. The Air Force became a separate Department on September 18, 1947, on equal terms with the Army and Navy, under the Secretary of Defense. The first Secretaries of the Air Force were Stuart Symington, then Thomas K. Finletter, and the first Chiefs of Staff, with rank of General, were Carl A. Spaatz, then Hoyt S. Vandenberg. In 1953 Harold Talbott became Secretary of the Air Force and General Nathan F. Twining became Chief of Staff.

When the fighting broke out in Korea in 1950, the Air Force took on wartime duties as an independent branch of the armed services. It controlled the sky over Korea throughout the fighting, though there were times when bad weather prevented the Air Force from supporting the ground troops as well as they expected. The most widely followed air action during this fighting was the battles between U. S. Air Force Sabrejets and Russian-built MIGs. Official reports show that the Sabrejets downed 800 MIGs while losing only 58 planes.

The principal work of the Air Force during and after the Korean fighting was development of new planes to maintain the air supremacy that it had won during World War II.

Standard Oil Co. of New Jersey

All kinds of things are sent by airmail. Even puppies can be shipped now by air.

airmail

People have become accustomed to airmail; a letter can be carried anywhere in the world by air, and usually gets to its destination from one day to five or six weeks earlier than it would if it went by regular mail (over land or by a ship). The cost of sending an airmail letter in the United States has ranged from five to eight cents, and a letter weighing no more than half an ounce (which is about as much as most letters do weigh) can be sent overseas for ten to twenty-five cents. It has become sure that nearly all mail will eventually be sent by air, except for packages and some kinds of mail on which there is no rush. In 1953, the United States Post Office began sending regular mail by air between New York and Chicago,

and between New York and Washington, even when no airmail stamp had been put on (of course, much of this mail also went by train, and it was necessary to put on an airmail stamp to make sure the letter would go by air).

Mail was first carried by air in 1870 when the French used balloons to send mail out of Paris after the Germans had surrounded the city. In the United States, Army planes, then a branch of the Signal Corps, first began carrying the mail between New York, Philadelphia, and Washington in 1918. A year later service was started between New York and Chicago, and still a year later it was extended to San Francisco. At first the planes flew only in daylight hours, the mail continuing by train at night. In 1924, however, airmail planes began to fly at night as well as during the day.

Airmail helped a great deal to advance aviation in the United States. When the airlines were young, and were having trouble getting enough passengers to pay expenses, the Post Office Department made large payments to them for carrying airmail, and this helped them through the early years. These payments were first authorized by an Act of the United States Congress, the Carey Act, in 1925. Earlier than that, flying the airmail had given valuable training to Army pilots.

This Boeing Model 40 was one of the first planes designed to carry passengers and mail. It made its first trip on July 1, 1927, and is now preserved in the Smithsonian Institution.

Smithsonian Institution

These Cub Scouts are learning how a propeller keeps an airplane moving forward.

airplane

The airplane is by far the most widely used of all the various aircraft men have developed. Ninety-nine out of a hundred flights are made in airplanes.

In the article on FLIGHT, you can read an explanation of why an airplane flies. Every airplane must have the same basic parts: a fuselage or body; wings; tail; engine; and landing gear.

THE FUSELAGE

The body, or fuselage, is usually long and narrow—to provide less resistance to the wind. It may be large, so that many passengers may be carried inside, as in an airliner, or small, so that only a pilot is carried, as in a fighter plane. The pilots' seats are usually placed on the top side and toward the front, so that they may see better. Cargo when carried also goes in the fuselage.

Long ago, in the early days of flying, the fuselage was merely a framework of wood with cloth stretched over it. Metals had not been developed that were light enough, especially since the engines of those days were not very powerful. But for 30 years and more, fuselages have been made all of metal, usually some alloy of aluminum, which is light but strong.

Usually there is only one fuselage. Historically this has also been true, although the AF F-82 of 1953 had two fuselages, and the AF C-119 had a fuselage that split into two booms as it neared the tail—similar to the old P-38.

Lockheed

The fuselage of the P-38 is divided into two parts, joined by the tail and by the cockpit. Each of the two side sections has a motor.

Lockheed

A transport plane with a cigar-shaped fuselage. This is a four-motor passenger plane. Its fuselage is about 114 feet long.

Lockheed

This low-wing monoplane shows one type of airplane wing. It is used on commercial planes to allow clear vision to the pilot.

Boeing Airplane Co.

A plane with this wing structure was called a biplane. The biplane has been completely replaced by the monoplane.

Boeing Airplane Co.

This is a "double-decker" passenger transport. On the lower deck, where the two portholes show, there is a lounge and snack bar.

Air Force Photo

The engine of a jet plane is very different from the conventional internal-combustion engine. Jets need no propellers.

Pratt & Whitney Aircraft

A propeller engine of this type has a regular piston-driven motor, like the motor of an automobile. This is a "radial" type motor.

Aero Service Corp.

The landing gear of a seaplane looks like little rowboats hanging from the wings. Actually, they are floats called pontoons.

Pratt & Whitney Aircraft

The modern aircraft factory has assembly-line production but every operation is done much more carefully than on an automobile.

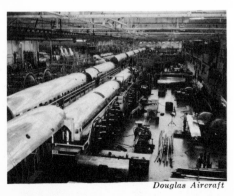

Douglas Aircraft

Assembling airplane fuselages is done by mass production methods, but most workers in aircraft factories are skilled experts.

Pratt & Whitney Aircraft

Propellers are given severe tests to make sure the metals in them are strong enough to stand the severe strains they will undergo.

THE WINGS

A very important part of the airplane is the wing, for it is by means of the air blowing over it that the lift is produced by which the plane rises or flies. At the outer ends of the wings are the ailerons, by which the pilot keeps the plane level, banks it, or rolls it. Also located on the wings are the flaps. By using them the pilot can make the plane climb or glide more steeply. The wings often contain the gas tanks. Wings are attached at about the middle of the fuselage, except in small planes and flying boats with high wings.

There is usually only one wing on each side, attached near the bottom of the fuselage, where it will not interfere with the pilot's view. Every plane with one wing is called a monoplane, although many people only think of a monoplane as having its wing attached to the top of the fuselage. In the olden days there were many biplanes—planes having two wings, one above the other. By 1953 they were no longer being manufactured, because the two wings created too much added drag, and with high-powered engines were no longer needed to provide lift.

THE TAIL

Another necessary part of the airplane is the empennage or tail section. This is attached to the back of the fuselage, and is composed of two parts. The *fin.* Hinged to the back of the fin is the *rudder.* It steers the plane to either side. The fixed horizontal part is called the *horizontal stabilizer.* It helps the wings and ailerons keep the plane level. Hinged to the back of the horizontal stabilizer is the *elevator,* which steers the airplane up and down.

THE ENGINES

The engines for multi-engine planes are usually on the forward edge of the wings or just beneath them. If a plane has only a single engine it is located at the front end of the fuselage. Those with rear propellers are *pushers.* Engines may be all jet, all conventional, or propeller engines, or a combination of both. The B-36, for instance, has six conventional engines and four jets. Before 1940 there were some tri-motored planes (three engines). Two were on the wings, the third in the nose. But with the growth in size of the airplane engine there was no longer room for one in the nose. Therefore all multi-engine planes made after 1940 have had an even number of engines.

THE LANDING GEAR

Finally, there is the landing gear of the airplane. This has to be one of the strongest and heaviest parts. If you should fall from a window 10 feet high, you would be going 17 miles per hour when you hit the ground—and it would give you quite a jolt. You can imagine how big a jolt it is on the landing gear when an airplane weighing many tons comes down at more than 100 miles per hour.

There are two types of landing gear: conventional, with which the plane sits in a three-point attitude on the ground with tail down; and tricycle, with which the airplane rests in a level position. By 1953, all planes being manufactured, except for a few small types, were of the tricycle type. This arrangement enables the pilot to see better while taxiing, since the plane is level.

Most landing gears are also retractable. That is, they can be drawn up into the fuselage while the plane is airborne, so as to reduce drag and thus gain higher speeds. (In 1949, the British Navy began experimenting with planes without landing gear, since without the additional weight greater performance could be obtained. They landed them on rubber mats on carriers, and catapulted them for take-off.)

The seaplane is similar to the land plane, except in landing gear. The difference is that the bottom of the fuselage is shaped like a boat's hull so it can land and take off from water. Some seaplanes though, instead of having hulls, have one or two pontoons attached to the bottom of the fuselage.

The amphibian is a plane that may use either land or water to take off or land. It usually has a hull with wheels attached on the outside or inside of it, and the pilot may lower the wheels if he wants to come down on land.

An airplane may have any number or combination of these parts, but by 1953 their number and combination had become fairly standard.

AIRPLANE MANUFACTURE

Airplanes are manufactured, much the same as automobiles are, on a mass production basis. They are constructed from a lightweight aluminum, which is especially treated to make it stronger, since airplanes are subject to greater stress forces than cars. Joints are riveted instead of being welded, because that gives them greater strength. From drawing board to the first test flight sometimes takes a long time; for the AF B-52 it was eight years.

See also the articles on PILOTING AN AIRPLANE, FLIGHT, and AVIATION.

airplane engine

There are two types of airplane engine commonly used: the jet engine; and the reciprocating or conventional engine, which is an internal combustion engine like the engines of automobiles. There is a separate article on INTERNAL-COMBUSTION ENGINES, and one also on JET ENGINES.

An airplane engine differs from an automobile engine in power and in weight. The most powerful automobile engine in 1954 had about 250 horsepower, which is another way of saying that if it operated at full power it could pull 50 tons a distance of one foot in one second. One very powerful internal-com-

bustion airplane engine has 3,500 horsepower, and the J-57 jet engine of 1954 developed 10,000 pounds of thrust, which is about 16,000 horsepower.

Airplane engines deliver much more power per pound than automobile engines. Most airplane engines are built to deliver one horsepower for each pound they weigh. Automobile engines can supply at the most one-third of one horsepower per pound. Since a Superfortress bomber often weighs fifty times as much as an automobile, its engine must deliver approximately that much more horsepower. Each 25 pounds of airplane must have one horsepower to keep it in motion.

Normally an automobile hardly ever uses more than 25 to 35 percent of its full horsepower. An airplane needs its full horsepower for takeoffs and climbs, and normally cruises at 65 percent of its power capacity. It is easy to see that airplane engines do more work than automobile engines over a longer period of time. The biggest problem in building airplane engines is finding metals that are strong enough to stand the high heat and pressure (especially in the case of the jet engines) and which at the same time are light enough. Various alloys of aluminum, nickel, chromium, and steel are most commonly used in constructing airplane engines.

TYPES OF AIRPLANE ENGINE

There are two types of internal-combustion airplane engines. One is the in-line water- or air-cooled engine which is very much like the engine an automobile employs. (However a liquid that does not freeze as easily as water—somewhat like the antifreeze used in automobiles—is used instead of water to cool the airplane engine.) An in-line engine has cylinders mounted one behind the other in a line. Most in-line airplane engines used today are air-cooled.

Liquid-cooled engines have not been widely used in American airplanes because they are too difficult to repair in emergencies; when used in military planes and hit by bullets, their liquid spills out and causes the engine to "freeze"—that is, to stop because it gets so hot that the moving parts can no longer move.

By far the most widely used type of airplane engine is the radial air-cooled engine. Here the cylinders are arranged in a circle around the driveshaft (the shaft that turns the propeller). This arrangement is called a bank of cylinders. Normally an airplane engine has two banks of nine cylinders each. The largest engine of this type has four banks and thirty-six cylinders. The banks are "staggered"—arranged so that each cylinder is not directly in line with the one ahead of it. This lets air come through and cool each cylinder. Additional cool air is blown onto the rear banks of cylinders through ducts (pipes) that lead back from the front of the engine. These banks of cylinders and the accessory section behind them (containing the carburetor, electric generators, etc.) are covered with a metal sheeting, called the cowling.

air plants

There are some plants that grow without having roots in the ground. They are found mostly in tropical countries, not so much because it is warm but because the air in those places has a lot of moisture in it, as it has in places farther north on a very hot, "sticky" summer day. Plants need water, and when they cannot draw it through their roots from the ground, they must take it in from the air through their leaves and, in some cases, roots that they grow hanging in the air.

Most air plants grow on other plants. That is, they are attached to the other plants, sometimes to trees. But they do not take their food from the plants they attach themselves to, as do some other kinds of plants called parasites. All of

Air plants usually grow on other plants, as shown here. This air plant is an orchid.

the food of an air plant comes from the air and from the sunlight.

Many air plants have beautiful flowers, and one kind of orchid, which many people consider the most beautiful flower of all, is an air plant.

air pockets

An airplane flying through the air will often hit a "bump," or air pocket. These bumps are sometimes frightening to inexperienced travelers by air, but they do not bother experienced travelers, who know there is nothing dangerous about them. A bump can either lift the plane in the air, or cause it to fall suddenly through the air, because it can be caused by either a rising or a falling current of air.

Just as cream floats to the top of milk, because it is lighter than milk, hot air rises because it is lighter than cool air. When the ground below the plane is very hot, the warm air from the ground will rise, which causes the cool air to rush downward and carry the plane down with it. Also, moving air tends to follow the earth's surface. As a plane passes the top of a mountain, it is likely to hit a descending current of air going down the side of the mountain, and to bump downward with this current. Descending currents of air, causing air pockets, will also be found near thunderstorms, because warm air will be rising. The plane neither falls nor rises very far when it strikes an air pocket, and is immediately leveled out to continue on its way.

airport

An airport is a place specially built for airplanes or other aircraft to land or take off. It may be on the land, or on the water, or even on a building. Generally, though, it is thought of as being a particular piece of ground with runways and with special equipment for guiding planes when they land or take off, and for servicing them.

The modern airport came into being about 1935. It is a necessity as well as a convenience, since large planes must land on strong concrete runways, and since it offers a central place for passengers to begin their trips, just as a railway station does.

There are military airports, large and small commercial airports, and small private airports. Basically these are all the same. The smaller ones simply have less equipment, sometimes being no more than a level grass field.

WHAT AN AIRPORT NEEDS

First of all, strong runways are needed. Most modern planes are too heavy to land in grass fields, as their wheels would sink into the ground and upset them. A DC-6 or a Constellation weighs about 75,000 pounds, or as much as about 30 automobiles, so the runways must be stronger even than highways.

Normally the length of a runway is about 6,000 feet, though they may be as short as 4,000 feet, or as long as 10,000 feet. The width is usually about 200 feet, though at military fields they are about 300 feet wide so that single-engine planes can land on either side. This way, a group of planes can land or take off more quickly.

Planes don't really need runways that long but they are built that way for the sake of safety. Pilots say: "The first third (of the runway) is to land on, the second third to taxi on, and the last

A modern airport like LaGuardia Field in New York provides for both comfort and safety.

The control tower in a large airport tells pilots when they may land and take off.

third is life insurance." Planes can generally take off and land in one-third to one-half of a 6,000-foot runway. Jet planes require somewhat more space, since they accelerate and decelerate more slowly. Most multi-engine planes (that is, planes with more than one engine) usually have reversible propellers (propellers that can be made to push the plane backwards and so help it to stop) and also brakes on the wheels, so they can land in even shorter space.

WHY THERE ARE SEVERAL RUNWAYS

Planes always land and take off into the wind, for reasons explained in the article on PILOTING AN AIRPLANE; so at any airport there are as many runways, usually five, as there are directions from which the wind is likely to blow. Runways are numbered by the first two digits of their magnetic compass heading. A runway that is on a course of 320 magnetic would be called 32, and the number is painted at the end of the runway. Also, the length of the runway is painted

on it and is shown by means of a white painted bar for each 1,000 feet, big enough so that the pilot can read it from the air. Other marks are painted at the one-third and two-third distances. For planes without radios a tetrahedron (◁) which may be moved by the wind or mechanically, or a wind sock, tells the direction of the wind.

At the large fields there are always several fire trucks, a crane, and an ambulance for use in case the pilot has an accident while he is landing or taking off. If the plane catches fire, or if anyone has been hurt in the crash, help is right there waiting.

To get to the runway from the hangars, parking areas, or passenger terminal, there is a taxi way, which is just like a driveway for a car.

THE TOWER

Every large field has a central tower in which one or more men direct the traffic of planes at the field. When a pilot wishes to taxi from his parking place, he calls the tower on his radio, and the tower tells him which runway to use, the one that is most nearly in line with the direction of the wind. The man in the tower also tells him the altimeter setting—the barometric pressure at the moment. (See the BAROMETER article.) The altimeter is the instrument for telling how high he is above sea level. He sets the current barometric pressure, and if the airport is 100 feet above sea level, since he is on the airport, his altimeter, when set correctly, will also tell him that. When the pilot gets to the starting end of the runway, after he was warmed up the plane and checked to see that everything about the plane is working right, he asks the tower for permission to take off, and if no one else is landing or taking off, the tower tells him to go ahead.

The procedure is just reversed for landing. The pilot calls when he is about ten minutes away from the airport. Landing planes have priority, since they are usually low on fuel when returning. The tower gives the pilot instructions on his radio where and when to land. The men in the tower also have a gun that shoots colored lights, by which they can give more instructions to the pilot.

Planes without radios or at least without receivers usually don't land at crowded airports, because it is too hard for them to get directions.

HELPS TO LANDING

At night the runways are lit up with a row of white lights on each side two-thirds of the way down, and yellow lights for the last one-third, so that pilots will know they are coming to the end. There are four green lights at each end, and the taxi ways have blue lights. Rotating lights on the tower tell the pilot which runways are being used.

Airports also have blind-landing devices that guide the pilot from some position over or near the airport to the end of the runway when he is unable to

At Tempelhof Airport in Berlin, the planes are taxied under a shelter for passengers.

see it because of bad weather. There were two such devices in use in 1953: GCA, Ground Control Approach, in which men in a truck located about half-way down on the side of the runway use radar to guide or "talk" the pilot down; and ILS, Instrument Landing System, which is a series of radios that transmit signals to an instrument in the plane by which the pilot can guide himself down. For various reasons the military favors the former, the airlines the latter.

"OPERATIONS"

In addition there is at every airport a place which is most commonly called "operations." This provides information on three things: weather, navigation, and clearance.

At the weather desk a pilot can find out the weather where he is going, and all along the way. He then can tell whether he will have to direct his plane by instruments, or whether he can do it by merely watching the ground.

At the navigation table he figures out the compass headings to fly, allowing for any wind present, and also the time it will take him. Thus he knows whether he will have enough fuel, since he already knows how much the plane uses per hour.

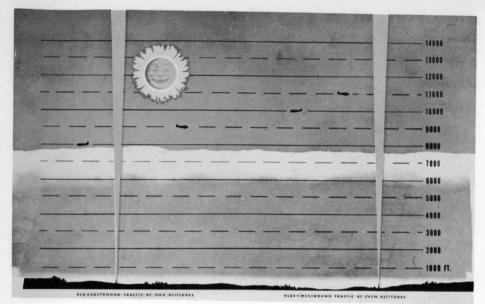

Eastbound and westbound planes can never collide head on. That is because planes flying eastward stay on odd-numbered altitudes, such as 15,000 feet, while planes flying westward stay on even-numbered altitudes, such as 16,000 feet. They can fly above clouds or bad weather, as shown in this picture. The picture also shows how radio beams are sent up to guide them. See the article on piloting.

At the clearance desk, he must file a clearance if he is going to fly on instruments, called IFR, Instrument Flight Rules. This means he will be flying in the clouds without looking at the ground. The CAA (Civil Aeronautics Administration, a branch of the United States government) can then coördinate his path with that of other planes so that they won't bump into each other. If he is going to fly VFR, Visual Flight Rules, by looking at the ground, a flight plan is not required, though he may file one, saying when he expects to reach his destination. When he arrives he merely tells the CAA, who take care of the flight plans, that he is there; otherwise, if he should become an hour overdue, they would begin to look for him.

THE HANGARS

Large airports also have hangars, or large garages, where planes may be stored and repaired. There are also park-ing spaces outside of the hangars, either concrete or asphalt, where planes may be tied down, since small planes are easily blown by the wind.

THE TERMINAL

Passenger airports have in addition a building called a terminal, where passengers buy tickets, check their baggage, and get on and off the planes. Restaurants and stores are often found there, just as they are in railroad stations. There is usually a post office for the government. There are also places to handle air cargo or freight.

At military fields there are places for the officers and men to live and eat, plus recreational equipment.

SEA AIRPORTS

Water airports, or "sea ports," are the same as land airports except that the runways are the water, which is marked out by buoys. There are also

American Airlines

This man is about to release a weather balloon. As it floats up, a telescope with a recording device will report to the ground observers how it behaves in the upper air. This tells the airline's weather service how the weather is up where planes will be flying.

concrete ramps on which a plane may taxi out of the water if it is an amphibian (a plane that has wheels as well as a hull or float), or if the plane is made so that wheels can be attached to it while it is still in the water, so that it may be towed out. Most seaplanes are made this way. In addition, a small boat patrols the water runways, taking away logs and other debris that would punch holes in a hull or pontoon and make the seaplane sink.

SOME AIRPORT RULES

Civilian planes are forbidden to land at military airports unless they are in some kind of trouble, lost, almost out of gas, or having engine trouble, and can't make it to a civilian field, or if they have special permission beforehand from the commanding officer of the field. Military planes, however, can land at any airport that is large enough, and at any military airport.

A private plane is charged a fee for landing at an airport, much as a private automobile is charged at a garage. The fee may range from a few dollars to $50 or more, depending on the size of the airport and the size of the plane.

Information a pilot may need about airports, such as field elevation, radio frequencies, location, and so on, can be found in charts put out by the government.

Many large airports, such as La Guardia Airport in New York City, conduct tours on which many of the things described here can be seen.

Trucks at the airport refuel planes quickly.

Standard Oil Company of New Jersey

air rifle

An air rifle must not be thought of as a toy. It is a real gun, except that it uses the force of compressed air instead of gunpowder. Though gunpowder is more powerful, if you will read the articles on AIR COMPRESSION and AIR-BRAKE you will learn that compressed air can stop a railroad train or a heavy truck or bus, and that is enough power to make an air rifle a very dangerous weapon.

Some air rifles shoot bullets, and shoot them with such force that they can be used in hunting. The air guns that boys know best are usually called "BB guns" because they shoot little balls of lead or other metal called BBs. Little ball-shaped pellets of this sort are called *shot,* and shot comes in different sizes. Each size is called by a different number or letter to show exactly how big it is. For example, No. 12 shot is very small, and No. 3 shot is considerably bigger. BB shot is one of the biggest. It has a diameter of eighteen hundredths of an inch (written .18"), which means that five BBs in a row would measure almost an inch.

Parents have different ideas on how old a boy (or a tomboy) should be to have a BB gun. Most of them seem to think twelve years old is about the earliest age, and some make it fifteen. At least, he must be old enough to follow these rules:

The gun must never be pointed at anybody. It must not be used or even loaded in the city. It must not be fired unless you can clearly see everywhere the shot might possibly go. When carried it must be pointed downward and slightly forward (away from your own feet).

The picture below shows what goes on inside a BB gun. All the different parts are numbered, so that you can understand how the gun works, and why, and what you must do to fire it.

First you drop a number of BBs through the hole in the front of the *muzzle* (21). You have the gun pointed upward, so they will fall through the *barrel* (19) to the *shot follower* (17) and into the *magazine* (15). The magazine in a gun is the place where bullets are kept for use as needed. This BB gun need not be loaded every time. It will continue to fire as long as there are BBs in the magazine. One BB at a time will drop into the *firing chamber* (13).

Now you pull back the *handhold* (16). This forces back two *cocking levers* (8) and (14). These move a *cocking arm* (7) that is attached to the *trigger* (3) by a *safety bar* (4). At the same time they move a *piston* (10) that compresses the *spring* (9) and later compresses air in the *chamber* (11). The cocking arm forces back a *plunger* (5) and hooks it over the top of a *sear* (2). The *stock* (1) is placed against the shoulder; the gun is aimed by lining up the *sights* (20) and (6); and the trigger is pulled. This releases the spring, which flies forward and pushes the compressed air through a small hole in the *air tube* (12), and forces the BB out through the *shooting barrel* (18).

Daisy Manufacturing Co.

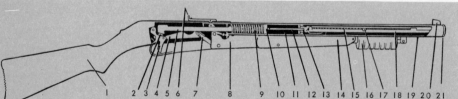

Air Transportation

air transportation

The carrying of paying passengers or freight by air is called air transportation. In present times, this business is done solely by airplanes. Giant dirigibles, or airships, tried to compete with the airplanes as recently as fifteen or twenty years ago, but airplanes proved to be faster and in the long run cheaper. Most of the business of companies engaged in air transportation is the carrying of passengers. Light freight and express is carried when it has to get to its destination in the least possible time, but most of the heavy freight is still carried by ships or railroads.

Air transportation is probably the fastest-growing business in the world. Since the railroad was invented, about 125 years ago, it has carried most of the passengers and freight overland throughout the world. It still does. However, in 1954 airlines in the United States alone carried passengers more than 12 billion passenger miles, as compared to 32 billion passenger miles for the railroads, more than a third as much, and the number of air passengers was growing every year. Since passengers take airplanes only for fairly long distances, while the bulk of the railroad business is done over short distances, the airlines had at least equaled the railroad companies in the number of passengers they carried over the same route.

The great advantage of airplane travel is the speed with which the journey is completed. Airliners, the giant luxury planes used for passenger travel, were going more than 350 miles an hour (and jet planes, in which the British were pioneers, were approaching 500 miles an hour). While a fast train might reach 100 miles an hour or even a bit more on a long, straight, level stretch, they had trouble averaging more than 60 miles an hour for a complete trip. The airline passenger could save anywhere from four-fifths to nine-tenths of the travel time if he went by air. On short trips, airlines were not yet able to compete with railroads, because it took so long for a passenger to get to the airport in the city he left and from the airport to the city he was traveling to. The aviation world thought this might eventually be overcome by having helicopters land in the very centers of cities.

FIRST-CLASS AND AIR-COACH TRAVEL

The airline passenger has a choice between first-class travel and air-coach travel. First-class travel is much more expensive. It is often a bit faster, but seldom more than a few minutes—perhaps as much as an hour on long trips. The difference is that in first-class travel there are fewer seats in the plane, and the passenger has more leg room (which is important to big men, but seldom to women and children); the first-class service includes meals served free if the traveling time is the same as a regular mealtime; and the first-class planes often take off and land at hours that are considered more convenient. Tourist (air-coach) flights have no round-trip discounts or "family plans" (when on certain days all members of a family except one may ride for half fare); they also

have limited stopover privileges, and there is no sleeper service provided. There is only one steward or stewardess instead of the usual two. If you make a tourist reservation you do not have the privileges of late pickup of ticket and last-minute cancellation that you do on first-class reservations. One first-class service plane even has a bar.

SCHEDULED AND NONSCHEDULED LINES

First-class service is offered only by the scheduled airlines. Tourist or air-coach service is offered by both the scheduled and nonscheduled airlines. The difference between these two types of airline is just what their names say. The CAA (Civil Aeronautics Administration) authorizes the scheduled airlines to land and take off at certain airports, to fly certain routes, and to have prearranged regular schedules for taking off, just like a railroad's. The nonscheduled airlines, or nonskeds, as they are called, are not allowed to provide regular service. They must wait until they have a planeload of passengers for a particular destination and then take off. Non skeds usually operate between places that are fairly far apart; for instance, from coast to coast, with one stop in the middle, or the length of a coast, as from New York to Miami.

Some people believe that the nonskeds are not as safe as the scheduled

The flight deck of a Stratocruiser is fitted with hundreds of instruments and dials.

The navigator on a plane checks constantly on the exact air position of his ship.

Pan American World Airways

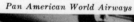

Pan American World Airways

A steward serves canapes and tiny sandwiches to the passengers on a trans-Pacific flight. The seats are large and comfortable, with foot rests. They can be tilted back so that passengers can lean back and sleep if they wish.

Pan American Airways

Children usually enjoy air transportation. They play games while in flight, and they are given meals especially designed for young people. Sometimes parents can arrange to send their children on plane trips alone, knowing they will be given excellent care by the stewardesses until someone meets them when the plane lands.

On many long-distance planes that fly all night, there are big berths in which two persons can sleep comfortably. There will be breakfast all ready for this little girl and her mother when they get up in the morning. The plane is air-conditioned, and soundproofed so that motor noises do not disturb the passengers trying to sleep.

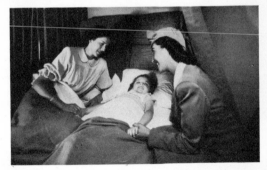

Flying in a big transport is almost like sitting in your own living room. These people are writing postcards to be mailed the next time their plane lands. There are lights and air circulators above each seat so that a passenger can have as much or as little air and light as he chooses. You can see the round light directors over the woman's head.

airlines. This is only partially true and only then as to some of the smaller nonskeds. The larger and wealthier nonskeds are in some cases even larger than the smallest of the scheduled airlines. The CAA requires all airlines, scheduled or nonscheduled, to maintain certain minimum standards as to the pilot qualifications, plane maintenance or repair, the load the plane may carry, and the weather conditions under which they may fly. But the airlines with large amounts of capital go far beyond these standards set by the CAA, because it helps them to give better service and maintain a better safety record. For financial reasons the smaller airlines—mostly nonskeds—are sometimes not able to go so far. They must, of course, comply with the minimum standards.

The cost of first-class service is fairly low—about on a par with first-class railroad fares. In some cases it is even lower.

RESERVATIONS

For all air travel, unlike railroad travel, the rule is that the passenger must make a reservation in advance. Airplanes have few seats and cannot accept any more passengers when full. (The largest airliner in use in 1953 carried only 88 passengers.) Whereas trains may have empty cars for last-minute passengers and pull empty cars and still make money, the airlines cannot fly empty airplanes and make a profit. However, a passenger can almost always get a seat at the last minute if he is at the airport. It is necessary to make reservations a little further in advance for tourist flights than for first-class flights, since there are fewer of them.

Passengers are allowed 40 pounds of personal baggage free, and 60 pounds if they are going out of the United States. Any excess baggage must be paid for at the rate of $\frac{1}{2}$ of 1 per cent of the fare per pound, thus making it very expensive to carry excess baggage.

RELIABILITY OF AIR TRAVEL

The scheduled airliners now make 97 percent of their scheduled flights. That is, bad weather or mechanical trouble

Passengers in a city terminal, about to board the special bus that will take them to the airport several miles away.

American Airlines

Before taking off, the captain-pilot finds out exactly what winds and weather conditions are at every point on the flight.

American Airlines

American Airlines

Fresh fruit flown by air freight will reach
your table a day or two after it is picked.

Air freight gets news films to television stations within a few hours of the event.

Standard Oil Co. of New Jersey

causes only 3 percent of them to be can-
celled. If a flight is unable to continue
after departing, the airline will always
pay for transportation to your destination, either on another airplane or on a
train if the weather does not permit flying.

AIR FREIGHT

Freight is also carried by air, along
with express packages and airmail. Besides the airlines that haul nothing but
freight, the passenger airlines carry some
freight in their passenger planes, and
many of them also operate separate
freight planes. The largest use of air
freight is in hauling goods that are
perishable and would be harmed by a
long railroad or truck haul. Some businesses have candy, fresh flowers, sea-
food, and some kinds of fruit regularly
delivered by air. Air freight is widely

used in emergencies to transport various articles needed quickly. The transportation of larger articles has been increasing, too. In 1952, an elephant was flown from North Africa to a zoo in the United States.

One further service that is available in air transportation is the charter plane. Just as one would charter a bus, a plane may be chartered. Both private companies and the scheduled and non-scheduled airlines provide this service.

By 1953, it had become safer to fly the scheduled airlines than to drive your own car; and the safety record of the railroads is only slightly superior to that of the airlines.

Aisne

Aisne is the name of a department (which is like a large county) in northeast France, near the border of Belgium. It is also the name of a river that runs through this county. One of the most famous battles of World War I was fought here. It was in May, 1918, and the Germans were losing the war but it was not then known. They opened a great attack against the Allies, crossed the Aisne River and almost got to Paris. Troops from the United States and Canada, as well as from the other Allies, were opposed to them. The Germans almost broke through the Allied lines, but finally they were stopped and driven back. It was the last great German attack of the war, and a few months later they admitted defeat and the armistice was signed.

AISNE. Area, 2,868 square miles. Population, 453,411. Capital, Laon, population 14,868.

Aix-la-Chapelle

Aix-la-Chapelle is the French name given to the German city of Aachen. The name is seldom used now but is remembered because two treaties were signed there and an important Congress (that is, a meeting) was held there.

The first Treaty of Aix-la-Chapelle, in 1668, ended a war between France on one side and England, Holland and Spain on the other. The Treaty allowed the French to keep some towns they had conquered, but they had to give back other territory. The second Treaty of Aix-la-Chapelle was signed in 1748. It ended a war, called the War of the Austrian Succession, that was fought over whether or not Empress Maria Theresa should be allowed to rule Austria. The Treaty permitted the empress to stay on her throne. The Congress of Aix-la-Chapelle was held in 1818. It was a meeting of high officials of England, Russia, Austria, and Prussia. These four European nations had kept armies in France since the defeat of Napoleon in 1815. The Congress decided to take the soldiers of the four nations out of France.

Ajax

Ajax was one of the great warriors in the Greek armies that fought Troy in the Trojan Wars, which are the subject of one of the most famous stories of all time. (There is a special article about the TROJAN WARS in a later volume.) He was a giant and very strong, but not very smart. He committed suicide after Achilles was killed.

Akron

Akron is a city in northern Ohio. More things made of rubber, such as tires and hoses and rubber balls, are manufactured in Akron than anyplace else in the world. It is also a center for building blimps, and two famous dirigibles, the Macon and the Akron, were built here. In early days, the Indians passed through on their freight route, and it was a station on the old Indian Portage Path.

AKRON, OHIO. Population, 274,605; urban area, 410,032 (1950 census). County seat, Summit County. On the Little Cuyahoga River. Settled 1807.

Alabama

Alabama

Alabama is a state in the "deep south" of the United States. Its nickname is "the Cotton State," because Alabama farmers used to raise so much cotton. Now they raise many other crops as well. The name Alabama came from a tribe of Indians who lived there before the white men came, and in their language alabama meant farmers.

In population, Alabama ranks 17th in the United States, with more than three million people living there. In area it ranks 28th, having 51,078 square miles. It became a state in 1819, and was the 22nd state admitted to the United States. The capital is Montgomery.

THE PEOPLE OF ALABAMA

Most of the people of Alabama used to be farmers. In the southern part of the state they still are, but in the center of the state, where the big cities are, there are many more who work in factories or who dig coal and iron ore out of the rich mines in this part of the state. In northern Alabama, which used to be a cotton- and corn-raising section, more and more factories are being built.

If you visit Alabama, and do not come from another southern state, one of the first things you will notice is that you see

almost as many colored people as white people. There are about a million Negroes in Alabama, and about two million white people. Most of the Negroes work on farms or are laborers in factories. For many years they were very poor. They lived in one-room cabins in the country, and in small shabby houses called shanties in the cities. They did not usually have bathrooms or running water or electric lights. Since World War II the Negroes have made more money and they can afford to live much better than they did. But they are still poorer than the white people.

Most of the two million white people in Alabama were born there, and their parents and grandparents were born there. They are proud that they are southerners and that Alabama was one of the states that formed the Confederate States of America in 1861 and fought against the Union in the Civil War. In Alabama you will see the old Confederate flag in many places, and monuments to soldiers who died in the Confederate armies. The Confederate President, Jefferson Davis, was from Alabama, and the capital of Alabama, Montgomery, for a short time was also capital of the Confederacy, back in 1861.

The churches are very important in the social life of people in Alabama. Nearly everyone goes to Sunday School and to church, and especially in the smaller towns people have their clubs and parties and picnics through their churches.

WHAT THE STATE IS LIKE

If you meet someone who comes from Alabama, you still can't be sure what

Mobile Chamber of Commerce

The Infirmary at Mobile, Alabama, one of the most modern hospitals in the world.

his home country looks like until you find out what part of the state he lives in. The southern, the central and the northern parts of Alabama are quite different.

The southern part is the "Black Belt" section. At the very southern end, of course, Alabama has a seacoast—a very short one, where long, deep, Mobile Bay runs north from the Gulf of Mexico to the city of Mobile, second-biggest city in the state. Near the seacoast there is sandy soil, as there usually is near the ocean; and there are forests of pecan and other trees; and there are swamps and marshes where many alligators live. A few miles above this region begins a "belt" of rich, black topsoil, twenty to fifty miles or more wide. This beltlike strip of land winds northward to the central part of the state. It is the blackness of its soil that gave it the name "Black Belt." Once it was considered one of the finest cotton-raising places on earth. But the farmers used to have such bad years when the cotton crop failed, or when cotton prices fell too low, that they now raise peanuts and vegetables and other crops, as well as cotton, and they are much better off than they were.

The central part of the state is the "Coal Mountain" section. Driving through this part, you are likely to see coal miners with axes on their shoulders and lamps on the fronts of their caps, just as you would in western Pennsylvania. There is much iron ore in those mountains, too, and other valuable minerals. In the center of this section is

1. The beautiful capitol at Montgomery, Alabama. It was built in 1845 and for three months in 1861 it served as the capitol of the Confederate States of America.

This statue of Vulcan was cast (in 1903) from pig iron produced in the district of Birmingham, Alabama. It is 53 feet tall and weighs 120,000 pounds. Just one of Vulcan's thumbs is 3 feet long. The statue stands on Red Mountain, overlooking the city, which is shown above.

Birmingham, the biggest city in the state and one of the biggest in the South. Birmingham is called "the Pittsburgh of the South" because it has great steel mills, just as Pittsburgh has. Only the Pittsburgh and Chicago areas produce more steel each year than Birmingham does.

The northern part of Alabama is the "Tennessee Valley" section. This means it is the valley through which the Tennessee River flows. In the northeast corner of Alabama, this great river enters the state. It flows all the way across the state, and in the northwest corner flows back into the state of Tennessee.

Northern Alabama is very beautiful. The river flows through the Cumberland Plateau (a plateau is a region that is high, like a mountain, but level, like a plain). On both sides of the river, as it flows through the state, hills and mountains rise. Many "mountaineers" live in these hills, as they do in the mountains of Kentucky and Tennessee and several other southern states.

Less than a lifetime ago, northern Alabama was nothing more than farming country, and much of it was not even much good for farming. Too much of the good soil had washed away. Then, in 1933, the Tennessee Valley Authority of the United States Government began to develop the river. Beginning at a part of the river called Muscle Shoals, which was a long section of rapids where the water flowed so fast and the river was so rocky that no boat could get through, the "TVA" built three great dams— Wilson Dam, Wheeler Dam, and Guntersville Dam. These dams made big lakes where before there had been only the river. Water flowing over the dams turned great generators, producing electricity to run factories and bring electric light and power to cities and farms in several states. The dams also put an end to the terrible floods that for many years had damaged towns and farms along the Tennessee River. After all this was done,

northern Alabama began to be as busy and prosperous as the rest of the state.

Many an independent nation could envy the state of Alabama. It is said that the most important things a country can have are fertile farmlands, so it can raise its own food; and forests, for wood; and coal and iron mines, to feed its factories; and rivers that can be dammed to produce electricity and navigated to transport goods; and a seacoast so that it can trade with other countries. Alabama has them all. The soil is rich, and the climate, though it often gets uncomfortably hot in the summer, is ideal for farming and cattle-raising, with an average temperature of 65 degrees and an average of 52 inches of rain a year. The mineral wealth in Alabama's mountains, and the power created by the Tennessee River, are the greatest in the South. Next to steel, the biggest industry of Alabama is textiles (cloth, yarn, and clothing, chiefly of cotton). Next to cotton, the chief agricultural product comes from the trees, which are cut not only for lumber but for paper-making.

Besides the Tennessee River in the north, Alabama has several big rivers in the south. Among these are the Coosa River, the Alabama River, and the Tombigbee River—all Indian names. The Alabama and Tombigbee run together and form the Mobile River, which flows into Mobile Bay.

Railroads and highways reach nearly every part of the state.

THE GOVERNMENT OF ALABAMA

Alabama, like most other states, is governed by a Governor, a Senate, and a Legislature. The Governor and members of both houses are elected to serve four-year terms. Judges are elected and serve six years. The capital is Montgomery. There are 67 counties in the state.

Everyone has to go to school through grammar school at least. There are more than three thousand public schools in Alabama. Nearly half the schoolchildren

All Photos Ala. State Chamber of Commerce

1. Cotton in an Alabama field. It is still a very important crop in Alabama, but not as much as it was a hundred years ago.
2. The Presbyterian Church in Eutaw, Alabama, built in 1824.
3. The first bank building in the state, in Decatur.
4. The first White House of the Confederacy, in Montgomery, is open to the public.
5. Southern Alabama has become important cattle country.

go to big consolidated schools, to which they are taken in school buses.

There are twenty-seven colleges and universities. Nine of these are free state institutions, and some of the others receive some help from the state. Among the principal state-operated colleges and universities are:

University of Alabama, at University. Enrollment, 6,119 in 1953 (4,266 men, 1,933 women). The medical and dental colleges are in Birmingham.

Alabama Polytechnic Institute, at Auburn. Enrollment, 6,750 in 1953 (5,136 men, 1,614 women).

Alabama State College for Negroes, at Montgomery. Enrollment, 2,374 in 1953 (586 men, 1,788 women).

Alabama Agricultural and Mechanical College (for Negroes), at Normal. Enrollment, 967 in 1953 (382 men, 585 women).

Tuskegee Institute, at Tuskegee, the world's first and most famous college for Negroes, is partly supported by the state. There is a separate article about TUSKEGEE in a later volume.

Among the principal private colleges are Howard College and Birmingham-Southern college, both at Birmingham.

CHIEF CITIES OF ALABAMA

The leading cities of Alabama, with populations from the 1950 census, are:

Birmingham, population 326,037, the largest city in the state. There is a separate article about Birmingham.

Montgomery, population 106,525, the state capital. There is a separate article about Montgomery.

Mobile, population 129,009, the second-largest city in the state, and its principal seaport, on Mobile Bay. There is a separate article about Mobile.

Gadsden, population 55,725, the fourth-largest city, manufacturing center, in the northeast part of the state.

ALABAMA IN THE PAST

When the Spanish explorer Hernando De Soto first entered what is now Alabama, in the year 1540, it was a land of the Creek and the Choctaw Indians, and De Soto had to fight and win a bloody battle from them before he could cross the state. The battle was fought in what is now Clarke County, and it is said that 11,000 Indians were killed, and only 82 of De Soto's Spanish soldiers. In later years, the English and French as well as the Spanish claimed Alabama, and the French held it for nearly a hundred years. For a time, Mobile was the capital of Louisiana. In 1763 France gave Alabama to the British.

When the United States won its independence, Alabama was considered as part of Georgia, but in 1798 it was made part of the Mississippi territory, and in 1819 was admitted as a state. Alabama became one of the principal cotton-raising states, and the "Black Belt" was filled with big plantations whose rich owners lived in fine mansions and owned hundreds of slaves to raise the cotton. Although only a small number of Alabama's people owned slaves, the slave owners had great power.

When Abraham Lincoln was elected President in 1860, and it appeared that the slaves would be set free, Alabama was one of the southern states that took the lead in seceding from the United States. Alabama seceded on January 11, 1861, the fourth state to do so. Jefferson Davis, who had been a Senator from Alabama, was elected the first president of the Confederate States of America, and the first Confederate capital was Montgomery (until July, 1861, when Richmond, Virginia, was made the capital). During the Civil War, Alabama contributed 122,000 men to the Confederate armies, and 35,000 of them were killed or wounded.

Alabama's cities and farms were badly hurt by Union armies in the Civil War, and after the war Alabama was very poor. "Carpetbaggers" controlled the state government and robbed it of millions. Gradually, the original citizens of the state got control of it back. Alabama

Ewing Galloway

Mobile Chamber of Commerce

Alabama Chamber of Commerce

Mobile Chamber of Commerce

1. This is Wilson Dam, one of the ten great plants that generate the electricity in the Tennessee Valley. It is located at Muscle Shoals, Alabama. Wilson Dam is 140 feet high and 4,111 feet long. Many tourists visit it each year.

2. Mobile, Alabama, is a shipbuilding center. The picture shows the launching of a barge, one of the boats on which freight is carried down the rivers of Alabama to the Gulf of Mexico, for shipment all over the world.

3. The port of Mobile, Alabama, is one of the busiest on the Gulf of Mexico. These ships are anchored at Alabama State Docks.

4. From the air, Mobile Bay looks like a giant sand flat, but most of it is quite deep. The busy city of Mobile, shown in the picture, is on the west side of the bay. This is the point where five rivers empty into Mobile Bay. They are the Mobile, Tensaw, Apalachee and Blakely Rivers.

Mobile Chamber of Commerce

The wood being hoisted by these giant cranes is Alabama pulp wood, used to make paper.

was always considered part of the "solid South," meaning that it never voted for anyone but a Democratic candidate for office; but in 1948 it voted for the "Dixiecrat" candidate instead of for President Harry Truman. In 1952 it voted Democratic again.

PLACES TO SEE IN ALABAMA

William B. Bankhead National Forest, 560,604 acres, in the northwest, about 30 miles from Decatur, west of U.S. Route 31. Beautiful forests, where deer roam through the underbrush; a favorite vacation spot for campers and hikers; hundreds of hunters come to the annual deer hunt every November; Natural Bridge is one of the principal scenic attractions.

Talladega National Forest, 200,000 acres, with two divisions in central and eastern Alabama, one on U.S. Route 82 about 45 miles from Selma; the other on U.S. Route 241, near Anniston. Robinson Creek Falls is an outstanding attraction.

Conecuh National Forest, 339,573 acres along the Florida border, on U.S. Route 29; has a large recreational area with a 50-acre lake and picnic grounds.

Cheaha State Park, 2,679 acres, near Anniston, on U.S. Route 241. Contains Cheaha Mountain, the highest point in the state.

De Soto State Park, 4,650 acres, near Mentone, in the northeast, east of U.S. Route 11. Contains many beautiful cascades and waterfalls; famous De Soto Falls, 120-foot waterfall, is outstanding.

Azalea Trail, in Mobile, in the south-west, on U.S. Route 90; a 17-mile road along which magnificent flowers bloom every spring.

Mardi Gras, in Mobile, a colorful celebration on each Shrove Tuesday (the day before Lent). It has been held for the last 250 years.

Boll Weevil Monument, in Enterprise, on U.S. Route 84. Perhaps the only monument in the world erected to an insect. When the boll weevil destroyed the entire cotton crop about 55 years ago, the farmers were forced to plant peanuts, which became such a successful industry that the people erected the Boll Weevil Monument in appreciation.

Mound State Monument, 12 miles from Tuscaloosa, in west central Alabama, east of U.S. Route 11. Made up of 34 Indian mounds, which cover 300 acres; once used by Indians as temples, houses, and community meeting places.

Statue of Vulcan, the Roman god of fire, in Birmingham, on top of Red Mountain. It is 53 ft. high, weighs 60 tons, and stands on a tower 127 feet high; it can be seen by people all over the city.

Ginko Tree, in Selma, in central Alabama, on U.S. Route 80. A rare tree from China that grows through the roof of a cotton warehouse.

Saltpeter Cave, near Scottsboro, in the northeast, on U.S. Route 72. Once a cave-dwelling for Indians; later a temporary courtroom of Jackson County while the first courthouse was being built; Confederate soldiers mined the saltpeter and used it for gunpowder during the Civil War.

Alabama's Gulf Coast is warm nearly all year 'round.

U.S. Forest Service

The lumber industry in Alabama has become very important. These boards have been dried and are stored in a lumber yard in Grayson, Alabama, awaiting shipment to builders.

The First White House of the Confederacy, in Montgomery, on U.S. Route 80. The home of Jefferson Davis, where he was sworn in as first President of the Confederacy; now a museum with many interesting Civil War relics.

Talladega, in the northeast, on U.S. Route 241. One of the oldest white settlements in the state; near the place where Andrew Jackson fought the Battle of Horseshoe Creek, and defeated the Creek Indians.

Ivy Green, in Tuscumbia, in the northwest, on U.S. Route 72; the birthplace of Helen Keller.

ALABAMA. Area, 51,078 square miles. Population (1950), 3,061,743. Capital, Montgomery. Nickname, the Cotton State. Motto, We Dare Defend Our Rights. Flower, goldenrod. Bird, yellowhammer. Song, "Alabama." Admitted to Union, December 14, 1819. Official abbreviation, Ala.

Alabama Claims

During the Civil War, the North had a big navy, while the South had no warships. So the Confederacy (the South) bought an armed ship named the *Alabama* from Great Britain, along with other armed ships. These were very successful in sinking Northern ships. When the war was over the United States (the North) claimed payment from Great Britain for the ships that the *Alabama* had sunk. England refused to pay. They decided to put the question up to other countries. Ambassadors from Italy, Switzerland, Brazil, Great Britain and the United States met in Geneva, Switzerland, in 1871, and they agreed that the United States was to receive 15 million dollars in damages from Great Britain. This dispute was called "the Alabama Claims."

alabaster

Alabaster is a kind of stone, like marble except that it is much softer. It is milky white and finely grained, and is easy to carve and polish. This makes it a favorite stone for sculpture, statuary, vases, and other carved stone decorations. The same softness that makes alabaster easy to work makes it easy to scratch, and it must be protected from damage by weather, stains, and scratches, just like fine wood. When we read about the ancient Greeks and Romans we often find alabaster mentioned, but this usually meant a much harder, firmer stone, which was a kind of marble.

When Aladdin rubbed the magic lamp the genie appeared and granted his wish.

Aladdin

Aladdin is a character in a story in the Arabian Nights. According to the story, he found an old lamp that didn't seem to be worth anything. He got a cloth and started to rub the lamp, to clean it, when there suddenly appeared an enormous jinni, or genie, a spirit with magical powers who had to do the bidding of whosoever possessed the lamp. Aladdin found that no matter what he wanted, he merely had to rub his lamp, and the slave of the lamp would immediately appear and do what he wanted. Aladdin had the slave bring him great wealth, and he married a princess and had many adventures.

Alamo

The Alamo is an old fort in San Antonio, Texas, that was made from a little church. It is dearly loved by the Texans because of a famous battle that was fought there more than a hundred years ago. At that time Texas was not yet a part of the United States, but belonged to Mexico and was fighting to become independent. A small group of 180 Texas soldiers was caught inside the Alamo by a large army of 4,000 Mexicans, led by General Santa Anna. The fort was strong enough to withstand cannon balls, and from inside the Texas sharpshooters could shoot the Mexicans. They held the fort for ten days, but finally they were too tired and hungry to fight, and the Mexicans attacked the fort and killed all of them. But their bravery had been so great that it made the Texans fight better. Six weeks later, at a place called San Jacinto, a Texas army fought the Mexicans and beat them, and their battle cry was: "Remember the Alamo!" The Alamo fell on March 6, 1836. Among the famous men who died there, besides the commander, Colonel William B. Travis, were James Bowie and David Crockett.

The Alamo can still be seen in San Antonio, Texas. It was built in 1718 by Franciscan (Catholic) priests and was called the Mission of San Antonio de Valero.

Aland Islands

The Aland Islands are a group of about 200 rocky little islands lying in the Gulf of Bothnia, which is a sea between Sweden and Finland. On most of the islands there is no one living at all, but people of Swedish descent live on some of them. These people do some farming and cattle raising. The most important thing about these islands is their harbors, which are seldom or never frozen over in the winter. Such harbors, called "ice-free," are very valuable for warships in time of war, so that Sweden, Russia and Finland have all tried to get possession of the Aland Islands. In 1921 the League of Nations ruled that they were to become part of Finland, but with self-government. After World War II, Russia and Finland agreed never to fortify them. The largest island is only 18 by 14 miles, and is called Aland. The capital is Mariehamn.

ALAND ISLANDS. Area, 581 square miles. Population, 23,056. Capital, Mariehamn, population 3,506 (1949 official estimate).

Alaric

Alaric was a name borne by two kings of the Visigoths, a savage Teutonic (German) people, about 1,500 years ago when the Roman Empire still ruled most of the civilized world, and the Germans, whom the Romans called barbarians, fought them constantly.

Alaric I, king of the Visigoths, invaded the Roman Empire several times but was driven out each time by the Roman general, Stilicho. In the year 408, when Stilicho was dead, Alaric surrounded the walled city of Rome and threatened to starve the people to death unless they paid him a ransom. He withdrew after the city paid him. In the year 410 his victorious army entered Rome and his soldiers robbed it for six days. However, he forbade his men to harm women or destroy religious buildings. A few months later he died and was buried secretly in the bed of the Busento River to prevent the Romans from ever finding his body.

Alaric II became king of the Visigoths in 484. He ruled over all of Spain and part of southern France. The wealth of his lands excited the jealousy of Clovis, king of the Franks, a German people who ruled much of France. Clovis killed Alaric II in a battle at Vouillé, France, and completely defeated the Visigoth army.

Alaska

Alaska

Alaska is a big peninsula (that is, a body of land that sticks out into the ocean) that became a Territory of the United States nearly a hundred years ago when the United States bought it from Russia. It is twice as big as Texas, which is the largest State. But not very many people live there—only about 130,000, which is no more than there are in a fair-sized city. Perhaps that is because Alaska is so far away from the United States. It is nearly 1,200 miles by sea from the nearest big cities of the American Pacific Coast to the cities of Alaska, and it used to take several days to get there on a ship, because there are no railroads to Alaska. Airplane travel has reduced the traveling time to a few hours, of course, and since the Alaska Highway was built during World War II it is possible to drive an automobile to Alaska, or to send big trucks loaded with goods.

There are many exciting stories about Alaska, because once there was a big "gold rush" that caused thousands of adventurers, both good men and desperate men, to seek their fortunes there. They lived a rough and often lawless frontier life. The poet Robert W. Service wrote some of his most popular poems, and Jack London wrote some of his best novels, about the gold-rush days in Alaska and in the Klondike region of the Yukon, the Canadian territory that touches Alaska on the east.

During World War II, the United States had to pay more attention to Alaska than ever before. If Japan could have captured it, the United States could easily have been bombed or even invaded. At the western tip of Alaska, across a narrow stretch of water called the Bering Strait, which is only about fifty miles wide in some places, lies the eastern tip of Siberia, which belongs to Russia.

THE PEOPLE OF ALASKA

The people who lived in Alaska earliest were some tribes of American Indians, and Eskimos, who are related to American Indians. These still live there. They trap bears and otters and foxes and other animals, for their furs and meat; and they fish in the rivers and in the seas around Alaska. These natives do very little farming, and many of them eat nothing but meat and fish, as their ancestors did. (There is a separate article on the ESKIMOS.) There are about ten thousand Eskimos in Alaska, and about ten thousand members of other Indian tribes. Many of these have adopted the white men's ways, live in the cities or near them, and work in the fishing or canning businesses of southern Alaska.

The white people in Alaska, somewhat more than 100,000 of them, are nearly all Americans. Most of them came to Alaska from the United States, and some from Canada. There are about fifteen thousand who came from Norway and other Scandinavian countries, and there are a few thousand whose ancestors were Russians and went to Alaska when it belonged to Russia.

These white Alaskans live chiefly in the southern and western parts, where the cities and towns are. Nearly half of them live in or near the cities or towns. Life there is very much as it is in any part of the United States, except that they do not do nearly as much farming and manufacturing as people in the States do. Their work is mostly fishing and canning (especially of salmon); the cutting of timber from the vast forests; and mining the rich deposits of lead, tin, and precious metals such as gold.

WHAT THE LAND IS LIKE

Alaska is not nearly as cold as you might suppose. In the southern and western parts, where most of the people live, it seldom goes below freezing. That is, it is warmer in winter than the northern part of the United States is, but neither is Alaska ever very warm in summer. The average temperature in summer is

The Sawyer Glacier, one of many "rivers of ice" in Alaska. See the article on GLACIERS.

Pan American World Airways

only 56 degrees; in winter it is about 32 degrees. In the central and northern parts of Alaska the winter temperature is usually a few degrees below zero.

There are two big mountain ranges in Alaska. In the southern part there is the Alaska Range, which includes Mount McKinley, the highest mountain in North America (20,300 feet high). Across the northern part of Alaska is the Brooks Range. Here the highest peaks are less than 10,000 feet high.

The big Yukon River runs through central Alaska and empties into the Bering Sea at the west. It is very long— about 2,100 miles—and deep, so that steamboats and smaller boats can travel almost its entire length. The Yukon is very important in carrying the products of the mines and forests to the sea, where they can be shipped to the United States and other countries.

There are very few railroads and highways in Alaska. In the winter, much traveling is done by dogsled as it was long ago, but in modern times the people do most of their traveling by airplane.

THE GOVERNMENT OF ALASKA

A Territory is much different from a state. All the people who live in a Territory are citizens of the United States, but their Governor is appointed by the President instead of being elected by the people, and they do not elect Senators and Congressmen to represent them in Congress as the people of a state do. Alaska has a "delegate" to represent it in Congress, but he cannot vote there. The people cannot vote for President of the United States.

The capital of Alaska is Juneau, and here the Territorial legislature meets to pass laws that govern Alaska. There is a Senate with sixteen members, and a House of Representatives with twenty-four members. They are elected by the citizens of the Territory. The courts are part of the Federal Court system.

In Alaska, as in all parts of the United States, education is free and everyone must attend school. There is one fine, modern university, the University of Alaska, which is near the city of Fairbanks. It is a small university, though. In 1953 its enrollment was 351, including 294 men and 57 women.

THE CITIES OF ALASKA

Though much of the population of Alaska lives in cities, these are small in comparison with cities in the United States. The chief cities, with population figures from the 1950 census are:

Anchorage, population 11,254; with suburbs, 20,000. The largest city in the Territory, a seaport, and a fishing and canning center, on Cook Inlet, an arm of the Gulf of Alaska, in the south of the Territory.

Juneau, population 5,956, capital of the Territory and its second-largest city. It is on the narrow strip of land that runs along the sea to the south of the Alaskan peninsula.

Fairbanks, population 5,771, the largest inland city, in the central part of Alaska.

Nome, population 1,876, the largest town in western Alaska. It is on Seward Peninsula, the part of Alaska that comes closest to Siberia.

Sitka, population 1,985, on Baranoff Island, near Juneau. Sitka was the capital of Alaska until 1912.

ALASKA IN THE PAST

Captain Vitus Bering, the great Danish navigator, discovered Alaska more than two hundred years ago (in 1741). He was sailing for Russia, not for his native Denmark, and Russia claimed the territory and in 1784 established fur-trading posts there. For many years, Alaska was called "Russian America." In those days, there were hundreds of thousands of sea otters on the Alaskan coasts, and the fur of sea otter is by many considered the finest in the world, even finer than sable and mink. The Russians were cruel to the natives and very unwise in their business. They killed so

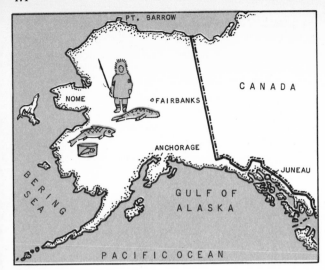

Alaska Steamship Co.

The map of Alaska at the top of the page shows some of the Territory's important cities. Juneau, part of which is shown in the picture below the map, is on the Gastineau Channel, separated by islands from the Pacific Ocean. The town across the channel is Douglas. The strange-looking figures at the right are on a totem pole made by Indian natives of Alaska. As you see, it has four sections. Each of the figures once stood for an individual god or protector of a family, and eventually became a symbol or seal of the family itself. For example, one family might decide to respect or worship the eagle. That would be the family protector, or god. After a while, it would become just an identification of the family itself. Other sections were added as children grew up and married into families or tribes with different protectors or gods. See the article on TOTEM POLES.

many of the sea otters that they almost wiped them out, and this valuable fur has been lost to the world ever since, except in very small quantities.

In 1867 the United States bought Alaska from Russia for $7,200,000. The purchase was made by William H. Seward, who was Secretary of State then, and Alaska was so far away and so undeveloped that the American people thought he had spent the Government's money foolishly. They called Alaska "Seward's Folly." But when gold was discovered in the Yukon in 1897, thousands of Americans passed through Alaska to get there; and they discovered more gold in Alaska than in the Yukon. Ever since, it has been known that Alaska is a rich and important territory, and Seward's "folly" turned out to be one of the best buys any country ever made. The people who went to Alaska to seek gold found it a good place to live in. They built cities and brought American civilization to the Territory. After

that, it was only a matter of time until Alaska would be admitted as a State of the United States.

PLACES TO SEE IN ALASKA

Tongass National Forest, 16,500,000 acres, on the southeast coast. Visitors spend their vacations there camping, canoeing, skating, and hiking.

Chugach National Forest, 5,000,000 acres, near Prince William Sound in the south; a vacation spot.

Mount McKinley National Park, 3,030 square miles, in central Alaska, 123 miles from Fairbanks. Second in size to Yellowstone National Park in the United States.

Glacier Bay National Monument, 1,820 square miles, near Juneau. Made up of vast and magnificent glaciers, which can be seen from a plane or boat.

Child's Glacier, in the northeast, near Copper River. A magnificent ice cliff, 200 to 300 feet high, about as high as the Capitol Building in Washington.

A dredge used for gold-mining in Alaska. It picks up sand from the bottom and washes it to sift out particles of gold.

Pan American World Airways

Sitka National Monument, 57 acres, in southeast Alaska. Contains an Indian stockade 150 years old.

Kasaan National Monument, 28 acres, on Prince of Wales Island. Contains the ruins of the former Haida Indian Village; one can see totem poles, Indian grave houses, and monuments that are very old.

Katmai National Monument, 1,700 square miles, in the southwest. Contains the famous Valley of Ten Thousand Smokes, filled with volcanoes from which pour great columns of white vapor.

Chief Shakes' Community House, on Wrangell Island, in the southeast. Contains a fascinating collection of household tools and works of art of the Tlingit Indians.

Yukon Trail, in central Alaska, the famous path taken by the miners in the gold rush almost sixty years ago.

White Pass and Chilkoot Pass, near Skagway, in the southeast. Dangerous

Pan American World Airways

An Eskimo girl of Alaska, wearing a coat and parka made by hand from reindeer skin.

Eskimos in Alaska are expert at spearing fish through holes cut in the ice.

Museum of Modern Art

mountain trails taken by the miners into the Yukon Territory.

Richardson Highway, a beautiful highway between Valdez and Fairbanks, along which can be seen the deserted towns known as "ghost towns," once filled with miners seeking gold.

Metlakatla, on an island in the southeast. A cooperative Indian village, where everything is owned by the people, including the great sawmill, and their canning and boat-building industries.

Ward's Cove, near Ketchikan, in the southeast. An excellent place for hunting bear and deer.

Mitkof Island, about 100 miles from Juneau. Mink- and fox-raising.

ALASKA. Area, 571,065 square miles. Population (1950), 128,643. Capital, Juneau. Flower, forget-me-not. Song, "Alaska, My Alaska."

The construction of the Alaska Highway required cutting paths through forests, and building roads where only wild animals had roamed. Powerful machines literally pushed the wilderness aside to make space for roads.

Alaska Highway

The Alaska Highway is the first road ever built to connect the United States, Canada, and Alaska. At first it was called the "Canadian-Alaskan Military Highway," and later it was called the "Alcan" highway, before it came to be known as the Alaska Highway. It starts at Dawson Creek, British Columbia, a town about 500 miles north of the United States border, and it ends in Fairbanks, Alaska, a distance of 1,527 miles. It is so long that if it started in Florida, it would end in Kansas, halfway across the United States.

The highway was built in 1942, during World War II, so that the American soldiers in Alaska could be supplied with food, clothing, and ammunition, by land. United States ships going to Alaska were in too much danger of being sunk by enemy submarines and airplanes. Seven regiments of United States Army Engineers, and more than 6,000 civilians, built the road in six months. That is very fast time, because it usually takes over two years to build such a road. They built a bridge across the Peace River, in British Columbia, down which the Cree and Beaver Indians used to paddle freight canoes full of precious furs to the Hudson's Bay Company trading post. The bridge is 2,130 feet long.

In Whitehorse, the capital of the Yukon Territory, there is a memorial to Robert W. Service, the famous poet who wrote about the Klondike Gold Rush days of the 1890s. This was wild country before the highway came through. It was forest wilderness, where the only people were Indians and a few trappers. Now there are gasoline filling stations, garages, restaurants, and motels (hotels where cars can be parked just outside the door) all along the way, while Fairbanks and Whitehorse are modern cities with big stores, churches, and movies.

The Alaska Highway is kept open all year, but travelers should carry blankets or sleeping robes if they drive over it in the very cold weather. Then if the car breaks down they can stay warm until help arrives. Most of the traffic is during the warm season, when tourists, vacationers, campers and sportsmen travel the highway by hundreds. In the spring and early summer there are large swarms of mosquitoes and other stinging insects, and travelers need protection against their bites, such as head-nets and mosquito bars. (These are nets that allow air to come through, but keep the insects out.) There are many kinds of wild animals in the woods along the highway—deer, moose, caribou, black bear, grizzly bear, and many small animals. The lakes and streams are full of such fish as grayling, trout, pike, and pickerel, while ducks, geese, ptarmigan, and other birds abound. The animals will not bother those who leave them alone.

Since the Alaska Highway came to the Northwest, travel and business have increased so much that it is like a new world.

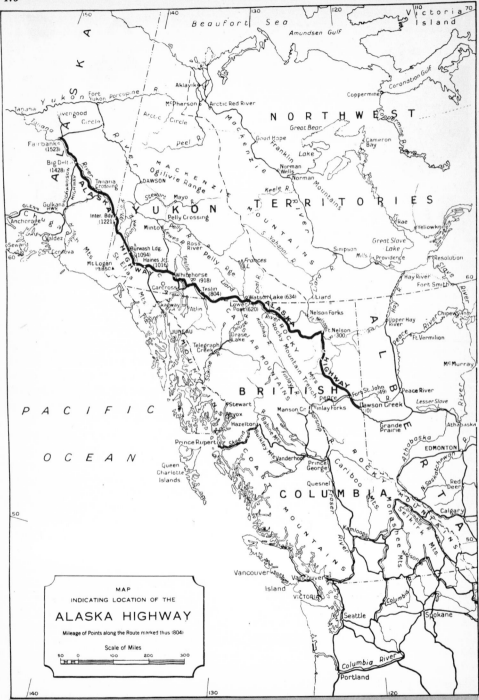

MAP
INDICATING LOCATION OF THE

ALASKA HIGHWAY

Mileage of Points along the Route marked thus (804)

Scale of Miles

Canadian Information Service

This map shows the route of the Alaska Highway, from Dawson Creek, British Columbia, to Fairbanks, Alaska. It is 1,527 miles long altogether, and winds through the Canadian Rockies where once only dog sleds traveled. The country is very wild and beautiful.

The queer word is "Albania" in the Albanian language.

Albania

Albania is a small country in Europe, not much larger in area than Maryland, which is one of the smallest states of the United States. Albania's population is not much more than a million people, which is only about one-half as many as Maryland has. In 1946 Albania got a Communist government and after that no one could find out much about what goes on there, but no one ever did know much about what went on in Albania. It is one of the oldest countries of Europe, yet it is one of the most mysterious.

Albania lies on the eastern shore of the Adriatic Sea, just across the narrow waters from the Italian peninsula and Rome. Two thousand years ago, Albania was called Illyria. It was a prosperous colony of the Roman Empire, which was then the center of the civilized world. Yet today Albania is a poor, backward land.

One reason, perhaps, is the high mountains that hem Albania in from its neighbors. Another reason may be that so many different conquerors have come to Albania to kill and oppress the people.

THE PEOPLE OF ALBANIA

Many of the people who live in Albania today are descended from the ancient Illyrians who lived there before written history began. They speak a language brought down through the ages from that ancient people. Other Albanian people came there, long ago, from Greece, which is Albania's neighbor on the south. The Turks, and Slavic people from different parts of what is now Yugoslavia, and Italians, have all ruled Albania at one time or another, and some of them have stayed there.

Most of the Albanians are poor, and they make their livings in the two oldest kinds of work known to man: farming, and tending cattle and sheep. Albania has some good farmland, but there is hardly enough of it, and besides the Albanians do not have modern farm machinery and do not use the best methods of farming. Sometimes they cannot raise as much food as they need, and have to buy some from other countries.

Nearly three out of four Albanians follow the Mohammedan religion. The Turks, who conquered the country five hundred years ago and ruled it until 1912, brought Mohammedanism with

them. The people who are not Mohammedans are Christians, belonging to
either the Greek Orthodox Church or the
Roman Catholic Church. Since Albania
has had a Communist government, which
is opposed to all these religions, Albanian Mohammedans and Christians alike
have had trouble keeping in touch with
the heads of their churches in other countries.

The people of Albania dress in the
eastern fashion, very much as the Turks
did thirty and more years ago, before
European customs of dress were introduced there.

According to law, education through
grammar school is required and is free,
but this law is often broken and it is
possible that as many as half of the
people cannot read and write.

WHAT THE LAND IS LIKE

Along the Adriatic Sea, Albania has
level land that has plenty of rainfall and
is good for farming. Behind this the
mountains rise steeply, and the Alpine
section in northern Albania has peaks
nearly 10,000 feet high. The climate is
warm in the south, as it is in southern
Italy, and temperate in the north, except
in the mountains, which are very cold
in the winter.

Every few miles, a river springs from
the mountains and flows through Albania to the sea. The principal rivers
are the Drin in the north, the Shkumbi
in central Albania, and the Vijosë in the
south.

The natural resource that has proved
most valuable to Albania so far is oil.
The best oilfields are in the low mountains in the south. The oil is carried by
pipelines to the seaport of Vlona. In one
way this oil has not been too lucky for
Albania, because in 1939 Italy, which
did not have enough oil of its own,
started a war against Albania to get it.

Albania has some coal mines, and the
mountains are believed to hold large
amounts of valuable minerals, but so

far they have not been mined. Albania
has neither the machines for mining nor
the railroads or roads to carry the minerals away. There are few automobiles.
Official travel between Albania and other
Communist countries came to be chiefly
by airplane after 1948 when Yugoslavia,
Albania's Communist neighbor, left the
Cominform.

THE GOVERNMENT OF ALBANIA

When World War II ended, Com-
munists were in control of Albania and
set up a dictatorship of the type known
as a "People's Republic." In this form of
government there is a parliament, and
members of it are elected by the people,
but the actual control is in the hands of
a presidium, or board of top-ranking
members of the Communist Party. This
board actually decides its own membership (which must be approved by the
powerful Communist organizations of
Russia and the Cominform) and members of the parliament vote as they are
told to vote. The people have no real
voice in their own government and there
is no personal liberty as it is known in
the United States.

The capital of Albania is Tirana, a
city of about 80,000 population, in the
central part of the country. There is a
separate article on TIRANA. The other
leading Albanian cities are:

Scutari, population about 30,000, the second-largest city, in the northern part of the country where most of the Albanians of Slavic origin live.

Koritsa, population about 30,000, in the southeastern section near the Greek border.

Durres, or Durazzo, population about 14,000, a seaport on the Adriatic Sea, in the central section near Tirana.

ALBANIA IN THE PAST

Albania has been ruled by one foreign country after another for more than two thousand years. Except for brief periods it was never really independent until the year 1912.

The Roman Empire made Albania (then called Illyria) a colony about 100 years before the time of Christ. When Rome fell to German invaders in the 5th century, Albania fell with it. After that, for about a thousand years, the Slavs of Europe and the East Roman emperor in Byzantium would occasionally fight over Albania, and one after the other would control it. Finally, in 1444, the Turks invaded Albania. A great Albanian hero named George Castriota fought them bravely, but they finally conquered. In the centuries that followed the Al-

banians adopted the Turkish ways that they still have, but from time to time they still fought for independence. Turkey finally became so weak that this had to be granted in 1912.

After World War I, a leader named Ahmed Zogu rose to power, and in 1928 he made himself King Zog. He is remembered in America partly because his queen, whom he married in 1938, was half American. In 1939, when Italy invaded and then annexed Albania, Zog had to flee with his wife and baby son, who was only two days old.

In World War II, while Albania was occupied by Italians and then by Germans, Albanian "partisans" fought them under the command of Enver Hoxha. He was a Communist, and was supported by Soviet Russia. After the war, it was easy for him to set up a Communist government.

ALBANIA. Area, 11,100 square miles. Population (1954 estimate) 1,200,000. Language, Albanian (an Indo-European language). Religion, about 75% Mohammedan, 25% Christian. Government, republic. Monetary unit, franc (gold franc used in foreign trade, worth 19.3 U.S. cents). Flag, red, with black double-headed eagle.

The market where farmers take their vegetables and livestock to sell in Tirana, the capital of Albania. Albania's only modern city is Durres (also called Durazzo), Tirana's seaport, 25 miles away.

Ewing Galloway

Albany

Albany is the capital of the state of New York. It is on the west bank of the Hudson River, and is 145 miles from New York City. Albany was first settled by Dutch people in 1624, only a few years after the Pilgrims landed in Massachusetts. It was called Beverwyck until 1664, when the English took it from the Dutch and named it Albany, which was an ancient name for Scotland. In colonial days many Indians brought furs to Albany to trade for cloth, knives, and other things they needed. Albany is far up the river, but it has always been considered a seaport, because ever since the days of the Dutch, seagoing ships have been able to sail up the Hudson all the way to Albany. This is because the river is deep enough for large ships.

The capitol, the building from which the state of New York is governed, is on the side of a steep hill, almost at the top. It is built of granite, and has spires at its corners but no dome as many capitols do.

ALBANY, NEW YORK. Population, 134,-995 (1950 census). Capital, New York State. County seat, Albany County. On the Hudson River. Settled 1624.

Albany Congress

The Albany Congress was a meeting of American colonies held in Albany, New York, in June, 1754. This was before the United States became an independent country. Representatives of New York, Massachusetts, Connecticut, New Hampshire, Rhode Island, Pennsylvania and Maryland were at the meeting. Their reason for meeting was that the Indians had been attacking farms and villages, and the colonies could fight the Indians better together than singly. Benjamin Franklin was the representative from Pennsylvania. He said there should be a colonial union, a government of all the colonies, that would protect the colonists from attack by Indians, collect taxes, and have its own army and navy. Franklin's plan was not approved by the colonies, nor by the British government that ruled the colonies. Still the Albany Congress was important, because many ideas in the Constitution of the United States were taken from Benjamin Franklin's plan.

albatross

The albatross is a large bird that lives mostly in the ocean regions, below the Equator, but is also found in the North Pacific. Most albatrosses are white with dark patches on their backs, but some are brown with white heads. The albatross has the greatest wingspread of all birds (12 feet from tip to tip). These long narrow wings make it easy for the albatross to spend most of its time flying over its ocean home. It comes to land only to mate and to lay a single egg in a clearing on sandy soil or on a rocky ledge.

The albatross feeds on the surface of the ocean, where it catches fish, and tiny shellfish that float on top of the water. Its beak is long and straight, with a sharp hook on the end. The albatross is a very greedy eater, and when it is full it has trouble getting into the air

An albatross may have a 12-foot wingspread.

New York Zoological Society

again. It skitters awkwardly over the surface of the water for several hundred yards before it can take off.

The albatross likes to follow ships. If you were on a ship being followed by an albatross, you would see the bird circling around and around high above. The albatross can glide and soar for hours and hardly ever beat its wings. In the days when ships had sails, the sailors thought it was bad luck to kill an albatross. The English poet Coleridge wrote about this superstition in a famous ballad called *The Rime of the Ancient Mariner*.

Albert, King of the Belgians

King Albert is a great hero to the people of Belgium, because he had the courage to defy the great, powerful German army though Belgium is a very small and much less powerful country. This was in World War I. King Albert, who was born in 1875, was only 39 years old and had been king of Belgium only five years when World War I broke out in 1914. For nearly a hundred years—since 1830—the great European countries, Germany and France and England, had agreed that if there was a war in Europe no one would invade Belgium, and Belgium had agreed not to take sides in such a war. Then

Belgian Gov't. Information Center
King Albert was a great Belgian hero.

in World War I, Germany went to war against France and England. Because they could reach France easier by going across Belgium, the Germans broke their word and sent their armies into Belgium. But King Albert would not break his word and let them through without a fight. He knew Belgium had no chance against Germany, but he knew that honorably they had to fight, and they did. All the people of Belgium agreed with him and fought the losing fight with him.

King Albert stayed with his soldiers all through the war, even though almost all of Belgium had been conquered. His wife, Queen Elizabeth, left her palace during the war and went to work in a soldiers' hospital, where she scrubbed floors and bandaged wounded soldiers. After four years, when Germany finally retreated before the armies of England, France, and the United States, King Albert led his little army back through his country and helped to defeat Germany. When the war was over he gave food and houses to the lost and wounded people of Belgium.

As a boy, King Albert had studied engineering, being especially interested in ships and airplanes. He died in 1934 when he fell while mountain-climbing, a sport he loved. He was 59 years old.

Albert, Prince

Prince Albert was the husband of Queen Victoria of England, one of the most powerful rulers of all time. He was not a king, because a man does not become a king by marrying a queen, though a woman becomes a queen when she marries a king. Prince Albert was called the prince consort, the word *consort* meaning a husband or wife.

Many times kings and queens have had to marry persons they did not love, because their advisers thought it would be good for the country for them to do so, but this was not so in the case of Vic-

Prince Albert was handsome and popular.

Alberta

Alberta is one of the provinces of Canada. It is in the western part, and the Canadian Rockies run through it, so it is known as "Fifty Switzerlands in One" because of the many high mountains and lofty peaks. Its beautiful scenery has made it a popular place for people to go on their vacations. Alberta ranks fourth in size among the Canadian provinces, having 255,285 square miles, which is bigger than any state of the United States except Texas. In population it also ranks fourth in Canada, nearly a million people living there. The province was named after Princess Louise Caroline Alberta, a daughter of Queen Victoria of England. It became a province in 1905. The capital is Edmonton.

toria and Albert. Theirs was a real love match. Victoria had become queen when she was only eighteen and a year later she met Albert, who was a prince in a little German kingdom called Saxe-Coburg-Gotha. He was her first cousin. She fell in love with him and he with her, and it was lucky for both of them that the British government thought it would be good for the country for them to marry. When they were married, each of them was only twenty years old. This was in the year 1840.

Prince Albert was a devoted husband and a very wise adviser to the queen. The English people liked him very much. He and Queen Victoria had nine children. But in 1861, Prince Albert suddenly died. He had been born in 1819, so he was only 42 years old. Queen Victoria was heartbroken then, and she lived for forty years more and always mourned for Prince Albert.

He was a tall, handsome young man, with reddish hair and a reddish mustache. A long coat that he made popular is still called a "Prince Albert."

THE PEOPLE OF ALBERTA

The people of Alberta originally came from many different countries to seek their fortune in the vast, rich country of Canada. More than half the Albertans came from Great Britain. Others came from European countries, especially Austria, Russia, and the Scandinavian countries. A smaller number were French Canadians from the eastern part of Canada; these still speak French and observe many French customs. There are some Indians, who live on reservations. Two hundred years ago the Indians were the only people living in Alberta.

The first settlers of Alberta were cattle ranchers. Raising cattle is still a leading industry, but many more Albertans are

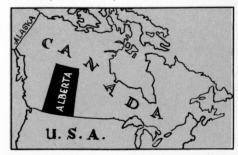

now farmers and raise millions of bushels of wheat, oats, and barley. They also raise sugar beets and potatoes, in the southern part of the province. In the northern part, like the Indians who lived there before them, they trap such fur-bearing animals as squirrel, beaver, and fox; they cut timber in the great Albertan forests; and they work the rich coal mines of the Rockies, producing more coal than any other province.

More than half the people of Alberta live in the country. The rest live in the cities, Edmonton and Calgary and others. They work in meat-packing plants, flour mills, and dairies. Others have jobs in canneries and beet-sugar factories in and near Raymond.

Once, when Alberta had a very small population, the people could not support a lot of different churches. They joined with people in other western provinces and formed the United Church of Canada. This is the largest church of Alberta, but there are Anglican, Roman Catholic, Presbyterian and Baptist churches.

WHAT ALBERTA IS LIKE

A visitor to Alberta will find that various parts of the province look quite different. In the north are the great forests, which extend over more than half of Alberta. From these forests logs are shipped to sawmills on the Peace River and the Athabaska River. In the northeast is Lake Athabaska, the largest of Alberta's many lakes. Part of the lake is in the neighboring province of Saskatchewan.

The central part of Alberta is mostly farm land where the people raise grain and cattle. In the center of this section is Edmonton, the capital and largest city of the province. It is a busy manufacturing center with petroleum-refining plants, paper mills, flour mills, and meat-packing plants.

The southern part of Alberta is prairie, with excellent grazing land on which cattle can be raised. In the southwest are the magnificent Canadian Rockies with their valuable coal deposits and their beautiful national parks.

The people of Alberta live in a pleasant climate, particularly in the summer. The average temperature then is about 60 degrees. In the winter, however, it gets very much colder, and in the north, the temperature can drop to 20 degrees below zero.

There are railroads throughout most of Alberta, but in the north the rivers are the chief means of transportation. A highway links Edmonton with the Alaska Highway in British Columbia.

Canadian National Railways

The roaring Sunwapta Falls, in Jasper National Park in Alberta.

THE GOVERNMENT OF ALBERTA

The head of the government of Alberta is a lieutenant-governor, who represents the British Queen. He is ap-

All Photos Canadian Pacific Railways

1. People go to Banff, Alberta, for skiing and tobogganing in winter, and for camping, fishing, golf and riding in summer.
2. Supplies are carried into the forest sections of Alberta on pack horses, because there are no real roads in the wilderness.
3. The Canadian Rockies make beautiful scenery in Alberta. Many of the streams have no bridges and must be crossed by wading the horses.
4. Alberta helps to make Canada one of the most important wheat-producing countries. The Canadian Pacific Railway's line runs beside the grain elevators in the background.
5. In Alberta, the mountains make even the oilfields beautiful.

pointed by the Canadian government. The province is actually run by a Prime Minister. He is appointed by a legislature, which is elected by the people. The Prime Minister has a cabinet, just as the President of the United States has. He stays in office as long as he can keep the confidence of the majority of the legislature. The legislature is elected for a five-year term. Judges are appointed by the Canadian government in Ottawa, and hold office permanently. The provincial government is in the capital, Edmonton.

Everyone has to go to school between the ages of 6 and 16, and there are many fine grammar schools and high schools all through the province. The University of Alberta is the only university. In 1952 it had 3,608 students.

CHIEF CITIES OF ALBERTA

The leading cities of Alberta, with populations from the 1951 census, are:

Edmonton, population 159,631, the capital and largest city, a manufacturing center, in the central part of the province.

Calgary, population 129,060, second-largest city, a manufacturing center, in the southern part of the province.

Lethbridge, population 22,947, third-largest city, cannery center, in the southern part of the province.

Medicine Hat, population 16,364, fourth-largest city, center for pottery plants, in the southern part of the province.

ALBERTA IN THE PAST

When the first white traders from Quebec came to Alberta in 1751, in search of furs, they found various Indian tribes living in the country. Explorers and trappers were the only white men for many years in that territory. Gradually trading posts were set up by men like Peter Pond and Alexander Mackenzie, and by the Hudson's Bay Company and the North West Company, who were bitter rivals. By 1821 the Hudson's Bay Company was the most powerful fur-trading company in the territory.

In 1870 Canada paid the Hudson's Bay Company and the British for some of their rights in Alberta and made it one of the Northwest Territories. The Northwest Mounted Police were making this region safe for settlers, and more and more people came into the territory. More came after the Canadian Pacific Railway was finished in 1883. In 1905 Alberta became a province. Discoveries of important oil and natural gas fields have added to Alberta's prosperity.

PLACES TO SEE IN ALBERTA

Jasper National Park, 4,200 square miles, in the Canadian Rocky Mountains, western Alberta, 200 miles north of Banff, on Highway 16. Jasper, one of Canada's largest parks, has magnificent ice fields, deep canyons, and towering peaks. Snake Indian Falls, Miette Hot Springs, and Punch Bowl Falls are particular attractions.

Banff National Park, 2,585 square miles, in the Canadian Rocky Mountains, in western Alberta, on State Highway 1. A beautiful vacation spot, with high peaks, ice fields, lakes, and green valleys.

Watertown Lakes National Park, together with Glacier National Park across the southern border in Montana, form the International Peace Park, 204 square miles, on U.S. Route 89. Noted for its beautiful mountains, trails, waterfalls, and lakes.

Buffalo National Park, 197 square miles, in eastern Alberta. This park, established in 1908, became a part of Wood Buffalo National Park in 1922.

Elk Island National Park, 75 square miles, in central Alberta, 25 miles from Edmonton, on State Highway 16. Buffaloes, elks, deer, and moose, under protection; a large recreation area for tourists.

Nemiskan National Park, 8 square miles, in southern Alberta, near Leth-

Skiers at Banff, Alberta, ride a "chair lift" to the top of the long hill where the ski trail begins.

Canadian Gov't. Bureau

A farmer in Alberta does his spring plowing with a team of oxen, while apple blossoms bloom overhead.

Canadian Pacific R'w'y.

bridge, on State Highway 4. An area set aside for the protection of a herd of pronghorn antelopes.

Wood Buffalo National Park, 17,300 square miles, in northern Alberta and the Northwest Territories. A large preserve of forests and open plains, where buffaloes, bears, beavers, moose and waterfowl live.

Banff, a popular winter and summer resort in the Banff National Park. Attracts mountain climbers and skiers.

Lake Louise, in the "Lakes in the Clouds" region of the Banff National Park. A famous tourist resort; the very beautiful blue lake reflects the snowy mountains, cliffs, forests, and sky.

ALBERTA. Area, 255,285 square miles. Population (1951), 939,501. Capital, Edmonton. Coat of arms, the cross of St. George at the top, a view of the Albertan mountains and fields in the middle, and a field of wheat at the bottom. Flag, this coat of arms on the flag of Canada. Flower, wild rose. Admitted to Dominion in 1905. Official abbreviation, Alta.

Pan American World Airways

One of Australia's unusual animals is the cuscus. This one is an albino.

albino

Living things—plants and animals —normally contain certain pigments, or coloring matter. One of these pigments is *melanin,* which gives a dark color to people's skin, hair, and eyes; and there are many other pigments. When a living thing does not have the pigments that are natural to its kind, it is called an *albino.* The condition of being an albino is called *albinism,* and it is not a disease because it seldom does any harm, except to give the person or plant a whitish look.

Human albinos have hair that is nearly white, and as a rule is soft and silky, and skin that is very fair and is often rough and scaly. Their eyes are somewhat pink, because of the blood showing through, and they can usually not bear strong light—because it is

the coloring that protects our eyes from too much light. Negroes have a lot of melanin in their skins, and blonds have very little. When a person stays in the sunshine a great deal, his skin stores a lot of melanin and he becomes darker. It is said that he is "tanned."

There are many albinos among animals, for example, white mice, white rabbits, white crows, and the sacred white elephant of Siam.

Albion

Albion is another name for England. It is what the ancient Greeks and Romans called the entire island of Britain. To them, the word meant "white" and it is sometimes said that Britain got this name because of the great cliffs of chalk along the English Channel, especially near Dover, but it is doubtful if that is the reason. Scotland was often called Alban, or Albany, and American cities or towns by that name take their names from Scotland. California was first called "New Albion"; it was given this name by Sir Francis Drake, the great English explorer, when he first visited there in the year 1579. There are several American towns called Albion, and there is a Methodist College, Albion College, in the city of Albion, Michigan.

albumin

Albumin is a sticky substance that is found in living things. The white of an egg is almost pure albumin (but here it is spelled album*e*n). There is albumin in your blood, and when you cut yourself the albumin helps make your blood clot (get hard and dry). Albumin is also present in vegetables and in milk as well as in eggs. Although albumin dissolves in water, it coagulates (becomes solid) when it is heated. When you cook an egg you can see how the colorless, watery part of the egg becomes solid and turns white. The sticky quality of albumen is what makes it possible for you to whip or beat the white of an egg into a fluffy froth. Because of this stickiness, albumin is used in making paste. Albumin in dry powder form will keep for a long time without spoiling. In liquid form it spoils rapidly. There is a small amount of sulfur in albumen; it gives rotten eggs their bad odor, and causes silver forks and spoons to turn black when we eat eggs with them.

Albuquerque

Albuquerque is the biggest city in New Mexico. It is on the banks of the great Rio Grande river, and it is a very beautiful place, with wide streets, gleaming white buildings, and palm trees and lovely flowers all year. Many people go there during the winter because it is always warm and sunny. It is about 5,000 feet above sea level, and the air is so dry that even on the hottest days it is comfortable.

Spanish people settled Albuquerque first, more than 200 years ago, in 1706; the name Albuquerque is Spanish. Mexico is only about 200 miles away, and there are many Mexicans in the city. They wear gay, bright-colored shirts and bandannas. There are usually cowboys around, too, because there are many large ranches outside of Albuquerque. The Pueblo Indian Reservation is nearby.

Though its population of 96,000 does not seem large in comparison with eastern cities, Albuquerque is the main shopping center for people who live on ranches and in smaller towns for miles around.

ALBUQUERQUE, NEW MEXICO. Population, 96,815 (1950 census). On the Rio Grande. Settled 1706.

Alcatraz

Alcatraz is an island in San Francisco Bay, off the coast of California. The island is small and very rocky. Only one thing makes it important. It is a prison island. The prison is run by the Federal government of the United States. In its cells are kept some of the most dangerous criminals in the country. Many of these men were arrested by the agents of the Federal Bureau of Investigation, the famous G-men. Alcatraz is also known as "The Rock." Escape from The Rock is almost impossible. The prisoners are closely guarded, and the waters around Alcatraz are patrolled regularly. Even if a prisoner could escape the guards and the patrol, he would likely drown in the rough waters around the island.

alcazar

An alcazar is simply a castle, in the Arabic language. We think of an alcazar as a castle or palace in Spain, built in the years (before Columbus discovered America) when Spain was under the control of Mohammedans. The ALHAMBRA, about which there is a separate article in this encyclopedia, is the most famous of the alcazars.

alchemy

Thousands of years ago, when very little was known about the science of chemistry, there were men in ancient Egypt who believed there was a wonderful material called the "philosopher's stone" that could change common metals like iron or lead into gold. They believed also that this philosopher's stone, or some other chemical, could make men live forever without ever becoming old.

These men were called alchemists, and the experiments they performed in trying to find the philosopher's stone were called alchemy. Today we know that there is no philosopher's stone that will make men young forever, and nobody has ever discovered a way of changing iron into gold. But though the ancient alchemists could not find what they were looking for, they did learn a little about chemistry, and they made some useful medicines for sick people.

The Egyptians passed their knowledge on to the ancient Greeks. The Greeks passed it on to the Arabs who lived in Palestine, Arabia, north Africa, and Spain. Men in Europe got their knowledge of alchemy from the Arabs. In western Europe during the Middle Ages, which lasted from about 1,000 years ago to about 1492, the year in which Columbus discovered America, alchemy was the only chemistry that men knew. The common people of those days, who could not read or write, often looked upon alchemists with fear, and thought they were magicians or wizards. Many scientists today feel that the an-

The alchemists of olden times used strange and mysterious-looking devices in their shops. They kept trying to turn cheaper metals into gold, and believed that they would some day succeed. They never did, but their experiments advanced chemistry.

cient alchemists were a great help to modern chemistry because they worked out ways of experimenting with chemicals.

Alcibiades

Alcibiades was a great commander of armies and navies in Athens, in ancient Greece, more than 2,000 years ago. He was born in 450 B.C.

In the days of Alcibiades each of the big cities of Greece was a separate state or country. These city-states were often at war with one another. The most powerful city-states were Sparta and Athens. For twenty-seven years (from 431 B.C. to 404 B.C.) they fought the Peloponnesian War for control of Greece. Alcibiades sailed with the Athenian fleet to conquer Syracuse, a city in Sicily, which is now a part of Italy but then belonged to Greece. He had enemies in Athens, and they accused him of crimes of which he was not guilty. He fled from the fleet to Sparta, and helped Agis II, King of Sparta, to defeat the Athenian fleet. But Agis distrusted Alcibiades, so Alcibiades fled once more, this time to the Persians in Asia Minor, who were the enemies of all Greeks.

Then a new government came into power in Athens, and Alcibiades went back there. Under his command the Athenian fleet gained several victories. But when one of Alcibiades's lieutenants lost a battle, Alcibiades lost his command. He left Athens forever, and without her best commander Athens was defeated by Sparta. Alcibiades again went to Asia Minor, but this time the Persians put him to death.

alcohol

Alcohol is a thin, colorless liquid that looks like water. It is used in medicine, in chemical products, in foods, and in drinks. It can be made from wheat, corn, potatoes, sugar beets, most starchy vegetables, and fruits. However, most alcohol is made from grain—such as corn, rye, and wheat—by the chemical process known as *fermentation*. (There is a separate article about FERMENTATION.) In the United States, a great deal of alcohol is made from petroleum, about as much as is made from grain.

Many beverages (drinks) contain alcohol. Whiskey, brandy and wines are called *alcoholic beverages*. Beer also contains alcohol, but in smaller amounts. It is the alcohol in alcoholic beverages that makes a person drunk (unable to control himself normally) if he drinks too much. This condition is also called *intoxication*. There is a disease called *alcoholism,* or *dipsomania* ("thirst craziness"), in which a person is unable to control his desire for alcoholic drinks.

When a person's temperature rises much above normal because of a fever, alcohol is often sponged on the skin. The reason for this is that alcohol dries very quickly. As it dries it carries heat away with it and thus gives a feeling of coolness.

Alcohol is very useful as an antiseptic—that is, to kill germs which cause so many diseases and infections. Alcohol is poured on small cuts and wounds to kill the germs.

Alcohol will not freeze even in the coldest weather known to man. Water will freeze at 32 degrees (Fahrenheit), while alcohol at 286 degrees below zero will only thicken slightly. For this reason it is sometimes used as an antifreeze in automobiles.

Alcohol is used as a solvent, because fats, oils, and some dry solids will dissolve in it. Drugs known as tinctures— for example, tincture of iodine—are dissolved in alcohol. Pure iodine is a dry, purplish-black solid. Alcohol is also an excellent fuel. It burns with a clean blue flame that leaves little or no soot. In an alcohol burner, a cotton wick, like a thick cord, soaks up alcohol from a container and burns just as the wick of a candle does. Alcohol is also an

excellent fuel for automobiles, and is mixed with gasoline in countries where gasoline is very expensive, because alcohol costs less.

Alcott, Louisa May

Louisa May Alcott was the author of *Little Women,* the most popular book for girls that has ever been written (nearly three million copies of it have been sold since it was published in 1868). Miss Alcott, whose family came from Connecticut, and who happened to be born in Germantown, Pennsylvania—a suburb of Philadelphia—while her father was working as a teacher there, lived most of her life in Concord, Massachusetts. This city was then the home of Ralph Waldo Emerson and other great American writers and was considered a center of education and learning for the entire United States.

Miss Alcott started to write when she was only a girl, and she usually wrote about people she actually knew. *Little Women* was a story about herself and her three sisters, as well as of their friends and neighbors in nearby towns in Massachusetts. Her other famous books were *Little Men, An Old-fashioned Girl, Eight Cousins,* and *Jo's Boys* (a sequel to *Little Women*).

She was born in 1832, and *Little Women* was published in 1868. She did some teaching, was the editor of a magazine for children, and wrote some stories and articles that were not for children. She died in 1888. Her father, Amos Bronson Alcott, was a famous teacher, born in 1799; he lived as long as his daughter did, dying in 1888. He was one of those who supported the BROOK FARM experiment, about which there is a separate article in this encyclopedia.

Alden, John

John Alden is most famous as a character in a long poem by Henry Wadsworth Longfellow, called *The Courtship of Miles Standish;* but actually he was a young man (not quite twenty-one years old) who sailed with the Pilgrims from England to Plymouth, Massachusetts in 1620, on the ship *Mayflower.* He was not really one of the "Pilgrim fathers," because he was hired to make the trip as a skilled worker, and did not come because of his religious convictions; but he stayed in Massachusetts and married Priscilla Mullens, daughter of one of the Pilgrims.

John and Priscilla had eleven children, and they were successful in living through the hard winters and periods when there was very little food and many of the settlers died. It has been estimated that more than one million Americans are descended from John and Priscilla Alden. The only other of the Pilgrims who might have more descendants is Governor William Bradford, who was the second governor of the Massachusetts colony.

Longfellow was one of the descendants of John and Priscilla, and that may be why he wrote his famous poem. In the poem, Captain Miles Standish, a more important member of the colony, asks John Alden to go to Priscilla and ask her if she would marry him (that is, if she would marry Miles Standish). But Priscilla liked John Alden, who was a younger and more handsome man, and she said to him, "Speak for yourself, John." When Captain Standish heard about this, he persuaded John Alden to marry Priscilla.

alder

The alder is a tree that grows best in moist or swampy soil. It is found in North America, Great Britain and northern Asia. The alder grows 30 to 60 feet high. It is a beautiful tree with dark green leaves and bark that is almost black. The wood is sometimes used for furniture, and makes an excellent charcoal for gunpowder. When men need to use a wood that will not

U.S. Forest Service

The alder leaf is about 4½ inches long. The leaves grow in this manner.

rot or weaken under water, they usually choose alder wood. The supports of most of the houses that are built over the canals in Amsterdam are alder wood poles that have been under water for many years. The bark of the alder is used in tanning leather, and is also used by fishermen to dye their nets.

Alderney

Alderney is a small island between France and England. It belongs to England, though it is much nearer to France. Alderney is one of four islands in a group called the Channel Islands (because they are in the English Channel). This little island is only one mile wide, and less than four miles long, but about 1,500 people live on it. It is very pretty, with beautiful green fields and pastures everywhere. The houses are small and neat looking, and many of them are hundreds of years old. It is famous for its cows, which give very rich milk. Alderney cows are small, and very pretty. They are usually brown and white.

Aldershot

Aldershot is a small town in England, in Hampshire county, only about 25 miles north of the English Channel. It is a name that comes up in books occasionally because for many years the British army had a big camp here, where the troops went into winter quarters during the time when transportation was too bad to carry on warfare in the winter. The soldiers of the regular British army also lived there when the country was not engaged in war. The city of Aldershot has grown to be a thriving business center with a population of more than 35,000, and the military camp is one of the principal camps in England for the training of the British army.

ALDERSHOT, ENGLAND. Population, 36,184 (1950 census). Military training center.

Aldrich, Thomas Bailey

Thomas Bailey Aldrich, who lived from 1836 to 1907, wrote many books of prose and poetry, but he remains best known for a book called *The Story of a Bad Boy.* Millions of American

children have read this book. It is really the story of Aldrich's own boyhood, which was spent mostly in Portsmouth, New Hampshire. In the book, he called the town Rivermouth and himself Tom Bailey. In many ways Tom Bailey would remind you of Tom Sawyer. He was not really a bad boy, but he was mischievous, and he had many adventures because of it.

Aldrich worked on several newspapers and magazines, and was the editor of *The Atlantic Monthly,* a very famous magazine. Other books of his that young readers still find interesting are *Marjorie Daw* and *Too Many Pets.*

ale

Ale is a kind of beer. In England it is just another name for almost any kind of beer. In the United States it means beer brewed in a certain way. It does not contain more alcohol than beer, though many people think it does.

Aleutians

The Aleutians are a long chain of islands that begin at the western tip of Alaska and reach into the Pacific Ocean for a thousand miles. There are more than a hundred islands in the Aleutians.

The people who live on these islands are called Aleuts. They are a kind of American Indian, related to the Eskimos. They are short and sturdy and have dark skin and black hair. The Aleuts are fishermen, and they also trap blue fox, seal and sea otter for their valuable fur.

There are no trees on any of the Aleutian Islands. The ground is very rocky and very little plant life grows on it. When you see the islands from the water they look like the tops of rocky mountains. On some of the Aleutians there are volcanoes that are still smoking and may blow up again some day.

An explorer named Vitus Bering discovered the Aleutian Islands more than two hundred years ago, in 1741. He was from Denmark, but he was hired by the Russians to find out what lay east of Siberia, the Russian part of Asia. Bering sailed toward the east and not only discovered the Aleutian Islands, but also was the first to reach Alaska. When the Russian Government learned of his discoveries, and how rich the islands were in fur-bearing animals, the Russians sent traders to the Aleutians. These traders forced the Aleuts to work like slaves for them and were very brutal, killing many Aleuts.

In 1867 the United States bought Alaska and the Aleutian Islands from Russia. New American laws made it easier for the Aleuts to live and go about their fishing and hunting. Most of the time Americans paid little attention to

The picture at the top shows how the Aleutian Islands begin at the tip of Alaska and stretch out (more than 1,000 miles) southwestward into the Pacific Ocean. An Aleut is pictured, and beside him another Aleut in his boat, called a kayak. Here and at the left center part you can see the snow-covered mountains of the Aleutians. The sailors are on a U.S. Navy ship anchored off the Island of Attu. At center right, the Aleutian mountains make a big Navy ship look as small as a rowboat. At the left, a Navy Quonset hut half hidden by the deep winter snows.

the Aleutian Islands, but when Japan became warlike the United States government woke up to the fact that the Aleutians are very close to Japan. The United States Navy built a naval base at Dutch Harbor, which is on an Aleutian island called Unalaska.

Shortly after the Japanese bombed Pearl Harbor, in 1941, they also bombed Dutch Harbor. At that time there were about 4,000 Aleuts living on the small islands. Since they were in danger, they were all taken to safer islands near the Alaskan coast. The Japanese occupied some of the western islands in the Aleutians, and it was feared that they would soon attack Alaska. American sailors and soldiers landed on one of the Aleutian islands, called Attu, and fought a bloody battle with the Japanese. After 19 days of fighting in the cold and fog, the Japanese forces were wiped out. After the war was over the Aleuts were moved back to their rocky, treeless, desolate islands, but they were very happy to be back home.

ALEUTIAN ISLANDS. Area, about 6,500 square miles. Population, about 6,000. Government, part of Alaska. Total, about 140 islands, chiefly: 5 Aleut or Near Islands (largest are Attu and Agattu); about 30 very small Andreanov Islands; about 31 Fox Islands (largest are Unalaska, Unimak, Umnak, and Akutan); about 15 Rat Islands (largest are Rat, Kiska, and Amchitka).

alewife

The alewife is a fish like the shad and herring, that lives in the ocean but swims up rivers to lay its eggs. At exactly the same time every year, millions of alewives used to swim up the rivers of Maine and Nova Scotia. The Indians and early settlers there could drop in a net any place and scoop out a whole netful of fish. Since the rivers have become unclean, there are not nearly so many alewives today, but they are still an important food fish.

Alexander, Tsar of Russia

For many years Russia was ruled by emperors, called tsars or czars (the word is taken from Caesar, which was the name of several great rulers in ancient Rome). The tsar was supposed to be an absolute ruler, whom everyone had to obey. Actually, the noblemen did not hesitate to kill or replace the tsars if they were not pleased, and most of the cruel acts charged to the tsars were actually done by the noblemen. Some of the tsars were quite nice men. Two of these were named Alexander.

The first one, Alexander I, was tsar from 1801 to 1825. During his time, Napoleon was fighting wars all over Europe and Alexander took part in several of these. Alexander was born in 1777, so he was a young man of 24 when he became Tsar, and he liked the ideas of democracy, even though there was nothing democratic about the Russian government. He was a very handsome and pleasant young man, and both the nobles and the people of Russia loved and admired him. For a few years he fought against Napoleon; then in 1807, he made friends with Napoleon and was his ally in war. But Napoleon became too powerful and Alexander I began to fear him. In 1812, Napoleon went to war against Russia. This is a very famous war, and the story of it will be told in the article about NAPOLEON. Napoleon beat Russia but lost the war.

During the last years in which Alexander I was the Tsar, he changed his earlier ideas and came to dislike democracy and to feel that the common man should have no freedom. He died in 1825, although there are some people who think he did not die in that year but disappeared to turn to a religious life and let someone else be the Tsar. At least, when they opened his tomb a hundred years later, it was empty.

Alexander II was the grandson of Alexander I. He was born in 1818, and became Tsar in 1855, when he was 37 years old. He is most famous because he is given credit for setting the Russian serfs free. The serfs were Russian farmers who were not much better off than slaves. They could be bought and sold along with the farms on which they worked. Alexander II signed a document in 1861, setting the serfs free and giving them ownership of small pieces of land on which they could grow their own food. There are many, however, who say he did this only because there would have been a revolution of the serfs if he had not. In any case, the revolutionists hated him, and in 1881 he was assassinated by one of them in St. Petersburg, which was then the capital of Russia and which is now called Leningrad.

Alexander the Great

Of all the kings of history who have tried to conquer the whole world, Alexander the Great was the earliest and he may have been the one who came closest to it. This was more than 2,300 years ago. Alexander was the king of Macedonia, a small country north of Greece. In those days, the Greek countries were the most civilized on earth. Before Alexander died, he made Macedonia the most powerful country on earth.

The father of Alexander was King Philip of Macedonia. Philip was a great warrior and wise statesman. When Alexander became king, his father Philip had already established the control of Macedonia over the great Greek states, though they did retain independent governments of their own. Greece was the center of learning then, and Alexander studied as a boy under the great Greek philosopher Aristotle. He was born in 356 B.C. and became king when he was only 20 years old. He was already given a great country to rule. He immediately set out to make it greater.

There are many legends about Alexander the Great, and this should be expected. When he lived, the gods of the ancient Greek mythology were still thought to have been real gods, and many stories were made up to make it appear that Alexander's great victories were caused by the blessings of the gods and not by his own skill. One story says that when he was only a boy, he tamed and rode the famous horse Bucephalus that no one else could ride. These stories usually have Alexander continuing to ride Bucephalus for 15 or 20 years, which is unlikely because horses do not remain young and strong that long even if they do live that many years. However, there had been a prophecy that the rider of this horse would be a great king of Macedonia, and the stories were told to prove that Alexander the Great deserved to be the king.

Then there was the old legend of the GORDIAN KNOT, about which there is a special article later in this encyclopedia. Whoever could untangle the Gordian knot was supposed to be the next ruler of all of Asia, and Alexander cut it through with his sword. It is probably true that he cut a representation of this knot with his sword, but he probably would have won his great victories in Asia anyway.

Like a great many successful rulers and generals, Alexander was able to be very severe when he thought he had

to be, and this was true even when he was a young king not more than 21 years old. He had been fighting the "barbarians" (as they were later called)— the Germanic tribes who occupied parts of Europe to the north of Macedonia. The Greek cities heard that he was dead, and one of them, Thebes, revolted. Alexander took his army back to Thebes, destroyed the entire city, and either killed or made slaves of nearly everyone who lived there. This was harsh treatment, but it made all the rest of Greece afraid to revolt against him.

Then Alexander led his well-trained army into Persia, where he conquered the great king of Persia, Darius, and made himself the ruler of that country. He next conquered Egypt, then one of the centers of the civilized world, and founded the city of Alexandria. His next goal was Asia, and he marched his armies through Afghanistan and into India, and conquered India. There was no other general who was as good. In most of Alexander's great victories the enemy had larger armies than he had, but he outsmarted the enemy commanders. He might even have gone on to conquer all of Asia, if he had lived long enough. But a fever overtook him, and he died when he was not quite 33 years old, at the city of Babylon in Persia.

The greatness of Alexander is partly in the way he spread education and culture to the countries he conquered. The Greeks were the great thinkers, the great architects, and the great builders.

Wherever Alexander went he left colonies that transplanted the beauty and knowledge of the Greek cities to places hundreds or thousands of miles away. Many scholars believe that Alexander the Great speeded up the civilization of the world by several hundred years.

Alexandria

Alexandria is a city in Egypt. In ancient times it was one of the great cities of the world; then it was destroyed, and rebuilt, and it became one of the great cities of the modern world, with a population of a million people; only five cities in the United States are larger. Since it is on the Mediterranean Sea near the mouth of the Nile River, Alexandria is also a great seaport. The modern city of Alexandria was built near the ruins of the ancient city.

THE ANCIENT CITY

Alexander the Great, conqueror of nearly all the civilized world, built Alexandria more than 300 years before Christ was born, and named it for himself. With the advice of his architects, who had built many of the beautiful buildings of ancient Greece, Alexander chose a site near the mouth of the Nile River, a fine natural harbor. Alexander loved the beauty of the Greek cities and wanted Alexandria to be just as beautiful. The city was built with straight streets lined with trees. From the center of the city one broad avenue ran north and south and another broad avenue

Clipper Line, Malmo

The rug market in old-time Alexandria (above) does not look much like the present-day city (in the photo at the left) with its tall, modern buildings and its traffic lights.

Deane Dickason from Ewing Galloway

ran east and west. The main buildings were of marble. They had graceful columns and beautiful sculpture.

A great lighthouse was built on an island in the harbor of Alexandria. The island was called Pharos and the lighthouse became known as the Pharos. It stood 300 feet high and was known as one of the Seven Wonders of the World. A long causeway (a strip of land that serves as a bridge) was built to connect the island of Pharos with the mainland. The causeway held back the sea and made an inner harbor.

Alexandria was a great center of trade, but it also was for several hundred years the greatest center of knowledge. The library at Alexandria was the largest in the world. It contained all the knowledge then known to man. There were over 700,000 books in the library and they were written in all the important languages. (They were not books like the one you are reading, but rolls of papyrus, the paper of those times.)

The great library of Alexandria was destroyed by an army of Saracens, who were Mohammedans, in the year 640 A.D., nearly a thousand years after Alexandria was first built. It is said that the scholars begged the king of the Saracens not to destroy their famous library. "Why?" he asked.

"Because it contains all the knowledge of the world," they answered.

"But the Koran (the Mohammedan Holy Book) contains all the true knowledge of the world," he replied. "So why is the library needed?" And he had all the books burned.

Nothing is left today of that great library nor of any of the other beautiful buildings of ancient Alexandria. One enemy after another attacked the city and destroyed a part of it. Today it is a mass of broken stone and ruins.

THE MODERN CITY

The modern city of Alexandria is a busy seaport built near the ruins of the ancient city. A mixture of many types of Mediterranean people scurry about their business in the warm sunshine. Ships from all over the world enter the fine harbor.

In World War II Alexandria became an important place. Of course, it is an Egyptian city, and Egypt was not in the war, but Alexandria controlled the approach to the Suez Canal which the Germans wanted to capture. The German Marshal Rommel and his famed

Afrika Corps tried desperately to seize Alexandria. Once they almost succeeded, but they were finally beaten back after a great battle against the British at El Alamein, a town a few miles west of Alexandria. This was in October 1942. The Germans never threatened Alexandria again.

ALEXANDRIA, EGYPT. Population, 919,024 (1950 census). Capital of ancient Egypt. On the Nile River. Founded 332 B.C. by Alexander the Great.

alexandrite

Alexandrite is a semiprecious stone used in jewelry, and often considered the birthstone for June, along with the pearl and moonstone. It is found in various parts of the world, including Mexico, and is usually in the form of smooth pebbles left on the ground by streams of water. Alexandrite looks like colored glass that is one color in daylight and another color under electric light—it may be blue with red lights in the daytime, and lavender with blue lights under the electric lights. This makes it very pretty for jewelry.

alfalfa

Alfalfa is a plant somewhat like clover, green and sweet-smelling, with small flowers of yellow, blue, or purple, when it blooms. Many farmers plant alfalfa in their fields to give them a rest from growing vegetables, because the alfalfa will help to nourish the field and make it right for growing vegetables again, and besides alfalfa makes wonderful hay to feed to cattle. In fact, the word alfalfa means "the best fodder," that is, the best food for cattle. It is cut when it is about three feet high. Originally, alfalfa grew wild in Europe. In England, they call it lucerne.

Alfonso, King of Spain

There have been many Spanish kings named Alfonso, which is a popular name in Spain, but the one remembered best today is Alfonso XIII, who was the last king of Spain. One remarkable thing about Alfonso XIII is that he became king the minute he was born, which was in the year 1886, because his father had died before he was born. He grew up during a period in which the Spanish people had become tired of kings and wanted to have a republic. King Alfonso was a brave and clever man who was very well liked by those who knew him, but he was not a good ruler. He turned the government over to a dictator, General Primo de Rivera, but that only made the people more dissatisfied. They were very poor and did not have enough jobs or enough to eat, and there were many secret revolutionary groups that plotted against the king and his bad government. Several times the Spanish army had to be called out to stop a revolution, and in January, 1931, it began to seem that even the army could no longer be depended upon to control the people. A few months later, in April, 1931, Alfonso saw that he could no longer be king, and he abdicated and left the country. Spain became a republic. Read also the article on SPAIN.

Alfred the Great

Alfred the Great was a wise, brave king in England about a thousand years ago. He defended his people against terrible enemies and brought peace and order to his country, which was the southern part of the island of Great Britain. (There were several kings in England then.) Alfred's people were called the West Saxons.

In those days the most terrible warriors were the Danes, who often sailed across the North Sea from their home in Denmark to rob and kill the West Saxons. Alfred became king in the year 871. The first time the Danes invaded his country after that, he drove them out. A few years later they came back and this time they beat Alfred's army and the king had to hide in a swamp.

King Alfred the Great.

King Alfred did not give up. He wandered among his people in disguise. Slowly he gathered his scattered army together again. Once he stayed at the home of an old woman who told him to watch some cakes she was baking. When he fell asleep before the fire and let the cakes burn, the old woman, not knowing he was the king, scolded him and called him a good-for-nothing. But finally Alfred gathered his army together and defeated the Danes in a great battle.

Alfred set up a good government, passed wise laws, and brought peace and order to his country. In those days most of the people could not read or write, and the few who could write used only the Latin language. Alfred brought teachers and learned men from all parts of his country and from other lands in Europe, to write books and teach the people. King Alfred helped to write the books. Instead of Latin he used the language of the people, Anglo-Saxon, which came to be the English language we speak today.

In 892 the Danes attacked again and after fighting them for four long years, Alfred defeated them again. He died in 899, when he was about 50 years old.

algae

Algae are special kinds of plants that grow in water. There are several thousand different kinds of algae. The green scum you may find in your fish bowl, or on the surface of a pond, is a form of algae. Most of the many kinds of seaweed are algae. Some seaweeds grow to a length of 200 feet. Seaweed has been called the grass of the ocean. Without algae there would be no fish, just as there would be no animal life on land if there were no plants for animals to eat. Algae have no roots, stems or leaves. Some float freely on or near the surface of the water. Have you ever squeezed the little pods on a piece of seaweed and heard them pop? The pods are filled with air to help the seaweed float. They must float in order to get the sunlight that they need to grow on.

Most algae are green, but some are other colors. The Red Sea gets its name from the red algae that grow there. In many parts of the world people have found uses for seaweed. The Japanese eat certain kinds and also use it to fer-

Some algae are water plants so tiny they can be seen only under a microscope.

American Museum of Natural History

tilize their crops. Other people who live near the sea also use it for fertilizer. From some seaweeds iodine is made, and other seaweeds are used to make medicines that are good for upset stomachs. Some forms of algae contain a substance that is put in ice cream to make it smooth.

algebra

Algebra is a way of figuring, just as arithmetic is. Both algebra and arithmetic are branches of the science of mathematics. Algebra is the branch of mathematics that is studied next after arithmetic. It begins as a kind of shorthand. Suppose you have the simple job of adding 4 and 2 together:

$$\frac{\begin{array}{r} 4 \\ 2 \end{array}}{6}$$

You could also write this:

$$4 + 2 = 6$$

and if you spelled out the numbers, it would look like this:

$$\text{Four} + \text{Two} = \text{Six}$$

In algebra you might write

$$F + T = S$$

—using the first letters of the words to stand for the numbers, just as George Arthur Jones might write his name G. A. Jones.

Now suppose you knew that F meant 4, and S meant 6, but you didn't know what T meant. You could easily figure out that T must mean 2, because no other number could be added to 4 to make 6. But this would not be easy to do in your head if F and T were numbers like 3,471 or 142,857. The purpose of algebra is to put calculations into a form that makes it just as easy to solve problems with big numbers as with small ones, and with numbers you don't know as with numbers you do know.

We will go back now to the first ex-

ample, in which F stood for Four and T stood for Two and S stood for Six. E would stand for Eight. Now we could write:

$$S - F = T \quad (6 - 4 = 2)$$
$$F \div T = T \quad (4 \div 2 = 2)$$
$$F \times T = E \quad (4 \times 2 = 8)$$

In algebra, instead of $F \times T = E$ you would write $FT = E$, because the multiplication sign is not used when two symbols are placed side by side.

All of these are called *equations*. An equation is a statement that two things are equal. There are many rules governing equations, and when you know them you can "solve" problems by finding unknown numbers.

Algebra goes on to study *powers*, *roots*, and *series* of numbers.

A *power* of a number is the product, or result, you get when you multiply the number by itself, one or more times. It is expressed by an *exponent*, a small number written after and higher than the number. Thus, 3^2 (when you read it aloud, you say "three squared") means 3×3, or 9; 2^5 means $2 \times 2 \times 2 \times 2 \times 2$, or 32 (it is read "two to the fifth power").

A *root* is the opposite of a power. It is a number that must be multiplied by itself to produce a given number. It is written with a *radical sign*, as $\sqrt[3]{64}$ (read "the cube root of 64"); the answer here is 4, since 4^3 ($4 \times 4 \times 4$) is 64. When the sign is used without a little number, it means *square root*, as $\sqrt{25} = 5$.

A *series* is a group of numbers related by some rule. In an *arithmetic* series, such as 1, 4, 7, 10 . . . , a constant number (here, 3) is added to each term to give the next. In a *geometric* series, such as 1, 2, 4, 8 . . . , each term is multiplied by a constant number (here, 2) to produce the next. Series often provide the best way to find out the value of important unknown numbers in physics and other sciences.

Alger, Horatio

Horatio Alger, Junior, was an American writer who wrote at least a hundred books for boys. Millions of copies of his books were sold, during his life and long after his death. All of them were books about boys who started life in humble circumstances, perhaps as orphans or as poor boys, but who worked hard and were honest and eventually became very successful. The critics did not think Horatio Alger's books were good, but the American people loved them because they were the perfect expression of the American democratic ideal in which a boy can be born in a

became a minister in the Unitarian church, then moved to New York City and did some work helping the poor boys who sold newspapers, worked as shoeshine boys, and did other things that hardly paid them enough to live on. Many of his books were written about boys who found themselves in just those circumstances. Sometimes he would have his poor boys defended by rich Harvard graduates, since he had himself gone to college at Harvard, and in many ways he used the experiences of his own life in his writing. His titles were catchy ones, like *Luck and Pluck,* or *Sink or Swim,* or *Ragged Dick.*

The cover of a Horatio Alger story, showing a poor boy leaving his home in the country to seek his fortune in the big city. Every Alger hero was poor but honest.

log cabin and still become President of the United States as Abraham Lincoln did.

The writing of Horatio Alger, Junior, was begun about a hundred years ago. He was born in Revere, Massachusetts, a suburb of Boston, in 1834. He

Horatio Alger, Junior, was certainly a good man himself, and he worked hard, but his recipe for success did not work so well with himself. In spite of the millions of copies his books sold, he never made much money out of them, and he died poor in the year 1899.

Algeria

Algeria

Algeria is a large country in North Africa, across the Mediterranean Sea from France and Spain. Its coast on the Mediterranean Sea is the famous Barbary Coast. Fierce Mohammedan pirates used to attack ships and capture Christians to be held for ransom or sold as slaves. For more than a hundred years, Algeria has belonged to France. In size it is about four times as big as France, but its population of about nine million is small for that big a territory. Many thousands of American soldiers were in Algeria during World War II. They fought there or passed through there during the first United States campaign in the European fighting, in 1942 and 1943.

WHO LIVES IN ALGERIA

People of many different races and origins live in Algeria, more different kinds than can be found in many countries. Those who have been there longest are the Berbers (and it is from them that the name "Barbary Coast" came); they speak their own language, a very old one, but like the people themselves it has been mixed because of the many times other peoples with other languages have conquered Algeria. One of these peoples were the Arabs, and there are many Arabs living in Algeria, speaking the Arabic language. Many of the Arabs are nomads ("wanderers") who have no permanent homes but live in tents. There are probably more than three million Berbers and more than three million Arabs in Algeria.

The other people of Algeria include many Negroes, who long ago were brought from the heart of Africa and sold as slaves, but who have been free ever since the French came to control the country. There are about a million Europeans, mostly French, Spanish, and Italian. The rest of the population is made up of Jews, many of whom went to Algeria hundreds of years ago, and Turks, who once conquered the country. Since many of these different races married one another, there are mixtures of races in a large part of the population, just as there are in the languages spoken.

Most of the people of Algeria, except the Europeans, follow the Mohammedan religion.

HOW THE PEOPLE LIVE

Most of the European people living in Algeria earn their living by farming in the fertile valleys and plains along the northern coast. This section is called the Tell ("hill"), and was famous for its rich soil as long ago as Roman times. The native farmers were very poor, be-

schooling is very difficult because they do not stay in one place very long. Children are taught either by a traveling teacher, or simply by their mothers.

WHAT KIND OF PLACE IT IS

Algeria is a mountainous country, crossed by the high Atlas Mountains which divide Algeria from the Sahara Desert in the south. On the mountain slopes cedar and oak trees grow, sometime to gigantic size. Until the country was built up, the people were not able to make use of the wood of these trees because they had no good roads or railroads to carry the timber to the cities. Now roads and railroads have been built and it is a flourishing industry.

Most of the rivers in the mountains are not very useful. The most important is the Chéliff, which is about 400 miles long and empties into the Mediterranean. In the rainy season, which is from October to March, it becomes swollen and dangerous as it rushes down from the mountains. In the center of Algeria there are also large marshes. Once it was very unhealthy to live near these, but the government has drained them and turned them into prosperous farmland where the Algerians can raise oranges, grapes, vegetables, and tobacco.

In the south is the hot desert. This is uninhabited and barren, except for spots, called *oases,* where there is water. Some of these oases are natural springs, but many have been made by irrigation. More than 10,000 palm trees have been planted in these areas.

It might be supposed that Algeria would have a hot climate because it is in Africa. However, because of the mountains, the climate varies a great deal. People living in the north have a comfortably warm climate like that of Florida. In the desert, south of the mountains, it is very hot. In the mountains themselves it is cool in summer, with severe winters. The coldest month in Algeria is January; the hottest is August.

cause they did not know modern methods, and used tools that were out of date, until the French took over the country. The French introduced modern machinery and new methods. Today, the Algerian farmers grow large quantities of wheat and other grain, olives, figs, and many fruits, including grapes, from which they make wine.

Most of the villages of the natives are on the slopes or mountainsides. The Berbers work at farming and cultivating fruit trees; the Arabs raise cattle, which is the other important occupation next to farming. The greatest possession of the Arabs is their sheep, but the horse and mule are also noted for their excellence.

In the cities, the modern Algerian— whether native or European—lives and dresses like the people who live in cities in the United States. Some of the Mohammedans still wear their native dress, and the women wear veils over the lower part of their faces. To an American, the cities of Algeria are a strange mingling of the familiar and the unusual. Most of the people, though, do not live in the cities, and their lives are more backward and simple.

Education has grown slowly in Algeria. The Mohammedans do not like to send their children to French schools. But more and more, Christian and Mohammedan children are going to the same schools. Among the Arab nomads,

The Algerian children in the picture at the left are wearing European clothes, but the older woman wears the costume of her ancestors and keeps her face veiled. In the picture above, the man at the right is a scribe. He earns his living writing letters for people who don't know how to write.

The native section of Algiers is called the Casbah. There the people live as their ancestors have lived for hundreds of years. In the narrow streets are merchants' stands, and skilled workers such as the weaver and sandal-maker (in the picture at the right) sit on the sidewalks outside the buildings. Visitors go to the Casbah and buy their artistic handiwork.

French Gov't. Tourist Office   *TWA*

Harvesting Algerian grapes (left). At the right, the entrance to the (French) Governor's Palace in Algiers.

Every year, from May to September, there are great wind storms called siroccos. The hot wind from the desert blows across the country, filling the air with fine sand. But Algeria has, on the whole, a healthful climate.

The lions and other wild beasts that used to live in Algeria, as they still do in other parts of Africa, have disappeared as the country became more settled, and now it is quite safe there.

HOW THE PEOPLE ARE GOVERNED

Algeria is now officially called a French government-general of the French Union, and this means it is considered almost as though it were a state in France. It sends its own elected representatives to the French Parliament in Paris, three Senators and six Deputies (which are the same as Representatives or Congressmen in the United States). Within Algeria, there is a governor-general, in somewhat the same position as the governor of a state in the United States except that he is appointed by the French government and not elected by the Algerian people. Algeria also has its own legislative body, the Assembly, with two houses (like the Senate and the House of Representatives in the United States government). Each house of the

Assembly has sixty members. They make laws that apply to Algeria only, but these laws must have the approval of the governor-general.

A large part of the population of Algeria still does not have the right to vote. These are the Mohammedans, most of whom have not fulfilled certain requirements made by the French. The French government has an office called the "Bureau of Arab Affairs" that makes rules for the Mohammedan peoples, especially the tribes living away from the cities, so that their customs and religion can be maintained without interfering with the European type of government that is now there. Since 1914, Mohammedans have been permitted to hold any position in the government or in the armed forces.

Algeria is divided into three departments, or states, each having the same name as the biggest city in it. These are called:

ALGIERS. The city of Algiers is the capital of Algeria. There is a separate article about it, the next article after this one.

ORAN. This is a big city, with a population of more than 250,000, on the Mediterranean Sea. The French navy has a big naval base here (the base being

Ewing Galloway

1. El-Oued, a village in an oasis surrounded by miles of sand dunes in the Algerian Sahara Desert. The center of the photo shows the village market place, and camels resting.

2. The cathedral at Algiers is a beautiful building with domed roof. There are more Christians than Mohammedans in Algiers.

3. At Djemila, a few miles from Constantine, stand the ruins of the Arch of Caracalla. Caracalla was a Roman emperor, about 200 A.D., when Algeria belonged to Rome.

4. The suspension bridge over the Rhumel near Constantine, Algeria, is as much as 700 feet above the Rhumel River. The highway is tunneled through solid rock.

Trans-World Airlines

also called Mers-el-Kebir, which is the name of the district next to Oran). When the Germans occupied France during World War II, the British fleet in the Mediterranean sailed up to this naval base and destroyed most of the French warships in it, so that the Germans could not get them.

CONSTANTINE. This is the largest inland city of Algeria. It has a population of more than 100,000.

ALGERIA IN THE PAST

There have been people living in Algeria for many thousands of years, but during most of this period it has been a colony of some other country. It was a thriving colony of ancient Rome, for about 500 years, from before the time of Christ until Rome, and then its colonies, fell to German invaders about 1,500 years ago. The Romans called the colony Numidia, and called the native Berber people Numidians.

St. Augustine, one of the greatest figures in the history of the Christian church, was the bishop of Hippo, a city in what is now Algeria. Hippo has long been nothing but ruins, but the modern Algerian city of Bône, with a population of more than 100,000, is near the place where Hippo stood. Bône is a seaport on the Mediterranean.

From about the year 440 on, Algeria was conquered many times. First the Germans came. Then came Mohammedan invaders, the Arabs and later the Turks. Ever since, Algeria has been a Mohammedan country. About the year 1700 it became an independent country, under a ruler whose title was Dey. It was under the Deys that Algeria became a home for pirates.

In 1830, a French consul in Algiers insulted the Dey, whose name was Hussein. The Dey became angry and hit the consul. Because the consul, like any diplomatic officer in charge, was a representative of the king of France, this was considered the same as though the king

of France himself had been struck. France went to war angrily, conquered Algeria, and made it a French colony. An Arab leader named Abdul Kadir, and other leaders since, led revolutions against the French but none of them was successful.

Although the Mohammedan population of Algeria has had many complaints against the French, under French rule there has been much development of the country that probably would not have come so soon under the previous governments. The Algerians have been encouraged not only to improve their farmlands, but also to build roads and railroads, which now stretch across the country. Disease has decreased, hospitals have been built, and schools have been growing. The Algerians are becoming a more prosperous and independent people.

ALGERIA. Area, 836,124 square miles. Population (1952 estimate), 9,251,000. Languages, French, Arabic, Berber, and others. Religion, chiefly Mohammedan. Government, partly self-governing possession of France. Monetary unit, French franc.

Algiers

The capital and largest city of Algeria, with a population of more than 250,000, is Algiers. It is an important seaport on the Mediterranean Sea. Part of Algiers is a very modern French city. The other part is a native quarter, called the Casbah, in which the people are nearly all Mohammedans of Arabic and Berber ancestry, dressing in the native fashion that their people have followed for hundreds of years, and following Mohammedan customs. Algiers is more than a thousand years old, and was once the capital of Mohammedan rulers of northern Africa. Thousands of soldiers of the United States Army visited Algiers or were stationed there.

ALGIERS, ALGERIA. Population, 266,165 (1950 census). Capital of Algeria. On the Mediterranean Sea.

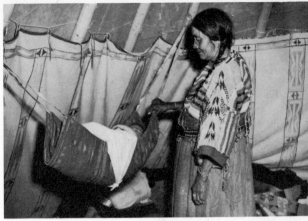

U.S. Indian Service, photo by Morrow

A Blackfoot woman rocking a baby in her tepee on the Blackfoot Reservation in Montana.

Algonquin Indians

The Indians of North America belonged to many different small nations or tribes. Each tribe spoke a different language, but in some cases there were anywhere from a dozen to a hundred different tribes whose languages were much alike. Scientists call these a "language group" or "family." The largest of these is the Algonquin family of tribes.

The Algonquin Indians lived mostly in the northeastern part of America. Their territory stretched from the Atlantic coast westward to the Mississippi River, southward as far as Tennessee and Virginia, and northward as far as Hudson Bay in what is now Canada. A few Algonquin tribes, such as the Arapaho and Cheyenne, lived on the plains. Another tribe, called the Blackfoot, lived as far west as the Rocky Mountains.

The first Indians met by the white settlers from Holland, France and England were Algonquins. There were about one hundred of these Algonquin tribes. They were always at war with one another. They would make raids to get scalps, which were pieces of skin with hair on them, cut from the heads of enemies whom they had killed. The more scalps a warrior brought back with

him from a raid on another tribe, the more he was admired.

Many of the Algonquin tribes were friendly to the white settlers when they first arrived, but they were soon at war with the colonists because the white men wanted the Indians' land for farming. In these wars the whites were just as cruel as the Indians. Both sides burned villages and killed women and children. In the French and Indian Wars, when England fought to control the New World, the Algonquins fought on the French side. But in the end the British destroyed most of the New England Algonquin tribes. Others were gradually pushed back into the forest by the whites and driven toward the west. Very often only a few Indians were left out of a tribe of several hundred. On their westward journeys they had to pass through the territory of unfriendly Indians who attacked and killed many of them.

Some of the most famous Indians in the early history of the United States were Algonquin. Massasoit, chief of the Wampanoags in New England, welcomed the Pilgrims when they landed at Plymouth. He taught them how to raise corn and signed a peace treaty with them. He never broke this treaty, even though the Pilgrims sometimes were cruel and unfair to his people. Another famous Algonquin was Pocahontas, who saved the life of Captain John Smith, leader of the first English settlement at Jamestown, Virginia, when he was captured by the Powhatan Indians. Later she married one of the English settlers, John Rolfe.

HOW THE ALGONQUINS LIVED

The Algonquin tribes lived in houses called wigwams, made of poles covered with elm-tree bark. In winter the poles were covered with mats woven out of cattail stalks, because these were warmer than bark. The floor was earth that had been stamped down with the feet. A fire was built in the middle of the floor and smoke escaped through a small hole in the roof. Raised platforms around the sides were used for sleeping and sitting.

The clothing worn by both men and women was usually made from deerskins. They wore soft shoes of deerskin called moccasins. The men usually wore only a breechcloth during the summer.

The women raised corn, squash, and beans, in small forest clearings. The men were forest hunters, and deer supplied most of their meat as well as fine skins for clothing. They made jugs and pots out of clay and knew how to make strong thread and twine from the inner bark of such trees as the swamp ash and linden. Until the white man came they knew nothing about metal, and made knives, needles and tools out of animal bones and stone. Their weapons were bows and arrows, knives, and battle axes called tomahawks. The arrowheads, knives and ax heads were made of stone. One of the best things made by the Algonquins was the birchbark canoe, a boat that was strong enough to carry three people yet light enough to be carried by one man. It was made of a framework of light strong wood tied tightly together and covered with birchbark. Using a canoe, the Algonquin Indian could travel swiftly and silently through the forests for long distances.

Their medicine men knew a great deal about healing herbs and roots, and many of the white settlers called upon them for help when they were ill.

Algonquin Indian women had their own beauty aids. They used bear fat to keep their hair glossy, and wore their hair long, since this was considered beautiful. They put fish oil and eagle fat on their faces to keep the skin soft. Sometimes they mixed red color into the fat to give color to the face, just as women do today when they put rouge on their faces. The men took even greater care of their hair than the women. They dressed it with bear fat every day and even mixed soot into it to make it look blacker than it was. They shaved their heads except for a ridge of hair in the middle of the head from front to back and often tied all sorts of ornaments like bits of shell and stone into it. They also painted pictures of animals and birds on their bodies and carried bags of paint about with them as part of their toilet kit. Both men and women liked to wear an embroidered band of skin around the head. In this they often stuck a row of feathers, but the big feathered headdress so often seen on Indians in the movies was not worn by Algonquin Indians but mostly by the Sioux, a tribe of the western plains.

Each tribe had a chief who was the leader in peace and war, but serious problems were discussed by a kind of mass meeting of all the people of the tribe. This meeting was often called a powwow, a word now used in the English language also. At the powwow a big fire was built and everybody sat around it and ate food. Some sang sacred songs and offered prayers. There was much pounding of drums, shaking of rattles, singing, and dancing. In between the singing and dancing there was a discussion of the problem. This might go on for days until a decision was made.

Algonquin tribes living along the Atlantic coast were the Abnaki, Algonkin,

Delaware, Mahican, Massachusetts, Micmac, Narraganset, Neskapi, Pequot, Powhatan, and Wampanoag tribes. Algonquin tribes living around the Great Lakes were the Cree, Illinois, Kickapoo, Menomini, Miami, Ojibway, Ottawa, Potawatomi, Sauk and Fox, and Shawnee.

Alhambra

The Alhambra is a palace in Granada, a city in the south of Spain. It was built when the Moors and other people of the Mohammedan religion had conquered Spain and ruled there. The Alhambra was built mostly by Christians who had been made slaves by the Mohammedan rulers. It took over one hundred years to build the Alhambra. It is such a big place that it covers 35 acres, which is as much as 16 or 17 city blocks, or about the size of the usual farm.

The Alhambra is not one building, but many. There are several palaces, and a strong fortress that looks like a castle, with high towers and walls. The palaces are very different from anything we have in the United States. If you were to walk in the Alhambra you would see bright colors everywhere; even the roofs of the palaces are painted red and blue and

The Court of the Lions is perhaps the most admired portion of the Alhambra. The lions may be seen around the fountain. The windows and arches look like lacework.

brown and gold. You would look out of windows made of wood carved to look like lace; under your feet you would see marble and painted tiles arranged in patterns and pictures. Painted tiles cover some of the walls and even part of the ceilings, and the wooden parts of the walls and ceilings are painted white and gold. There are many marble columns and archways. Some of the palaces are built in the shape of a square, with a garden in the center. In the gardens there are pools with live goldfish, carved fountains, and bright flowers, many of which can grow only in a warm country, like southern Spain.

In 1492, the same year that Columbus sailed on his voyage to discover America, the Spanish people drove the Moors out of their country. In the fighting they destroyed much of the Alhambra. Three hundred years later a king of Spain named Ferdinand VII, who loved the beauty of palaces and gardens, had the Alhambra rebuilt and restored. Washington Irving, a great American writer, wrote a book about the Alhambra.

Ali Baba

The story of Ali Baba and the Forty Thieves is found in the *Arabian Nights Entertainments,* sometimes called *The Thousand and One Nights.* Ali Baba

Spanish State Tourist Office

The Alhambra is on a hill overlooking Granada. The lower of the towers shown at the left is called "the Boudoir of the Queen." The Sierra Nevada mountains of Spain are in the background.

When Ali Baba spoke the magic words "Open Sesame" before the robbers' cave, the door flew open. He was breathless with astonishment at the sight of the treasures inside.

was a poor woodcutter. One day a band of forty robbers came by where he was working, and he hid from them. He heard them say "Open, Sesame," and these magic words opened the door of the cave where they kept their stolen treasures. After they had gone away, he hurried to their cave, and said the magic words. The door opened, and Ali Baba carried away so much gold and jewels that he became a rich man.

The forty thieves found out that Ali Baba had taken their treasure, and went to Ali Baba's house to get it back. With the help of a slave girl, Ali Baba outwitted them and wiped out the entire robber band. Then he married the slave girl and remained a rich man.

Alice in Wonderland

Alice's Adventures in Wonderland is the name of a book about a little girl who dreams she is in another world, and has many amazing things happen to her there. The book was published nearly a hundred years ago, in 1865, and is loved as much by adults as by children.

Its author was not a writer by profession, but a mathematician and professor. His name was Charles Lutwidge Dodgson, but he is known to all the world by the name of Lewis Carroll, which he signed to this book. He wrote the story to amuse some young friends, one of whom was named Alice. Later he wrote another book about Alice, calling it *Alice Through the Looking Glass*. The two books, "Alice in Wonderland" and "Through the Looking Glass," are usually read together and considered as one book.

Alien and Sedition Laws

These were laws passed by the Congress of the United States when this country was only a few years old and the people of the United States could still remember fighting the Revolutionary War in which they won independence for their country and freedom for themselves. The Alien Laws gave the President the right to send an alien (that is, a foreigner) out of the United States if the country went to war. The Sedition

Laws allowed the government to put a person in jail if he criticized the government.

All of these laws took away rights that the people felt the Constitution of the United States had given them. They hated the laws so much that they would not reëlect President John Adams, who was President when the laws were passed in 1798. Two states of the United States, Virginia and Kentucky, passed "resolutions"—that is, official statements by their legislatures—saying that the laws were unconstitutional. None of these laws was used very much, and they ended in 1801. You can read more about them in the article on President JOHN ADAMS.

alimentary canal

The alimentary canal is a sort of pathway all through the body. Along this pathway, food travels from the time it is swallowed to the time the unused part of it leaves the body as waste. Although it is called a "canal," it is really a series of big and little pipes, all connected together to form one tube about 30 feet long. It begins at the mouth and goes down through the neck and chest into the belly; there it winds around through the intestines and ends in a small opening at the back of the body called the anus.

The entire alimentary canal is lined with a thin, moist skin called a mucous membrane. A good example of mucous membrane is the lining of the mouth and inside of the nose.

The digestion of food takes place in the different parts of the alimentary canal. After food is chewed and swallowed it passes through the pharynx, a tube about 4½ inches long, and down into the esophagus, another tube about 9 inches long that connects with the stomach. The stomach is a pear-shaped bag about 11 inches long and 4 inches wide. In the walls of the stomach there are glands, or tiny sacs, that pour out

liquids called digestive juices. These help break down the food. In the stomach the food is only partially digested. It passes into the small intestine, a long narrow tube about 23 feet long, which takes up most of the belly or abdomen. It is in this long, winding tube that the digestion of food is completed.

What remains of the food now passes on to the colon, or large intestine, which is a bigger but shorter tube than the small intestine. The last eight inches of the colon is called the rectum. The waste matter of the body is stored here until it is forced out of the anus.

alimony

Alimony is the money paid by a husband to a former wife, from whom he is divorced. The law says that a husband must support his wife. When a husband and wife can no longer get along together, and want to end their marriage, they often get a divorce, but the husband must still support the wife and any children they had together. The judge in the court decides how much the husband must pay the wife. First he finds out how much the husband earns. Then he orders the husband to pay the wife a fixed amount of money every week or every month. This is alimony. Sometimes a wife receives no alimony if the judge thinks the break-up of the marriage was her fault. Sometimes a woman who is receiving alimony marries again. When this happens, her first husband no longer has to pay her alimony, but he may still have to pay for the support of their children.

alkalis

Alkalis are chemicals that are used in making many products. They may be liquids, gases, or solids. Some alkalis we know well are washing soda, which is used as a cleanser; bicarbonate of soda, or baking soda, which is mixed into dough to make biscuits light and fluffy; and caustic soda, or lye, which is often put into drain pipes in kitchens and bathrooms to clear them when they are clogged with grease. Lye, called sodium hydroxide by chemists, is also important in making paper, aluminum, glass, and soap (which is a mixture of lye with fat or oil).

There are weak alkalis, such as baking soda, and strong alkalis, such as lye. The strong alkalis are dangerous and can cause bad burns to the skin. If you should happen to drop a strong alkali on your skin the best thing to do is to wash it with a great deal of clean water and then pour on a weak acid like vinegar, which will neutralize the alkali. But if you drop a strong acid on your skin, you can avoid a burn by putting on an alkali, for example, by dipping your hand in soda water, if that is where the acid touched you.

Farmers sometimes have trouble with soil that has too much alkali in it, since it is hard to grow crops in such earth. Such soils have to be washed or flooded with water, and then drained, to remove the alkali.

alkaloid

Alkaloids are a group of chemicals made from plants and used in medicine and other drugs. Some of the best known of these alkaloids are morphine, opium, quinine, cocaine and nicotine.

Opium is a drug made from a flower, the poppy. Poppies from which opium can be made grow mostly in eastern Asia. Opium and drugs, such as morphine, that are made from opium, are used as pain killers, but they are very dangerous and can be obtained only by a doctor's prescription.

Quinine is a medicine made from the bark of the cinchona tree, which grows in Peru and in parts of southeastern Asia. It is used as a cure for malaria, a fever that attacks people in the southern part of the United States and in the tropical parts of Africa, South America, and Asia.

Cocaine is a pain killer made from the leaves of the coca plant in western South America. It is very dangerous just as are the drugs made from opium. Cocaine was once used by dentists, but novocaine, a substitute for it, is now used instead.

Nicotine is made from the leaves of the tobacco plant. It is very poisonous, but the amount of nicotine in smoking tobacco is too small to be very harmful. Nicotine is often mixed with water and other liquids and sprayed on plants, to kill insects that destroy crops.

There are several cases, besides that of novocaine, in which artificial drugs have been made to replace the ones made from plants. One example is atabrine, which is often used instead of quinine to prevent or control malaria.

Allah

Allah is the name given to God in the Mohammedan religion. Like the Christians and the Jews, the Mohammedans believe in only one God. They say this in the following way: "There is but one God and his name is Allah."

All-American

The name All-American is given to an athlete who has been chosen as one of the best in his particular sport. The first well-known All-American teams were football teams, and were picked by a man named Walter Camp. He had played football himself, and was the coach at Yale University. He knew a lot about the game, and could pick out the best players. Once each year, beginning in 1889, Walter Camp chose the All-American team. Every player on the team was judged to be the best at his position during the past football season. As long as Walter Camp lived, the team he chose was considered the official All-American football team. After he died, Grantland Rice, a famous sports writer, and then many others, began to choose teams, and today magazines and newspapers and radio stations all over the country choose All-American teams and there is no "official" All-American team.

All-American teams are chosen in many sports. The best college players in football, basketball, baseball, lacrosse, soccer, and other sports, are chosen each year. Many thousands of young athletes participate in college sports. The goal of every one of them is to be chosen on an All-American team.

Alleghenies

The Allegheny Mountains, or Alleghenies, are a small range in the eastern part of the United States. This range is the central section of the bigger mountain range known as the Appalachians. The Alleghenies stretch between the Catskill Mountains in New York and the Blue Ridge Mountains in Virginia and the Carolinas. The highest peak is the Peak of Otter, in Virginia. It is 4,000 feet high at its summit.

Many millions of years ago, before there were people living on the earth, there was a flat plain where the Alleghenies are today. On that plain were a great many plants. No such plants grow today. Some of them were like ferns but as big as trees. They made a huge, extremely thick mat that gradually became packed down, and grew harder and harder until it eventually turned into coal. Later, when the earth's crust wrinkled because it was cooling inside, mountains were pushed up, with the coal deep inside them. Miners dig both hard and soft coal out of these mountains today, in Pennsylvania and West Virginia.

allegory

An allegory is a story in which a character represents an idea as well as a person. This can also be done in other forms of art, for example, painting and dancing. Father Time may appear as a character in a story or in a picture, an old man with a long gray beard, and we

When Death is pictured as a skeleton, it is an allegory, because a person is made to represent an idea. Death holds a scythe, which represents the cutting off of life, and an hourglass, which means that the old scholar's time is running out like the sands in the glass, but these are called symbols. When a thing represents an idea, it is called symbolism; when a person does, it is called allegory.

may read about him or see him as a person, but we know he represents the idea that everyone grows old. In dancing, a character named Death may appear as a skeleton, but we know that he represents the idea that everyone must die.

The allegory that is best known in English literature is *Pilgrim's Progress* by John Bunyan, a book that has been read by millions of persons both young and old. In this book, the hero is a man named Christian, but the idea is the fact that man is always looking for goodness, and God, and is trying to be as religious as he should be. The other characters in this book stand for ideas in the same way.

Another famous old English allegory, which is not very often read today but is still studied in schools, is the story of Everyman; this was usually put on as a play rather than as a story to be read.

Some of the fables of Aesop and other writers may be thought of as allegories if you consider the animals to stand for ideas, for example, the fox standing for cleverness, the bee for thrift, and the owl for wisdom.

The British kept Ethan Allen in a prison in Bristol, England, for six months.

Allen, Ethan

Ethan Allen was an American hero in the Revolutionary War. He was the leader of the "Green Mountain Boys" from Vermont, and he is remembered as Vermont's greatest man of his time, but he was not born there. Vermont was not a state (or separate colony) then, and very few people lived there. Ethan Allen was born in Litchfield, Connecticut, on January 10, 1738, nearly forty years before the Revolutionary War began. He fought for the British in the French and Indian Wars, just as George Washington did. After this fighting, when the Governor of New Hampshire offered good farmlands "across the Green Mountains" to some of the soldiers, Ethan Allen was one of those who went there and built himself a home in what is now Vermont. These settlers, though they called themselves the Green Mountain "Boys," were really men, as Allen was.

As leader of these Green Mountain Boys, Ethan Allen rebelled against British rule before the Declaration of Independence was signed. On May 10, 1775, he and his Green Mountain Boys, with the help of Benedict Arnold and some soldiers from Connecticut, attacked Fort Ticonderoga in New York State, held by the British, and captured it. Ethan Allen's words in that attack have become famous. "Surrender," he shouted, "in the name of Jehovah and the Continental Congress!"

The Continental Congress sent Allen to Canada, to see if he could persuade the Canadians to join the Revolution. On his second trip to Canada, he was captured by the British. They put iron shackles on his hands and feet and threw him into the hold of a ship. He was kept there for five weeks before the ship sailed. As soon as the ship left Quebec, the captain released Allen from his dungeon until they reached England. The British knew Ethan Allen was too valuable to kill. They sent him back to America and exchanged him for a British colonel who had been captured by the Americans.

The Continental Congress greeted Ethan Allen with the greatest honor, and Vermont made him a major general. After the Revolutionary War was won, he spent his time as a delegate to the Continental Congress, trying to persuade them to recognize Vermont as a state. He died in 1789, when he was 52 years old, thinking he had failed; but two years later Vermont became a state and he had succeeded after all.

allergy

You have an allergy when something you eat or breathe or even feel can make it seem that you have some kind of disease. The kind of allergy that is known best, and that may trouble the most people, is called hay fever. When a person with hay fever breathes in air that has the pollen of certain grasses and flowers floating in it, he will sneeze and his nose will run and he will have fevers and it will seem that he has a bad cold. But he does not have a cold. He is simply allergic to the pollen in the air.

Filter the pollen out of the air he breathes and he will stop sneezing, his nose will stop running, and he will not have a fever any more.

Different people are allergic to different things. Some people seem not to be allergic to anything. No one knows, yet, what causes allergies. All that is known is that they exist. Strawberries can make one person's lips swell or his eyes puff out. A new puppy in the house may cause another person to cough or to itch. Even the fear of reciting in public might make your skin break out as if you had touched poison ivy.

When a person is allergic to something, eating or touching it will probably cause his body to produce large amounts of histamine. There is a separate article about HISTAMINE in a later volume. It is a substance produced by the body, and it can make the skin itch or the nose run or the stomach feel upset. Some people are allergic to certain medicines, such as penicillin or aspirin.

A skin doctor, called a dermatologist, can test to see what sort of thing you might be allergic to. He puts a number of different patches on your skin. Each patch has a little of a different substance on it. After a few days the doctor takes the patches off, and your skin will show if you are allergic to any of those substances.

There are several drugs that have been developed to help people who suffer from allergies. They do not work on everyone, but the doctor will usually try one or more of them, and often one can be found to help the person who has an allergy.

Allies

In World War I, when the fighting broke out in 1914, Great Britain, France and Russia fought together against Germany and Austria-Hungary (which was then a large, powerful nation in central Europe). Great Britain, France and Russia were called "the Allies," and Ger-

Dow Chemical Corporation

Ragweed, the chief cause of hay fever, thrives in vacant lots. Many cities have it sprayed with weed-killers, as shown in the picture at the top. Center: The plant on the left has not been sprayed. The one on the right shows how ragweed dies when it is sprayed. Bottom: The doctor is testing to find out what makes his patient sneeze. All the bottles hold different substances to which she may be allergic.

many and Austria-Hungary were called "the Central Powers."

The name Allies became popular, and when World War II began in 1939 it was again applied to Great Britain and France. The United States, when it joined the war during World War I, was known as one of the Allies, and again in World War II when Russia and later the United States went in, they were said to have "joined the Allies," but generally the word means Great Britain and France fighting on the same side against an enemy, usually Germany.

alligator

The alligator is the largest reptile of the United States. (Snakes, lizards, and other crawling, egg-laying animals are reptiles.) The alligator looks like a big lizard, but it is not a lizard. It is related to the crocodiles, but has a broader snout and a bigger tail. It spends most of its time swimming, or sunning itself on shore. A fully-grown male alligator may be as much as 13 to 16 feet long and may weigh up to 500 pounds, but most of them are smaller—up to 10 feet long for males, and 7 or 8 feet for females. This includes the tail. An alligator's tail is about as long as his body.

Alligators live in freshwater streams

The alligator looks like a big lizard.

New York Zoological Society

in the southern part of the United States, from North Carolina to Texas. Once they were thought to live to be 100 years old, but actually 20 to 30 years is closer to it. The alligator is one of the few reptiles that have voices. It can bellow or roar loudly.

Female alligators build nests of leaves and other material that they scrape up along the shore. They lay up to 38 eggs, 2 to 3 inches long. The young alligators are 8 to 10 inches long when they hatch, and grow about a foot a year at first, then more slowly. Young alligators are often captured as "pets," but this is very foolish. They seldom live in captivity, and if they do they soon become dangerous.

An alligator eats other animals. It captures them, drowns them in the water, then swallows them. Alligators are timid and seldom attack men, but if they do they are dangerous. They often swing their big, strong tails in fighting. Some men like to risk death by riding on the backs of alligators. The greatest value of alligators is that their skins make very fine leather.

alligator pear, another name for the avocado. See AVOCADO.

alliteration

Alliteration is the use of two or more words that begin with the same letter or sound. You are using alliteration when you say "tried and true," "safe and sound," "hale and hearty," or "in the merry month of May." When words are rhymed, the ending sound is the same, as in "moon" and "June." When you use alliteration, you make the beginnings of words sound the same. "Peter Piper picked a peck of pickled peppers" is alliteration.

A thousand years ago, poets who wrote in the Old English language used alliteration *instead* of rhyme. In the article on ANGLO-SAXON, you can read an example of this. A poet today often uses both rhyme and alliteration, but alliteration is used more in humorous poetry than in serious poetry. In the unusual example shown below, the poet Swinburne was writing "nonsense poetry." Many of the lines don't make sense, and were not intended to. His only intention was to use as much alliteration as possible.

THE BEST ALLITERATION EVER WRITTEN

NEPHELIDIA, by Algernon Charles Swinburne

From the depth of the dreamy decline of the dawn through a notable nimbus of
    nebulous noonshine,
Pallid and pink as the palm of the flagflower that flickers with fear of the flies as
    they float,
Are they looks of our lovers that lustrously lean from a marvel of mystic miraculous
    moonshine,
These that we feel in the blood of our blushes that thicken and threaten with throbs
    through the throat?
Thicken and thrill as a theatre thronged at appeal of an actor's appalled agitation,
Fainter with fear of the fires of the future than pale with the promise of pride in the
    past;
Flushed with the famishing fullness of fever that reddens with radiance of rathe
    recreation,
Gaunt as the ghastliest of glimpses that gleam through the gloom of the gloaming when
    ghosts go aghast?
Nay, for the nick of the tick of the time is a tremulous touch on the temples of terror,
Strained as the sinews yet strenuous with strife of the dead who is dumb as the
    dust-heaps of death:
Surely no soul is it, sweet as the spasm of erotic emotional exquisite error,
Bathed in the balms of beatified bliss, beatific itself by beatitude's breath.
Surely no spirit or sense of a soul that was soft to the spirit and soul of our senses
Sweetens the stress of suspiring suspicion that sobs in the semblance and sound of a sigh;
Only this oracle opens Olympian, in mystical moods and triangular tenses —
'Life is the lust of a lamp for the light that is dark till the dawn of the day when
    we die.'
Mild is the mirk and monotonous music of memory, melodiously mute as it may be,
While the hope in the heart of a hero is bruised by the breach of men's rapiers,
    resigned to the rod;
Made meek as a mother whose bosom-beats bound with the bliss-bringing bulk of a
    balm-breathing baby,
As they grope through the grave-yard of creeds, under skies growing green at a groan
    for the grimness of God.
Blank is the book of his bounty beholden of old, and its binding is blacker than bluer:
Out of blue into black is the scheme of the skies, and their dews are the wine of the
    bloodshed of things;
Till the darkling desire of delight shall be free as a fawn that is freed from the fangs
    that pursue her,
Till the heart-beats of hell shall be hushed by a hymn from the hunt that has harried
    the kennel of kings.

Republic Steel Corporation

This 70-ton electric furnace produces the finest alloy steels.

alloy

An alloy is a metal made by melting two or more pure metals together in a very hot furnace and mixing them together. When they cool and harden, they form a new metal. This is an alloy. Other alloys are made by mixing a melted metal with small amounts of a chemical that is not a metal.

There are so many alloys made by man today that it would take a very thick book to list all of them. Usually an alloy is better for some special use than a pure metal would be. One of the first alloys made by man was bronze, a mixture of copper and tin. Thousands of years ago, long before man discovered iron, bronze was used for knives, swords, shields, and tools. Ancient man had found that copper was too soft for knives and other cutting tools. Then he learned that by adding a little tin to copper he could make a metal that was harder than either tin or copper. Brass is another alloy made with copper. It is made by adding zinc to the copper and is much harder than either of these metals. There are many different kinds of brass, depending on how much zinc is added to the copper.

Some of the strangest alloys are amalgams, which are mixtures of mercury with other metals. These alloys are made without melting either metal. There is a separate article on AMALGAM.

Steel is one of the most important alloys in common use. It is made by melting iron and adding small amounts of pure carbon while the iron is still a hot liquid. Carbon is not a metal. Coal and charcoal—wood that has been burned black—are examples of carbon. Pure iron is a fairly soft metal. With enough carbon added, it becomes very hard. Stainless steel is made by mixing two metals called chrome and nickel with the hot melted steel. These metals will not rust, and so the entire alloy will not rust.

Very few pure metals are used by modern man. Even the silver dimes, quarters, and half-dollars we use have a little copper added to them to make them harder. Pure silver is a very soft metal and would wear out very quickly. Not all alloys are intended to make a harder or stronger metal. Sometimes a softer metal is needed. Solder is an alloy of tin and lead. It is useful because it melts at a very low temperature. When a stick of solder is touched to a hot iron, the solder quickly melts and drips down where needed. It hardens almost immediately, and will plug up a hole, or join pieces of metal together.

Scientists called metallurgists work constantly to develop new and better alloys. Some of the best known have special "trade names" given to them by their inventors. Duralumin is one of these. It is an alloy of aluminum and it was invented because modern airplanes needed a metal that is both lighter and stronger than pure aluminum. Carboloy is another. It is a mixture of carbon with two metals called cobalt and tungsten, and it was made to be the hardest alloy known, so as to make tools that would cut even the toughest steel alloys. Read the separate articles on METALS and on the different metals such as IRON, COPPER, and so on. New alloys are being created all the time.

All Saints' Day

All Saints' Day is a religious holiday. On this day, Catholics honor all the blessed persons who have died and reached heaven. The holiday falls on November 1 each year. All Saints' Day used to be called All Hallows' Day ("Hallow" means bless). The night before was called All Hallows' Eve. Now we call this night Hallowe'en.

All Souls' Day

All Souls' Day is celebrated the day after All Saints' Day. On All Souls' Day, Catholics pray for those who have died. Their prayers are to help those who have died to enter heaven. On All Souls' Day, special services are held in the churches. Some people also observe the day by going to a cemetery, and putting flowers on the graves of those who have died.

allspice

Allspice is the berry of a tree that grows on the island of Jamaica, in the West Indies. Another name for the berry is *Jamaica pepper*. Allspice gets its name because it is supposed to combine the flavor of several other spices, such as cinnamon, clove, and nutmeg. The berries must be picked before they become ripe. If they ripen on the tree, they will become spoiled and bitter. After the berries are picked, they are dried in the sun. Usually the berries are then ground to make a powder that can easily be sprinkled on food that is being cooked, to flavor it.

Allston, Washington

Washington Allston was one of the finest American painters of portraits and other pictures, about a hundred and fifty years ago. He was born in the little town of Waccamaw, South Carolina, in 1779, when the Revolutionary War was being fought, and he was named for General George Washington. After going to college at Harvard, he studied art in London, Paris, and Rome. He was a close friend of Samuel Taylor Coleridge, the English poet; Washington Irving, the American writer; and other great men of his time. His portraits and his paintings of scenes from the Bible may be seen in many art galleries, especially in London and Boston. They called him "the American Titian" because he used rich colors as the artist Titian did. One of Washington Allston's pupils was Samuel F. B. Morse, the inventor of the telegraph. He died at Cambridge, Massachusetts, in 1843, when he was 64 years old.

Washington Allston at work, as pictured by another artist of his time.

N. Y. Public Library

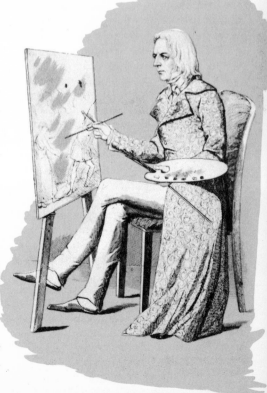

almanac

An almanac is a book published once each year to give many useful facts and to be a complete calendar for the coming year. If you have an almanac, you can know beforehand many things that will happen on each day of the year. It will tell you what time the sun will rise and when it will set, and how full the moon will be, on each day. If you live near an ocean, the almanac will tell you at what times the tide will be high and when it will be low. Some almanacs also try to predict the weather in advance, but this cannot be done scientifically so far in advance.

The first almanac was probably made in ancient Egypt, thousands of years ago. The Nile River overflowed its banks every year, and the Egyptian people wanted to know about when this would happen. The priests studied the movements of the stars and the moon. They knew that so many full moons would have to appear after one flood before the next one came. The priests then told the people when to expect the next flood.

Almanacs became popular in Europe during the Middle Ages, about six or seven hundred years ago. Some almanacs gave more information than others. There were almanacs that predicted wars, the death of kings, earthquakes, and fires. Each year the people rushed to buy these almanacs. They forgot that last year's predictions had been mostly wrong.

One of the earliest and most famous American almanacs was begun in 1732 by Benjamin Franklin. He called it *Poor Richard's Almanack*. Poor Richard was a name that Franklin used for himself. Franklin not only gave the usual kind of almanac information; he also included many witty sayings. Surely you have heard "Early to bed and early to rise makes a man healthy, wealthy, and wise." It was first written by Franklin for *Poor Richard's Almanack*.

Farmers in America read almanacs. Among other things the farmers want to know when to plant and when to harvest their crop. *The Old Farmers' Almanac,* started in 1766, is still read by many farmers in New England. Today several almanacs are published every year by large newspapers and by book publishers. These almanacs give more than information about the coming year. They also tell what happened during past years, and list many interesting kinds of information.

almond

The almond is a tree that grows in warm climates. It is related to the peach tree. The almond tree has lovely light-pink blossoms and fruit that looks like peaches but is not eaten. Inside each fruit is a shell, and inside the shell is a nut. When we say "almond," we usually mean the nut.

When the fruit of the almond tree ripens, it becomes leathery and hard, and peels away from the nut. There are two kinds of almond. One is sweet and the other is bitter. The nut we eat is the sweet almond. The bitter almond is like the nut you will find inside a peach pit. It should not be eaten, as it may make you very sick. Many almonds are grown in the warm valleys of California. Frost can ruin the almond crop, and smudge-pots are used to prevent this. The fires in the smudge-pots warm the air enough to keep the almonds from freezing.

The almond (upper left in the picture) has a soft shell you can break with your fingers. Also shown are branches and the flower of the almond tree.

Netherland West Indies Tourist Committee

The aloe is a small plant that can be grown in a flowerpot (left). Its leaves are crushed and the juice used to make medicine. At the right, above, a man is harvesting aloes in a field. Below: a West Indian distills the juice to make medicine.

aloe

Aloe is the name of a plant that grows best in tropical countries, where it is very hot. African natives use the fibers of the leaves to weave nets. The plant is best known as the source of a drug called *aloes*. This drug is contained in the juice of the aloe leaves. It has a very bitter taste. It is used in medicine to help in cleaning out the stomach. In South America some people use the dried stems of the aloe as tinder to start fires. The leaves of the aloe have sharp, spiny points. The aloe plant was brought to South America and Mexico by the Spaniards, hundreds of years ago.

alpaca

The alpaca is an animal that lives in the Andes Mountains of South America. It is related to the llama, the guanaco, and the vicuna, which also live in South America. All these animals are members of the camel family, but do not have humps, nor are they as large as camels. The alpaca looks very much like a sheep with a long neck. It is usually brown, but may also be grayish, white, black, or a mixture of these colors. It is a valuable animal because of its long, woolly hair. This hair is used in the weaving of fine woolen cloth.

The Indians of Bolivia and Peru keep herds of alpacas. The animals graze on pastures high in the Andes Mountains. Some alpacas live 15,000 feet above sea level. The Indians weave colorful blankets of alpaca hair. The alpaca is sheared once a year, and the wool is mostly sent to England and America. The alpaca, unlike the llama, is never used as a beast of burden.

alphabet

An alphabet is a system of using certain marks, which we call "letters," to stand for particular sounds. There are many different alphabets in the world today, and it has taken thousands of years to develop them. The English alphabet of twenty-six letters is also called the "Roman alphabet," because we got it from the ancient Romans, who had gotten it from the Greeks. We call it *alphabet* because the first two letters of the Greek alphabet were called *alpha* and *beta*—in others words, calling it the alphabet then was exactly the same as calling it the ABC's today.

The simplest way of putting an idea down on paper is to draw a picture, and that is how men first began to write, six thousand years ago or more. Our alphabet has come to us gradually from picture-writing of this sort. The picture-writing from which our alphabet is descended was done in ancient Egypt; it was called hieroglyphic writing. Picture-writing was able to express ideas as well as objects. For example, a little picture of a man could represent the word "man," but a picture of a man lying on the ground with a spear in him would represent the idea "death." The Chinese and even the American Indians developed methods of writing in pictures. But there was not much that could be said this way, and it would have taken hundreds of thousands of pictures to express everything—many more than a person could hope to learn in a lifetime.

Out of the early picture-writing came the use of pictures to stand for syllables. Suppose a picture of a pole or stake in the ground were used to represent the word "pole," and a picture of a lamp burning to represent the word "light." Putting the two together, you would have pole-light, which could mean polite— an idea that could never be expressed by a picture. Using pictures in this way to represent sounds instead of things, men were able to increase the usefulness of their writing by many times. The Chinese still use this kind of writing in syllables. The trouble is that there are so many different syllables, it takes a

scholar years to learn them all. In the Chinese language, there are more than fifty thousand and most of these are being used even today. A Chinese student does not master the writing of his language until he is beyond the age at which an American student may have graduated from college—say, twenty-five years old. In comparison with his thousands of characters, the American schoolboy has to learn only twenty-six letters.

Therefore the next step in the development of the alphabet was to have a symbol, or letter, for each sound that was used in the language being spoken. There are many more sounds that a human being can use than we have in our alphabet, and the alphabets used for other languages have in them certain letters that we do not need in writing the English language. But also we have some letters that they do not need. No alphabet needs more than thirty or forty letters. A child can master these in a year or two.

Writing with letters instead of with pictures is more than five thousand years old. Just as we got our alphabet from the Greeks, they got theirs from the Semitic peoples—the Phoenicians and the Jews and other ancient peoples who spoke Semitic languages. But, like most Oriental peoples, they wrote from right to left. When the Greeks took their alphabet, they changed the direction of writing and wrote from left to right as we do today. In doing this, they turned the letters around. You can see, in the first article in this encyclopedia—the article on the letter A—how we got our present letter by the turning around of the ancient letters. The exact form of our capital letters was developed chiefly by the ancient Romans. Our small letters, and our handwriting, were developed because with them it is possible to write faster.

The English alphabet, like other alphabets that are used throughout the world, is very far from perfect. There

Ephron Gallery—Margot L. Wolf

The Egyptian alphabet was written in pictures instead of letters. This is a stele, a slab of stone used as a tombstone. It was made for the grave of a king. The eyes at the top are supposed to keep away evil spirits. The picture letters are called hieroglyphics, and the two lines going up and down tell what the king did while he was alive. The man at the left is the king, eating; the figure at the right is his son. Below is a prayer that asks the Egyptian god Osiris to keep the king comfortable. The tombstone tells that this king died about 3,500 years ago. Our own alphabet grew out of the Egyptian alphabet.

are many people who are anxious to change it so that it will be easier to tell how a word should be pronounced the first time you read it. Reading is more difficult when a single letter, such as A, can be pronounced in six different ways. Still, the modern alphabet is one of the greatest works of the human mind, and has been at least as responsible as anything else man has done for the growth of civilization.

Alps

The Alps are a great chain of mountains in southern Europe. Parts of six European countries are in this great mountain range. The Alps run north from the Mediterranean coast and form the boundary between France and Italy. Then they turn east and run through most of Switzerland and through parts of northern Italy, southern Germany, and Austria. From here they turn south into northern Yugoslavia to the coast of the Adriatic Sea.

Several million people live in the Alps. They live in the valleys and on the lower slopes of the mountains. It would be impossible for anyone to live in the higher parts of the Alps. Above 8,000 feet, the snow and ice never melt. There are over 400 high mountain peaks in the Alps; many of them are over 10,000 feet high. The highest peak is Mont Blanc in France; it is 15,781 feet above sea level.

Some of the mountain peaks have strange names. Some of the best-known names are German, some French, and some Italian. The mountains known best by their German names are Jungfrau, Matterhorn, Finsteraarhorn, Grossglockner, Dufourspitze, and Wildspitze. Some of the French names are Grand Combin, Barre des Écrins, and Montgenèvre. Gran Paradiso, Marmolada and Bernina are Italian names.

The Alps are high but it is not difficult to cross through them. There are many long valleys and mountain passes. For hundreds of years people have used these valleys and passes in order to get through the Alps and travel from one country to another. First they used footpaths. Later, as the footpaths became wider, wagons and carriages were able to cross the Alps. Now you may cross the mountains in an automobile, driving on well-paved roads that curve through the passes. Railroad trains run through some of the passes and valleys. In some places, they go through long tunnels to get through the mountains. The longest tunnel in the Alps is the Simplon tunnel; it is more than 12 miles long, and was dug and blasted from the mountain rock between Switzerland and Italy.

CHEESE AND MILK CHOCOLATE

No one is quite sure how the Alps got their name. Some people think it comes from the Latin word *alba,* which means white. This could be true, because the snow-covered mountains do look white. Other people say that the name is taken from the German word *alp,* which means high pasture.

There are many high pastures in the mountains below the snow-line. At the beginning of every summer, the farmers drive their herds of cows up the mountains to these high pastures. There the cows graze during the warm summer months, while the farmers live in little stone huts on the mountain slopes. Toward the end of summer, the farmers cut hay. The hay is needed to feed the cows during the long winter months. When the summer is over, the farmers drive the cows back down the mountain to the valley farms. Swiss cheese is made from the milk of cows that graze in the high Alpine pastures. The milk chocolate made with the milk of these cows is famous throughout the world.

VACATIONS IN THE ALPS

Summer or winter, there are always tourists and visitors in the Alps. Many people come to see the beauties of the

German Tourist Office

1. This representation of Calvary is in a village in the Bavarian Alps.

2. The alpenhorn, used by cowherds in the Alps, makes a strange, loud sound that can be heard for miles.

3. Flocks of sheep graze high in the rocky stretches of the Swiss Alps.

4. In the Alps wild crocuses cover whole fields with carpets of beautiful color.

5. A guide in his cottage in the Swiss Alps. He is making shavings to use as kindling.

mountains. In the summer, the snow-capped peaks are mirrored in beautiful blue lakes. The green pasture slopes are spotted with many colorful flowers. Many of the people who visit the Alps come to enjoy the sports and adventure in the mountains. In the summer they come to climb the high peaks. Native guides show them the best way to climb each mountain. In the winter, the Alps are famous for all kinds of winter sports. There are skiing, skating, and bobsled-racing. Almost all the people who live in the Alps are expert skiers. They start skiing on the snow-covered slopes when they are young children.

In the spring, the snow that covers the slopes of the Alps begins to melt. Small streams trickle from the high slopes. The streams flow into larger streams, and finally into rivers. Three great European rivers get their start in this way. From the Alps, the Rhine flows north to the North Sea, the Rhone flows south to the Mediterranean, and the Po flows east to the Adriatic. Alpine streams also help to make the Danube River one of the largest in Europe.

On the plains below the Alps, many people work in factories. The machines in these factories are run by electricity. The electricity is made by dynamos that are turned by the rushing waters that move down the slopes of the Alps.

Many kinds of animals used to live in the Alps. There were large numbers of bison, elk, wolves, and wild boars. They have disappeared from the mountains completely. A few harmless brown bears and foxes live in the lower forests of the mountains. In the high pastures there are field mice and meadow mice, and large numbers of marmots. The marmot is related to the groundhog and prairie dog. Mountain climbers sometimes see chamois in the high Alps. The chamois is a small antelope; it is one of the most sure-footed animals in the world. Because it has suction cups on its feet, it can cling to a small pinnacle of rock, or jump from rock to rock, without losing its footing.

A famous animal of the Alps is the St. Bernard dog. The St. Bernard is named for a monastery in the Swiss Alps. The monks who lived here trained the dog to look for lost travelers in the snow. The dog's keen sense of smell helped him to find a traveler. The monks used to tie a little keg of brandy around the neck of the St. Bernard. The brandy helped to revive and warm the frozen traveler. People may become lost in the Alps when there is a snowslide that covers the trails. The biggest snow-slides are called avalanches. Huge quantities of snow come piling down the mountainside, and sometimes bury whole villages.

Alsace-Lorraine

Alsace-Lorraine is a territory in Europe, between France and Germany. It is on the Rhine River and in a mountainous country that is rich in coal and iron, so it is a valuable territory to own and France and Germany have fought over it for hundreds of years. First one has owned it, then the other. Today it is part of France. When it is German territory, its German name is Elsass-Lothringen.

The people of Alsace-Lorraine are partly French and partly German, and

Alsatians like to dress up in the gay-colored costumes their ancestors wore.

A typical scene in a city of the Haut-Rhin department of France, in southern Alsace.

partly a combination of the two; many of them prefer to call themselves simply Alsatians. Most of them are farmers, clothmakers, or miners.

Originally, Alsace was one province, and Lorraine was another, to the north of Alsace. The biggest city of Alsace is Strasbourg, which is famous for its fine geese (from which *pâté de foie gras* is made, meaning "paste of fat goose," a food that is used as an appetizer and sandwich spread), and of course Strasbourg is famous also as a big and important city. The biggest city of Lorraine is Metz.

The Germans had Alsace-Lorraine most of the time until about two hundred years ago, when it became French. The people became accustomed to speak the French language. During the French Revolution, in 1792, the national anthem of France—La Marseillaise—was written in Strasbourg.

Then in 1871 the Germans won a big war from France, the Franco-Prussian War. They took Alsace-Lorraine away,

and they decreed that the children could no longer learn French in the schools and that German must be the official language. Sad stories were written and sad pictures were printed in France and other countries about how unhappy the Alsatians were when they had to give up French and become Germans. One of these famous stories was called "The Last Class," and was a story about the last time a school teacher could teach French to the children in his class.

In World War I, the French beat Germany and got Alsace-Lorraine back. In World War II, while the Germans were winning, they claimed Alsace-Lorraine again for a few years, but since they lost the war at the end the territory became French again. It is now divided into three departments (that is, counties) of France—Moselle, Haut-Rhin, and Bas-Rhin. If you look at a map made after World War II, you may not even see Alsace-Lorraine on it. Alsace-Lorraine has 5607 square miles and the population in 1946 was 1,767,131.

Altai Mountains

The Altai Mountains are a long range of mountains in central Asia. They belong to Russia and form part of the border separating southern Siberia from northern Mongolia. In some parts of the range, the mountains rise to almost 15,000 feet above sea level, but for the most part, they are below 10,000 feet. There are many beautiful lakes in the Altai, and three great Siberian rivers begin as streams in these mountains. The rivers are the Obi, Irtysh, and Yenesei.

Most of the people who live in these mountains are Mongols or Kalmucks. They are herdsmen, miners, and forest workers. The miners dig for gold, silver, and lead. Much lumber is cut in the dense forests in the Altai Mountains. People hunt in the forests for deer and rabbits, but they have to be careful, for there are many bears and wolves.

The ancient Chinese called the Altai the "Golden Mountains," because they knew there was much precious metal in the ground there.

altar

An altar is a bench or stand used in religious services. Usually an altar is used for the making of a sacrifice, or presenting of a gift, to God or to some object or being that is thought to be a god, as in primitive religions. Christians have used the altar for taking communion, burning candles as a form of worship, or kneeling in prayer. Most persons consider that an altar, though it is a stand of about the size and shape of a table, should be solid and should not have legs as a table does. Altars have often been beautifully carved and decorated.

alternating current

Electricity flows through a wire in the same way that water flows in a river, and just as the movement of the water in a river is called a current, the movement of electricity through a wire is called an electric current. When you turn on a light, electricity flows through a wire that leads from one of the two outlets of the plug, all the way through the electric lamp and back again through the other wire.

This electric current comes from a generator in a powerhouse. The generator is a big machine like an electric motor. It produces the current. Some generators produce current that always flows the same way. It will always flow into the lamp from one of the wires and out of the lamp through the other wire. Electric current that does not change its direction is called direct current. Other generators produce alternating current. First the current will flow through one of the wires, then it will flow through the other wire. It changes its direction in this way 120 times every second. The word *alternate* means change, so current that so changes its direction is called alternating current.

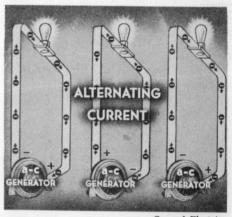

General Electric

Electric current from an alternating-current, or A-C, generator changes direction 120 times every second. This is about the time it takes to switch on a light. But since electricity travels about 186,000 miles per second, you never notice the change. The electricity goes into the wire from the side of the generator that is marked (−), lights the lamp, and returns into the side marked (+). The (−) side is called "negative" and the (+) side is called "positive."

When the current has flowed once in one direction and once in the other direction, it is said to have completed a cycle. If it changes direction 120 times in a second, it has completed 60 cycles.

Most of the electric current used in the United States is 60-cycle alternating current. The abbreviation for alternating current is A.C., and for direct current is D.C. The article on GENERATOR will explain why alternating current must change its direction.

altimeter

An altimeter is an instrument used in an airplane to tell the pilot how high above sea level he is flying. All dry land has to be above the level of the sea, or it would be covered with water, but flat land near the ocean may be only a few feet or a few hundred feet above sea level, while mountains are thousands of feet above sea level. An airplane pilot must know how high he is, especially when he cannot see ahead of him because it is cloudy or is nighttime, because otherwise he might run into the side of a mountain.

The altimeter used in most airplanes is a kind of barometer. This is an instrument used to measure air pressure. The article on AIR tells how the weight of the air presses down on the ground, so that at sea level the pressure of the air is more than fourteen pounds on every square inch of the earth. The higher you go into the air, the lower the air pressure is. An aneroid barometer is a device to tell what the air pressure is (you can read an explanation of it in the article on BAROMETER). An altimeter uses this air pressure to show how high the plane is.

But the altimeter does not show how high the plane is above the ground. A plane might be flying at an altitude of 15,000 feet, but it would be only a thousand feet or so above the ground if the land in that district happened to be 14,000 feet above sea level, as much of the mountainous part of the United States, in the region of the Rocky Mountains, may be. Therefore a pilot is always careful to fly higher than any land or mountains can be in the territory over which he is passing.

alumina

Alumina is a mineral composed of aluminum and oxygen. We see it in various forms that we would never think of in connection with the aluminum of our pots and pans or the oxygen in the air we breathe. One example that is almost pure alumina is corundum, which in its finest form is a precious stone—sapphire or ruby—and in less beautiful forms is found in such abrasives as emery. Alumina is also called *aluminum oxide*. In the form of a white powder, it is used in producing aluminum. See the article on ALUMINUM.

aluminum

Aluminum is a metal of a silvery gray color. It is an element, which means that it is not made by combining other substances. Aluminum is useful in many ways. It is much lighter than most other metals. It never rusts. Being soft, it is easily hammered, rolled or pressed into any desired shape. Aluminum is lighter than copper and is almost as good for conducting electricity. This makes it useful as electric wire and parts of electric machines. It can be rolled into sheets thinner than tissue paper, called *foil,* which are used to wrap foods, cigarettes, and other things that would be spoiled by dirt or water.

You see aluminum every day. Pots and pans are made of it. Its softness makes it good for toothpaste tubes. Because it does not rust and is so light, it is used for making airplanes, railroad cars, truck bodies, boats, and bridges. Its silvery color makes it attractive in paints, moldings, signs, Venetian blinds, and hundreds of other things.

Reynolds Metals Co.

Aluminum comes from bauxite, shown being mined in Arkansas. Arkansas produces more bauxite than any other state. The method shown is called open-pit mining.

HOW ALUMINUM WAS FOUND

Although there is more aluminum in the earth than any other metal, it was not discovered until copper, iron, tin, and other metals had been known for thousands of years. One reason for this is that such metals as copper and iron are much easier to separate from ore or rocks in which they occur. Primitive man probably discovered copper by accident when he piled rocks around a fire. Some of these rocks had copper in them and when they became hot the copper in them melted and flowed out. While nearly all common rocks contain aluminum, heating the rocks will not make the aluminum flow out. Not until man had learned a great deal about chemistry was he able to discover how to separate metallic aluminum from the rocks, clay and earth in which it was found.

Even then the chemical method of separating aluminum from its ores was so expensive that a pound of aluminum cost more than a pound of gold or silver. It was not until man learned how to make use of electricity that a cheap way of making aluminum was discovered.

In 1825 Hans Christian Oersted, a chemist who lived in Denmark, made a tiny amount of pure aluminum by heating certain chemicals together. Nobody paid much attention to Oersted's discovery. Several years later a German chemist named Friedrich Wöhler repeated Oersted's experiment in a slightly different form and obtained another very tiny amount of aluminum.

A chemist in France, Henri Sainte-Claire Deville, became interested in the new metal. In 1852 he improved on Wöhler's work. He produced a pound of aluminum for $545 (today a pound costs less than 20 cents).

Napoleon III, the French Emperor, heard about the marvelous light metal. He offered Sainte-Claire Deville a big reward if he could produce aluminum more cheaply and in larger amounts. The emperor wanted aluminum for his armies. Sainte-Claire Deville managed to bring the cost of aluminum down from $545 a pound in 1852 to $17 in 1856, but this was not cheap enough.

THE HALL PROCESS

Some years later a young American named Charles Martin Hall, 22 years old, began trying to find a cheap way of making aluminum. He experimented with it during his senior year at Oberlin College in Ohio. After graduation he continued his experiments in the family woodshed. Hall's idea was to mix alumina, a white powder known to chemists as aluminum oxide, with some liquid and then pass an electric current through the mixture to separate the pure aluminum from the oxygen. (See the article on ALUMINA, just before this article.)

Hall finally discovered that if he melted a rock called cryolite in a very hot furnace he could make alumina melt and mix completely with this liquid rock. When he passed an electric current through this mixture the alumina separated into pure aluminum and oxygen.

1. The man is stirring hot aluminum oxide that has been baked in this giant kiln (oven) to remove impurities. See the article on *alumina*.

2. Aluminum is so soft and workable that it can be rolled into sheets thin as tissue paper. First it is made into rectangular billets and then flattened into sheets.

3. These men are making aluminum rods out of the "pigs" shown in picture number 5. The rods go next to manufacturers. More than 4,000 different things are made of aluminum.

4. Melted aluminum is poured in liquid form from this big bucket into the containers you see lined up here. When it cools and hardens it will be in the shape called a "pig." These containers are called ingot molds. They look like large bread pans.

5. These are aluminum "pigs" ready to be shipped to manufacturers in all parts of the world.

Reynolds Metals—Alcoa

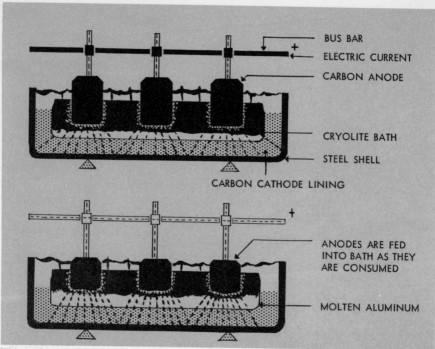

This is the "Hall Electrolytic Cell" in which aluminum is made. Look first at the diagram on top. There is a tank, lined with carbon. In this tank there is a liquid, or "bath," of a chemical called cryolite in which alumina, also called aluminum oxide (a compound of aluminum and oxygen), has been dissolved, much as sugar is dissolved in coffee to sweeten it. Electric current flows through a heavy metal bar (called a *bus bar*) and into blocks of carbon hanging from it. These blocks of carbon act as *anodes* (meaning they have a positive charge of electricity), and the lining of the tank acts as a *cathode*, which attracts the electricity from the anodes, and causes it to flow through the cryolite bath. The electricity, flowing through, separates the aluminum from the oxygen. The aluminum settles on the bottom of the tank in molten (melted) form, as shown in the diagram at the bottom. The process wears away the carbon anodes, but the bus bar lowers them gradually into the cryolite bath as they become smaller.

February 23, 1886, was the happiest day of Hall's life. On that day he discovered a cheap way to make aluminum in large quantities.

Strangely enough, another young man, a French youth named Paul Louis Toussaint Héroult, who like Hall was only 22 years old, discovered how to make aluminum by exactly the same method and only a few months later. Héroult made his discovery in France and neither of the two young men knew anything about the other's work.

The discoveries of Hall and Héroult brought the price of aluminum down to $8 a pound. By 1914 the cost was 34¢ a pound, and in 1950 the price had dropped to only 18¢ a pound.

HOW ALUMINUM IS MINED

The ore from which aluminum is obtained today is called bauxite. It is an earthy-looking material, and may be as hard as rock or as soft as clay. It may be pink, tan, yellow, red, white, or any combination of these colors. Bauxite is found in many different parts of the world. Most bauxite used in America comes from the island of Jamaica, in the West Indies; or from Dutch Guiana and British Guiana, in South America; or from Arkansas.

In some places the bauxite mine is underground, but usually open-pit mining is used. In open-pit mining, giant power shovels and other powerful earth-moving machinery remove bushes and trees and then dig away a layer of gravel and dirt. After that the bauxite is scooped out of the earth. It is a mixture of lumps and fine material when it is first removed from the mine. Crushing machines break up the big lumps. The bauxite is then dried in ovens called kilns, to drive off moisture. Then it is shipped by train or ship to the place where it will be refined or purified.

HOW ALUMINUM IS MADE

Most metals are made directly from their ores, and then purified. Bauxite must first be purified to separate the alumina from the iron and other impurities in the ore before the metal can be made.

Bauxite is refined by the Bayer process, invented by Karl Bayer, a chemist who lived in Austria. In this process, the crushed, washed and dried bauxite from the mines is further crushed and ground into powder. It is then mixed with certain chemicals, put into tanks called digesters, and strained through filters. The impurities that remain behind in the filters are called "red mud." What passes through the filters is *sodium aluminate* and is poured into giant tanks, each as high as a six-story building.

As the liquid in the tanks cools, fine white crystals of *aluminum hydroxide* settle to the bottom of the tanks. Aluminum hydroxide is aluminum oxide chemically combined with water. The aluminum hydroxide is heated until it is white-hot, in slowly turning giant kilns, to drive off the water. The result is the snowy white powder called aluminum oxide or alumina.

THE ELECTROLYTIC PROCESS

Now the process of changing the white powder into the silvery-gray metal begins. The alumina is taken to electro-

lytic cells. These are rectangular steel tanks lined with carbon. Coal and charcoal are good examples of carbon, but these are not quite as pure as the carbon used in electrolytic cells. Inside the tank is a bath of melted cryolite. Big blocks of carbon attached to metal rods hang down from above into the cryolite. Electricity passes down the metal rods. It runs through the blocks of carbon and the cryolite to the thick carbon lining of the tank. Alumina is fed into the tank and mixes with the cryolite. Pure melted aluminum separates from the alumina and lies at the bottom of the tank, while the oxygen escapes into the air. The strong electric current that passes from the carbon blocks to the carbon lining of the tank produces tremendous heat, so that the cryolite and the aluminum at the bottom of the tank remain in a liquid form.

From time to time, melted aluminum in the tank is ladled out with a long-handled dipper and poured into the hollow molds called "pigs," where it cools and hardens. The aluminum is now ready for use by industry and can be made into all the shapes that are needed.

Amalekites

The Amalekites were an ancient tribe who lived in Biblical times. They were fierce warriors who made their home in the desert south of Israel. The Amalekites were enemies of the Jews. They attacked the Jews that Moses had led across the Red Sea, and killed many of them. The Bible tells us of other times when the Amalekites attacked the Jews in Israel. But a prophet named Balaam predicted that the Amalekites would be destroyed, and they were, first by King Saul of Israel, and twenty years later by the Jews under David. The few Amalekites who escaped were later wiped out. An Arabian poet writes, "The race of Amlach (the Amalekites) has disappeared and there is left of it neither mean man nor mighty."

amalgam

Amalgam is the name given to a mixture of mercury and any other metal. Mercury is the only metal that is a cool liquid, instead of a solid. It mixes very easily with other metals, except iron and platinum. The best-known amalgam is used by dentists. If you have a cavity, your dentist may fill it with amalgam. The dentist makes amalgam by putting a drop of mercury in some silver powder. He mixes the two thoroughly. The dentist then stuffs the soft, doughy amalgam in the cavity and shapes it to fit. The amalgam soon gets hard and makes a long-lasting filling.

amalgamation

When two or more groups join together, they are said to amalgamate. Business firms often amalgamate because it costs less to run one big company than several smaller ones. General Motors Corporation is an amalgamation. Chevrolet, Oldsmobile, Buick and Cadillac automobiles used to be made by different companies. They joined together to form a new large company.

General Foods is an amalgamation of several smaller food companies. There is often amalgamation in labor unions too. The Amalgamated Clothing Workers Union is formed from what were once several smaller unions.

Amati

The finest violins ever made were made hundreds of years ago in the Italian city of Cremona. While science in other ways has advanced tremendously since then, no one has ever found a way to make violins better, or even as good, as the early violin makers of Cremona made them. The first great violin-making family of Cremona was named Amati. The first violin maker in the Amati family was named Andrea Amati. He was born more than 400 years ago, about the year 1530, and died in 1611. His sons Antonio and Geronimo were also great violin makers, and Andrea's grandson Nicolo was the finest violin maker of the family. He was also a great teacher of violin-making. Antonio Stradivari, by many considered the greatest violin maker who ever lived, was one of his pupils; another was Andrea Guarnieri. There are separate articles about the GUARNIERI and STRADIVARI families of violin makers.

Both the Guarnieri and the Stradivari violins are generally considered better than the Amati violins, but Amati violins still sell for thousands of dollars each. The Amati family also made cellos, violas, and bass violins. Nicolo Amati, who was born in 1596 and died in 1684, was the last great member of the Amati family.

Amazon

The Amazon is a river in South America, one of the greatest rivers in the world. It is about 3,900 miles long. The Nile in Africa, and the Missouri and Mississippi rivers together, in the United States, are slightly longer than the Amazon. The Amazon, however, has more water in it than any other river in the world. It flows from the Andes Mountains in Peru, all the way across Brazil to the Atlantic Ocean. Along the way, seventeen other large rivers empty into the Amazon. At its Atlantic mouth, the Amazon is 150 miles wide.

Through most of its length, the Amazon runs through some of the wildest jungles on the face of the earth. In these jungles there are still wild tribes of Indians. The jungles of the Amazon are called rain forests. It is always very damp and hot there. Most of the Indian villages are near the banks of the great river itself. The Indians who live in the jungle wear very little clothing, and their homes are crude, thatched shelters. They travel mostly by river in dugout canoes. It is almost impossible to travel far in the dense jungle. The Indians use

For hundreds of miles, the Amazon is 3 to 5 miles wide. Near the ocean it is so wide you cannot see across it. It is 100 to 200 feet deep. So that all its water will not flow into the ocean and be wasted, ditches like the one shown in this picture lead the water away to irrigate the country near by and make it good for farming. The map shows the network of rivers that form the Amazon. They drain an area almost as big as the entire United States, nearly 3,000,000 square miles.

big knives to cut their way through the undergrowth.

The Amazon is teeming with life. Big and little fish of all kinds swim in its waters. The jungles are noisy with the cries of animals and birds. The Indians are fishers and hunters. Life is full of danger for them. They must be careful when they go fishing because there are many alligators in the Amazon. There are fierce jaguars and cougars in the jungle. There is danger from other Indians, too. Some of them used to be cannibals and headhunters. In the headhunting tribes, a warrior was judged by the number of heads he had taken. These Indians shrank the heads and kept them.

Many strange animals live in the Amazon jungle. The capybara is the largest rodent in the world. The coati is related to the raccoon, but has a longer nose. The tapir is a hoofed animal about the size of a large dog. The sloth spends its life hanging upside down from a jungle tree. The armadillo has a hard shell and looks like a baby tank. Anteaters use their long, sticky tongues to gather their food. Many kinds of monkeys swing through the jungle trees. Colorful birds fly through the air. There are parrots and macaws and toucans. The Indians use blowguns to catch animals and birds. Some of the darts shot from the blowguns are poison-tipped.

We get many things from the Amazon region. Much of our coffee comes from there. We get tapioca from the cassava tree that grows in the jungle. From the Amazon region we get mahogany for furniture, indigo for dyes, sarsaparilla for flavoring, and quinine, a drug used to combat malaria.

Little by little, the Amazon region becomes more civilized. The more civilized it becomes, the more it can be used for farming purposes. Some day, perhaps, the Amazon will send food all over the world.

Amazons

The early Greek story-tellers told of a nation of women warriors called Amazons. These legendary women were supposed to have lived in a country on the Mediterranean Sea. They did not permit any men in their nation. The Amazons were strong and swift. They fought in battle against the men of other nations. Once each year the Amazons visited another country. The men in this country became the fathers of the Amazon children. The boy children were not kept by the Amazons. Some stories say they were put to death; others, that they were sent back to their fathers. The girl children were brought up and trained to become Amazons themselves. Nowadays you may hear some woman called an Amazon. This usually means she is big and strong.

ambassador

Representing one country in its dealings with other countries is called diplomacy, and a person who does this is called a diplomat. An ambassador is the highest-ranking diplomat, just as a general is the highest-ranking officer in an army, and an admiral is the highest-ranking officer in a navy.

An ambassador from the United States represents the President of the United States. The head of a foreign country is supposed to treat him as though he were the President of the United States. Actually, however, an ambassador simply follows the instructions of the department of his country that has the duty of conducting affairs with other countries. In the United States, this is the Department of State and the head of it is the Secretary of State; he instructs the ambassadors as to what they should do. In most other countries, this department is called the foreign ministry and the head of it is called the foreign minister.

An ambassador lives in the capital of the country to which he is sent. His title includes the name of that country. For example, the ambassador to France represents the United States in its dealings with France, and while he is ambassador he lives in Paris, the capital of France. The building in which he lives and has his offices is called the embassy. His full title is usually "envoy extraordinary and ambassador plenipotentiary." Envoy simply means that he is a person who was sent; the title "envoy extraordinary" does not have much meaning any more. But "plenipotentiary" means "full of power," and this means that the ambassador has the right to act for his country, for example, by signing a treaty to which the country must live up.

Supposedly an ambassador is sent only to the most important other countries with which a country must deal. To less important countries, it would send a lower-ranking diplomat called a minister. Today it is known that nearly every other country, large or small, is really important, and the United States sends ambassadors to most other countries. Read also the article on DIPLOMACY.

amber

Amber is a dark yellow, stonelike material that is used to make beads, mouthpieces of smoking pipes, cigarette holders, and many carved ornaments. Most of the world's amber comes from coasts of Germany and Russia on the Baltic Sea. Millions of years ago certain kinds of pine trees grew along the shores of the Baltic Sea. From time to time these trees gave off a brownish yellow liquid, resin, which dripped down into the ground. After millions of years in the ground the resin turned into a sort of stone, which we now call amber.

The ancient Greeks and Romans used to make jewelry and ornaments out of amber. They discovered that if a piece of amber is rubbed hard on cloth, bits of wool, cotton, dust and other fine particles will cling to the amber for a time. The Greeks and Romans did not know, as we do now, that this was caused by static electricity, but their name for amber was *electrum,* and it is from this word that we get our own word electricity.

ambergris

Ambergris is a fatty, waxlike material. It is found floating on the surface of the waters of tropical seas. Sometimes it is washed up on the beaches of countries in the tropics, where it is warm all year. It can also be found in some whales that are caught. Ambergris is gray, yellowish, black or a mixture of any of these colors, and has a very sweet pleasant smell. It is the result of a disease in the intestine of the sperm whale. The ambergris passes out of the body of the whale, along with other waste, but floats on the water because it is fatty. It has no particular shape or form and may weigh from half an ounce to as much as 100 pounds. It is tremendously valuable because it is very important in the manufacture of perfumes.

Amboina

Amboina is a small island in the East Indies, one of the group of islands known as the Moluccas. At various times, it belonged to the Portuguese, the English, and for many years to the Dutch. Now it is part of the Republic of Indonesia. Once the Moluccas were called the Spice Islands, because of the many kinds of spice grown there. Clove and nutmeg are important crops of Amboina, as well as coconut trees. The climate of Amboina is tropical, hot and wet all year. The people are Malayans and Polynesians. See INDONESIA.

ambulance

An ambulance is a car that is used to carry sick or wounded people from one place to another. Most of the time an ambulance takes sick people to a hospital. Most hospitals have their own ambulances. Day and night, they go out on hurry calls.

Suppose someone in your family were suddenly to become very sick, or suppose you were at the scene of an accident and help was needed quickly. What would you do? You would call for an ambulance. The easiest way to get an ambulance is to go to the telephone and dial the operator. Tell her where the ambulance should be sent. The telephone operator then calls a hospital, or calls the police and they call the hospital. At the hospital, a driver quickly jumps into the front seat and a doctor gets into the back. The ambulance travels at high speed. Policemen stop traffic to let it through. Its bell clangs and its siren wails; it goes through red lights and stops for nothing.

At the home of the sick, or at the scene of an accident, the doctor makes a quick examination. He gives first aid if it is needed. The sick or injured person is put on a stretcher and carefully placed in the back of the ambulance. The driver then speeds back to the hospital.

Ambulances are also used in wartime. Each army has its own ambulances. They are used to carry the wounded from the front lines and from the airfields to the base hospitals. Every military ambulance has a red cross painted on it. The red cross keeps it from being fired upon or bombed from the air. Jeeps are sometimes used as ambulances. Stretchers are laid across the jeep and tied down. Jeeps can be driven to places where larger ambulances could not get through.

The newest kind of military ambulances are airplanes and helicopters. The airplanes are used to carry the wounded back to their own countries. Helicopters are used to pick up wounded from the battlefield, particularly those who have to be flown to a hospital in a hurry.

ameba or amoeba

An ameba (also spelled *amoeba*) is a tiny animal. It is so small that it can be seen only through a microscope. If you take a drop of water from a river, swamp, or pond, and look at it through a microscope, you will see several strange shapes that look like splotches of clear jelly with a few dark dots inside them. These jellylike splotches are amebas. They have no legs, feet, arms, or head.

When an ameba wants to move, it pushes a part of its body forward like a long foot and the rest of it flows into this foot. Then it does the same thing all over again and in this way it can move in any direction. Scientists call the foot that the ameba pushes out a *pseudopod* (meaning "false foot") because it is not really a foot.

The ameba has no mouth. When it finds a tiny bit of food it pushes out pseudopods on both sides of the food.

This picture shows the entire single cell of the ameba. However, the picture is about four hundred times as long as an ameba actually is. The nucleus ("b") will later split in two parts and become two amebas. One of the "pseudopods" or "false legs" by which the ameba moves is shown at "e." Vacuoles containing waste matter are shown at "c" and "d," and food particles, on which the ameba feeds, are at "a." Though an ameba is the simplest kind of animal, it is the same substance—called "protoplasm"—that makes man and other highly developed animals.

American Museum of Natural History

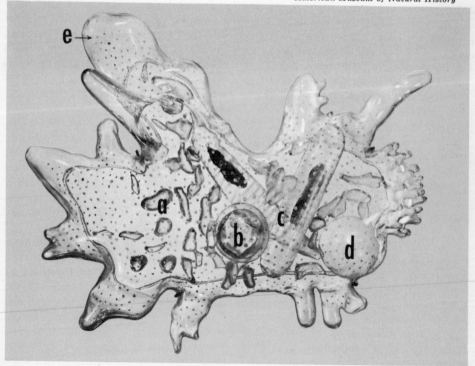

These slowly close around it until it is completely surrounded. The food is then drawn inside the ameba's body, where it is kept in a little pocket, called a *food vacuole,* until it is digested. The waste material that remains after the food is digested is kept in another little pocket or vacuole. After a time this vacuole rises to the surface of the body and explodes and sprays the waste outside.

The ameba has a dark spot inside its jelly called a nucleus which helps it grow and produce other amebas. There are no male or female amebas, and it does not lay eggs like insects and birds or produce young from a mother animal. Instead it just splits in two and then there are two amebas, each with its own nucleus and vacuoles.

Most plants and animals are made up of millions of tiny parts called cells, which can only be seen under a microscope. Human beings are also made up of millions of cells. An ameba has only one cell. There are many one-celled animals besides the ameba. However, ameba cells are different from those of plants, human beings, or the larger animals such as horses, cows, and dogs.

amendment

When a change is made in a law, the change is called an amendment. An amendment may be made in a law before it is passed, or after it has been in operation.

The best-known amendments are those that have been made to the Constitution of the United States. Constitutions are the most important laws of a state or a country. The Constitution of the United States, which is the highest law of the land, has twenty-one amendments. The amendments were passed from time to time. Some amendments changed parts of the Constitution; other amendments provided for things that were not in the original Constitution. Most of the amendments made the Constitution stronger.

An amendment to the Constitution must be approved by two-thirds of the Representatives and Senators in Congress. Then it must be approved by three-quarters of the states. In each state, the legislature votes on amendments to the Constitution of the United States. When an amendment has been approved, it becomes part of the Constitution.

America

One of the two chief patriotic hymns of the United States is named *America.* It is second only to *The Star-Spangled Banner,* which is the national anthem. *America* has the same tune as the British national anthem, *God Save the Queen* (or *King*). The words for *America* were written by a Boston minister named Samuel Francis Smith, more than a hundred years ago, in 1832. He found the tune in a German songbook and did not know it was the tune for *God Save the King.* It is not considered necessary to stand up when *America* is played, but most people like to, anyway.

American Federation of Labor

The American Federation of Labor, which is usually called the A. F. of L., is an organization to which many different labor unions belong. A labor union is a group of men who work at the same trade, and who form a society to fix the wages and working conditions of all of them; there is a separate article on LABOR UNIONS in a later volume of this encyclopedia. The two chief kinds of labor union are the *industrial union,* whose members usually work in factories, and the *craft union,* whose members practice a skilled trade such as plumbing or printing. Most of the members of the American Federation of Labor are craft unions.

The A. F. of L. was founded about seventy years ago, in 1881. Its first president was Samuel Gompers, and he remained president until he died in 1924.

Then William Green was president until he died in 1952. George A. Meany was elected president in 1953. When the A. F. of L. was formed, working men had very few rights. By strikes and some other means, the A. F. of L. did much to win higher pay and shorter working hours for American labor.

In the A. F. of L., every union is independent. It pays part of its dues each year to support the Federation, but it does not have to do everything the A. F. of L. wants done, and it can withdraw from membership if it wants to. It was the resignation of several A. F. of L. unions that led to the formation of the Congress of Industrial Organizations, one of the other big labor organizations in the United States.

American Indians, redskinned people who lived in North and South America before it was settled by white men from Europe. See the article on INDIANS, AMERICAN, and also articles on the important Indian tribes.

American Legion

The American Legion is the largest group of veterans in the United States. It was organized after World War I in Paris, France, by a small group of Americans who had fought in the war. In the next few years, more than a million other Americans joined the organization. The American Legion became very strong. It has groups called *posts* in cities and towns all over the United States. Each post is led by a commander, with other officers under him. There are state commanders and a national commander. After World War II, several million more veterans joined the American Legion.

The American Legion has become one of the strongest and most important organizations in the country. Naturally, it is interested in anything that has to do with veterans. The Legion was largely responsible for the creation of the United States Veterans Administration.

The American Legion parade is a big event on New York's Fifth Avenue. It lasts from early in the morning until after dark, often ten hours or more.

American Legion Photos

One of the Legion's greatest interests has been to keep the United States strong. It wants the country to have a large army, navy and air force, and strong defenses. It also has a "Back to God" movement to keep the country spiritually strong. This movement encourages church attendance, prayer, and religious education.

A member of the Legion is called a Legionnaire. He wears a military-looking uniform. On his cap is embroidered the name of his post. If a Legionnaire is or has been an officer of the post, his rank is also embroidered on his cap. Legionnaires attend post meetings to discuss the business of the post and to pass laws for the post. At the meetings they sometimes pass resolutions that approve or disapprove of what other people are doing. Legionnaires also meet for social purposes. They have dances and entertainments. They organize bands and have military drills. In most towns, the American Legion sponsors a boys' base-ball club. These clubs play games all over the country, and at the end of each season a tournament is held to pick the winning team.

The American Legion holds an annual convention. Delegates from all the posts meet in a different city each year. Prominent Americans make speeches to the delegates. Usually, the President of the United States speaks to the organization. The main business of each convention is the election of officers for the coming year. The new national commander and his staff are chosen by a vote of all the delegates. The final business of the convention is to choose a city where the next year's convention will be held.

If you live in a city where an American Legion convention has been held, you will know that the members do something besides attend to their Legion business. They usually bring their wives and enjoy all the amusements the convention city offers.

Two parades are held at each conven-

A wounded World War veteran salutes the colors as the Legion marches by.

American Legion Photos

Singer Eddie Fisher was the two-millionth veteran to join the American Legion in 1954.

American Legion Photos

tion. One is a formal military parade, with all the Legionnaires in uniform. The bands play stirring music, and the Legionnaires march with their buddies down the main street of the convention city. The other parade is held by a Legion group called the Forty and Eight. The Forty and Eight is named after French boxcars that many of the soldiers rode in during World War I. These boxcars were made to carry forty men and eight horses. The members wear funny and colorful costumes. Some of them ride in decorated floats, and others drive tipsy automobiles. The parade is a very noisy affair; bands play, guns boom, bells clang and whistles blow. Automobiles that have been fixed up to look like locomotives chug along in the parade. Usually they pull boxcars that are models of the French boxcars that the soldiers rode in.

American Revolution, the war in which the United States won its independence: see REVOLUTIONARY WAR.

Americas, the

Though you may most often hear "America" used to mean the United States, all the countries in the Western Hemisphere—including North and South America and the islands near them—are "the Americas." There are twenty-two independent countries in the Americas:

NORTH AMERICA	SOUTH AMERICA
Canada	Argentina
Mexico	Bolivia
United States	Brazil
	Chile
CENTRAL AMERICA	Colombia
Costa Rica	Ecuador
El Salvador	Paraguay
Guatemala	Peru
Honduras	Uruguay
Nicaragua	Venezuela
Panama	

ISLANDS
Cuba
Dominican Republic
Haiti

Canada is a kingdom, but the other twenty-one are republics. They have not always been friendly with one another. Especially the countries of Central and South America have often been afraid of the United States, because it is so much bigger than they are. These countries are called Latin-American countries because their people speak Spanish or (in Brazil) Portuguese, which are "Latin" languages.

During the present century, the countries of the Americas have seen the importance of getting along well together, and there has been a great improvement. They have had several conferences to decide matters that are of importance to all of them. These are called Pan-American or Inter-American conferences. In World War II, all the other countries of the Americas except Argentina took the side of the United States, and some of them entered the war.

In their 1954 conference at Caracas, Venezuela, the Inter-American countries united in opposing Communism.

See also the articles on PAN-AMERICANISM, the GOOD NEIGHBOR policy, and the MONROE DOCTRINE.

America's Cup

The America's Cup is a prize in international yacht racing. It is named for a yacht named *America,* which won a big yacht race held by England more than a hundred years ago. The *America* and every yacht that has held this cup since has been from the United States. Challengers have all been British except for one Canadian challenger. The principal British challenger was Sir Thomas Lipton.

The last three races, held during the 1930s, were all won for the United States by Harold S. Vanderbilt. The yachts are Class J, which means they are about 80 to 100 feet long. Since a yacht good enough to race for the America's Cup costs more than a million dollars, races cannot be held very often.

Courtesy Harold S. Vanderbilt

The *America* is shown in the drawing at the top. It was the fastest yacht of its day, and won the silver cup (since known as the America's Cup) offered by the Royal Yacht Squadron of England in 1851. The cup cost £100 then, worth as much as $2,500 in the 1950s. At the right is *Rainbow*, the defender for the United States in the 1934 races. Harold Vanderbilt's *Ranger*, shown in the picture above, was the best and most scientifically designed racing yacht ever built. Its mast, of Duralumin, was 165 feet high, and its sails covered an area of 7,546 square feet. It won the America's Cup races in 1937. All yachts that have raced for the America's Cup in this century have been sloops (having only one mast). The original *America* was a schooner (two-masted).

Amerigo Vespucci

America is not named for Christopher Columbus, who first discovered it in 1492, but for another explorer named Amerigo Vespucci, who sailed across the Atlantic Ocean a few years after Columbus and landed on the northeastern coast of South America in 1497 or 1498.

Like Columbus, Amerigo Vespucci was an Italian but made his voyage for Spain. He was born in Florence, Italy, in 1451, and was a businessman in Florence before he went to Spain and became an explorer. Between 1497 and 1502 he made three voyages across the Atlantic Ocean to South America. Vespucci wrote several letters to a friend about these voyages. The letters were printed and were read all over Europe. Most of the people who read them had not heard of Columbus. They thought that Vespucci had discovered the New World.

One man who read the letters was Martin Waldseemüller, a professor of geography in the city of Freiberg, Germany. He suggested that the new world be named America in honor of Amerigo Vespucci. After this, most geography writers used the name America when they wrote about the New World. Vespucci died at Seville, in Spain, in 1512.

amethyst

Amethyst is a stone used in jewelry. It is a semiprecious stone, which means it is valuable but not nearly as valuable as a precious stone like diamond or ruby. Amethyst is a clear violet or purple in color, and is a kind of quartz, a mineral that is found in great quantities all over the world. Many amethysts are found in the United States, in the region of Lake Superior, but the best amethysts for jewelry come from Scotland, Russia, India, and Ceylon.

The ancient Greeks believed that if a person drank wine from a cup carved out of amethyst, or if he dropped an amethyst in his cup, he would not become drunk, and that is where the amethyst got its name—from a Greek word that means "not intoxicating." The amethyst is the birthstone for February.

Amherst

Amherst is a town in the western part of Massachusetts. There are two colleges in this town. One is Massachusetts State College, and the other is Amherst College. A President of the United States, Calvin Coolidge, was graduated from Amherst College. It is a college for men only, and about a thousand men study there. The town and college were named after Lord Jeffrey Amherst, a British governor in North America in colonial times. Here is part of the famous Amherst College song:

"Oh, Lord Jeffrey Amherst was a soldier of the king,
And he came from across the sea;
To the Frenchman and the Indian he didn't do a thing
In the wilds of this wild country.
Oh, Amherst, brave Amherst
Was a name known to fame in days of yore,
May it ever be glorious
Till the sun shall climb the heavens no more."

AMHERST, MASSACHUSETTS. Population (1950), 10,086. County seat of Cumberland County. Founded 1750.

Amiens

Amiens is a city in northern France. In the oldest part of the city there are buildings that were put up hundreds of years ago. The cathedral in Amiens is one of the most beautiful in all Europe. It is almost seven hundred years old. The people of Amiens manufacture fine velvet, silk, woolen and cotton cloth, and carpets. A famous treaty was signed at Amiens in 1802, to end one of the NAPOLEONIC WARS, about which you can read in another volume of this en-

French Government Tourist Office

Although the town of Amiens was half destroyed in World War II, its beautiful old cathedral was miraculously left undamaged.

cyclopedia. More than a hundred years later, Amiens was the scene of a great battle of World War I. This battle was won by the Allies.

AMIENS, FRANCE. Population (in 1950), 79,807. Capital of Somme department.

Amish

The Amish are members of a branch of the Mennonite Church. They began as a small group of Protestant Christians who left Germany in 1683, came to America, and settled in what is now Pennsylvania. The Amish do not believe in baptizing infants. They refuse to take oaths or to carry weapons. The rules of their faith are based on the Bible only and their aim is to live as much as possible as the Christians did in the days of the Apostles. They live in small villages and towns of their own and are very successful, prosperous farmers. They wear strange old-fashioned clothing without buttons. The men wear broadbrimmed hats and often have beards. The women wear very plain, long dresses and their hats look like the sunbonnets women used to wear a hundred years ago.

Ammon

Ammon was one of the chief gods of ancient Egypt, thousands of years ago. The Egyptians pictured many of their gods as having animal heads. Statues of Ammon usually show him with a human head. At one time Thebes was the capital city of the Egyptian kingdom. The people who lived in Thebes worshipped Ammon as the supreme god. They built a great temple to honor him. The early Greeks believed Ammon to be the same as Zeus, their chief god. The Romans thought he was Jupiter, their chief god.

ammonia

Ammonia is a gas that has many uses. It is used to make ice, and in big refrigerators. It is also used in fertilizers for the soil and in some explosives. What is called ammonia in the home is actually a little of the gas mixed with a lot of water. Ammonia has a sharp, choking smell.

When ammonia is cooled, and then compressed (by the same process that you can read about in the article on AIR COMPRESSION), it turns into a liquid. This liquid is allowed to run through pipes into big refrigerators, such as those in butcher shops, and here it turns back into a gas and draws the heat out of the air around the pipes. This makes the room very cold. Ammonia also dissolves fats and greases, and that is why it is mixed with water and used as a cleaner.

When mixed with nitric acid, ammonia forms a chemical called *ammonium nitrate,* which is used in explosives and also in fertilizers. When added to hydrochloric acid, ammonia forms *ammonium chloride,* also called *sal ammoniac,* which is used in dry-cell batteries for radios and flashlights, and in some medicines.

Ammonia got its name because the ancient Egyptians, thousands of years ago, found the white powder ammonium chloride near the temple of Ammon.